C0-BXA-718

WITHDRAWN
HARVARD LIBRARY
WITHDRAWN

DISPUTING
CHRISTIANITY

DISPUTING CHRISTIANITY

■

THE 400-YEAR-OLD DEBATE OVER

RABBI ISAAC BEN ABRAHAM OF TROKI'S

CLASSIC ARGUMENTS

■

RICHARD H. POPKIN

HB

Humanity
Books

an imprint of Prometheus Books
59 John Glenn Drive, Amherst, New York 14228-2119

Published 2007 by Humanity Books, an imprint of Prometheus Books

Disputing Christianity: The 400-Year-Old Debate over Rabbi Isaac ben Abraham of Troki's Classic Arguments. Copyright © 2007 by the estate of Richard H. Popkin, edited by Peter K. J. Park, Knox Peden, and Jeremy D. Popkin. All rights reserved. No part of this publication may be reproduced, stored in a retrieval system, or transmitted in any form or by any means, digital, electronic, mechanical, photocopying, recording, or otherwise, or conveyed via the Internet or a Web site without prior written permission of the publisher, except in the case of brief quotations embodied in critical articles and reviews.

Inquiries should be addressed to
Humanity Books
59 John Glenn Drive
Amherst, New York 14228–2119
VOICE: 716–691–0133, ext. 210
FAX: 716–691–0137
WWW.PROMETHEUSBOOKS.COM

11 10 09 08 07   5 4 3 2 1

BL
2775.3
.P67
2007

Library of Congress Cataloging-in-Publication Data

Popkin, Richard Henry, 1923–2005
   Disputing Christianity : the 400-year-old debate over Rabbi Isaac ben Abraham of Troki's classic arguments / by Richard H. Popkin ; edited by Peter K. J. Park, Knox Peden, and Jeremy D. Popkin.
       p.   cm.
   Includes bibliographical references.
   ISBN 978–1–59102–384–5 (hardcover: alk. paper)
   1. Rationalism. 2. Christianity—Controversial literature. 3. Judaism—Apologetic works. 4. Jesus Christ—Jewish interpretations. 5. English, George Bethune, 1787–1828. Grounds of Christianity examined. 6. Troki, Isaac ben Abraham, 1533–1594. Chizzuk emunah. I. Park, Peter K. J., 1973– II. Peden, Knox. III. Popkin, Jeremy D., 1948– IV. Title.

BL2775.3.P67 2006
239—dc22
                                                                    2005032102

Printed in the United States of America on acid-free paper

CONTENTS

10/15/07 Amazon

PREFACE

Richard H. Popkin, Rabbi Isaac of Troki, and George Bethune English

By Jeremy D. Popkin

This new edition of George Bethune English's *The Grounds of Christianity Examined*, with an introductory essay about the sixteenth-century Hebrew polemic against Christianity that inspired it, makes a fitting conclusion to the scholarly career of my father, Richard H. Popkin, who died on April 14, 2005, at the age of eighty-one. George Bethune English, a young Unitarian minister trained at Harvard in the early years of the nineteenth century, is just one of many readers of Rabbi Isaac ben Abraham of Troki's *Chizzuk Emunah* ("The Strengthening of the Faith") whose life was changed by an encounter with this text. *The Grounds of Christianity Examined*, originally published in 1813 to explain why Bethune English had given up his clerical career, gave American readers their first introduction to the Rabbi's powerful criticism of Christian claims for the divine inspiration of their religion. Always on the lookout for a chance to demonstrate the influence that authors and ideas outside of the mainstream had had on the making of modern thought, my father spent the last months of his life eagerly putting together the story of how a sixteenth-century Lithuanian member of the Jewish Karaite sect had come to set off a major controversy among New England Protestants more than two centuries after his death.

The story of Rabbi Isaac's critique of the New Testament and its influence over the centuries brought together themes that had been central to Richard Popkin's work throughout his long career. The Rabbi's tract stimulated skepticism about the truth of the Bible and thus con-

7

tributed to the emergence of modern thought, a part of the process my father had explored in his major work, *The History of Scepticism*.[1] At the same time, the influence of the Rabbi's tract demonstrated how closely the Jewish and Christian worlds interacted during the early modern period. The fact that religious groups, both Jewish and Christian, continue to debate and republish this work, originally written in 1593, shows that the controversies of the past are still very much alive today. These were issues that my father pursued in innumerable books and articles over the course of his scholarly life.

Richard Popkin did the research for this project under conditions that would have stopped most scholars. In the last years of his life, he was almost blind. Severe emphysema meant that he had to take an oxygen tank with him everywhere, and he could leave his apartment only in a wheel-chair, making it impossible for him to work in libraries. From the computer terminal in the corner of the dining room in his condominium in Pacific Palisades, however, he continued to pursue one scholarly project after another, forcing my mother, Juliet Popkin, to fight a daily battle to keep enough space on the dining table clear of scholarly papers so that they could eat their meals. A succession of devoted research assistants read aloud to my father, typed what he dictated, and helped him use the Internet to track down the often obscure sources for his various projects; in the course of their work, they received extraordinary training in historical scholarship. My father's worldwide network of scholarly friends was always ready to come to his aid, visiting libraries and archives he could no longer reach and sending him the information he sought. Even in his last weeks, his astounding memory still enabled him to call up passages from books he had read years earlier and to make connections that no one else would have imagined. His enthusiasm never waned, and as my father excitedly filled me in on the latest developments in his work during our regular telephone conversations, Rabbi Isaac and George Bethune English came to seem almost like members of the Popkin family.

Much of the research for this project was carried out with the assistance of Peter K. J. Park, now assistant professor of history at the University of Texas–Dallas; Knox Peden, a PhD candidate in history at University of California–Berkeley; and Jonathan Zorn, a recent graduate of Wesleyan University. When his final illness hit, my father had dictated some thirty pages of an introductory essay for this volume to Knox Peden and had indicated where he intended to put explanatory notes in the Bethune English text. Unfortunately, Richard Popkin was never able to put this essay into publishable form. With the help of Peter K. J. Park and Knox Peden, I have edited and rearranged the material my father dictated, and, following the suggestions my father had made, I have attempted to fill in a few parts of the argument that he had not yet elaborated and to supply the notes he intended to include. The ideas in this introductory essay are unmistakably those of Richard Popkin: no one else had the vast fund of information about the philosophers, theologians, millenarians, and other characters whose often surprising interactions make up this story. The research is also mostly his, drawn from the hundreds of files of notes he had accumulated in his work on the subject. Along with the text of *The Grounds of Christianity Examined*, we have included the biographical article about George Bethune English published by his friend Samuel Lorenzo Knapp in 1833, the most complete account of the life of a man who was clearly one of the great American eccentrics of his time.

There is much more to be learned about Rabbi Isaac, the *Chizzuk Emunah*, and George Bethune English, and my father certainly hoped that his work would inspire others to follow up on these subjects, but I have resisted the temptation to turn this into a research project of my own. Nevertheless, because my father had to dictate his words to others, and because he never had time to complete and revise this essay, it has unavoidably been necessary to rephrase much of what he had put down, to rearrange some of the material, and to eliminate repetitions. My father never took kindly to having his work edited: he liked his writing to have the easy flow of his conversation, and he hated academic jargon and stylistic nitpicking. I hope that the introductory essay published here preserves something of his spirit and of his uniquely accessible way of putting things.

Jeremy D. Popkin
Professor of History, University of Kentucky
June 25, 2007

NOTE

1. Richard H. Popkin, *The History of Scepticism: From Savonarola to Bayle* (New York: Oxford University Press, 2003).

INTRODUCTION

Four Centuries of Influence:
Rabbi Isaac ben Abraham of Troki's Chizzuk Emunah

By Richard H. Popkin, edited by Jeremy D. Popkin,
with the assistance of Peter K. J. Park and Knox Peden

Originally published in 1813, George Bethune English's *The Grounds of Christianity Examined* was one of the strongest critiques of the truth claims of Christianity to be circulated in the early United States. In explaining why he had given up his post as a minister, its author, a former divinity student at Harvard College, understood that he was testing the limits of the young republic's toleration of freedom of speech. "*Our* country is the *only one* which has not been guilty of the folly of establishing the ascendancy of one set of religious opinions," he wrote. Echoing the famous defense of press freedom made by the poet John Milton in the 1640s and anticipating the arguments that the British philosopher John Stuart Mill would make fifty years later in his classic essay *On Liberty*, Bethune English insisted on the importance of allowing radical opinions to be heard. "As it is every man's *natural right*, and *duty* to think and judge for himself in matters of opinion; so he should be allowed freely to bring forward, and defend his opinions, and to endeavour, when he judges proper, to convince others also of their truth."[1]

Bethune English needed to make a strong argument for freedom of speech because *The Grounds of Christianity Examined* challenged the religious beliefs held by almost all Americans of his day. His critics blamed him for endangering the very basis of society. "Does it prove that a man ought to speak what he thinks, if he perceives that the moral consequences of thus speaking are infinitely pernicious?" one of them asked.[2] Although earlier rationalist and Unitarian writers had questioned some aspects of Christianity, Bethune English was the first to introduce American readers to the ideas of an obscure Jewish rabbi whose writings had already been affecting European thinkers for more than two centuries and whose attack on the New Testament continues to exert an influence even today. "I do not claim to have originated *all* the arguments advanced in this Book," Bethune English told his readers. "A very considerable portion of them were selected and derived from ancient and curious Jewish Tracts, translated from Chaldee into Latin, very little known even in Europe."[3] In fact, Bethune English took most of his ideas from a work written in Hebrew, not "Chaldee." That work was the *Chizzuk Emunah*, "The Strengthening of the Faith," written in Lithuania in 1593 by Rabbi Isaac ben Abraham of Troki.

George Bethune English had encountered Rabbi Isaac's tract in the Harvard College Library, which possessed a copy of a Latin translation first published in Germany in 1681. Reading the *Chizzuk Emunah* was a transforming experience for him. He had previously put his Christian faith to the test by examining the deist and rationalist critiques and concluded that "their objections were not insurmountable," but Rabbi Isaac's work convinced him, "by proofs he could neither refute nor evade, that how easily soever Christians might answer the Deists, so called, the Jews were clearly too hard for them." As he explained to his readers, "Either the Old Testament contains a Revelation from God, or it does not."[4] In either case, the basis of Christianity collapsed: if the Old Testament was true, Christians were wrong to change its dispensations, and if it was false, the very foundation of Christian claims disappeared.

The *Chizzuk Emunah*, the book that changed George Bethune English's life, had been written in 1593 in the small Lithuanian town of Troki. Throughout the Middle Ages and the Renaissance, there had been few explicit Jewish critiques of Christianity. Jewish authors had to fear that the Christian authorities would suppress such works and possibly also their authors. Occasionally in the Middle Ages, Christian authorities would force a disputation between Jewish leaders and Christian leaders, but these rituals were held under ground rules that more or less foreclosed the possibility of a real debate. The Jewish participants were fearful for their lives and tried to be extremely cautious and evasive.

But a new situation had developed in the sixteenth century in Poland and Lithuania, which were then parts of the same kingdom. The political authorities there had invited a wide spectrum of religious groups to help develop modern Poland. By the middle of the sixteenth century, this area was probably the most tolerant on the planet at the time. At the same time that Jews were forbidden to reside in England and France, in Spain and Portugal, and in many parts of Italy and Germany, they could freely practice their religion in Poland and Lithuania. They were flourishing in a world in which many kinds of Christian belief were being practiced, and in which radical Christians were challenging the dogmas of the Catholic and Orthodox churches, in which forms of Socinianism were being set forth and even forms of Judaized Christianity.[5] The breakup of the Byzantine Empire to the south, the expansion of the Ottoman Empire in the Balkans, and the conflicts between the Protestants and Catholics and between different kinds of Catholics (Greek and Russian Orthodox) and Uniates, meant that there were groups with many divergent views about the nature of religion, the Godhead, and the religious organization of society living in the region. The interaction of these many cultures, belief systems, and ways of life produced a very exciting intellectual and cultural world. There were also Turco-Calvinists, that is, Calvinists living in the Ottoman Turkish areas, as well as the reverse, Muslims living in Christian territory, and Jewish groups who had escaped persecutions in Germany and elsewhere.

Rabbi Isaac came from a small heretical group within Judaism called the Karaites. This group had been expelled from the mainstream Jewish community in the eighth and ninth centuries because they refused to accept any religious teachings other than what was in the Bible. They rejected the authority of the Talmud and other rabbinical commentaries. After their expulsion from the Jewish community, they had survived on the fringes of Muslim territory and later began moving into Poland and neighboring lands. During the late Middle Ages, Karaites existed in enclaves in the Crimea, Turkey, Lithuania, and Egypt. In the sixteenth century, the Lithuanian town of Troki became their main center. When they learned about the Karaites, Protestants, who were calling on Christians to make the Bible their sole authority, seemed to have hoped that this dissident Jewish group would prove to be proto-Protestants who could be won over to the whole Scripture as soon as they learned of it. The Karaites found themselves in tune with some of the attitudes of the Protestant reformers and the anti-trinitarians and Socinians, a varied group of thinkers who had come to the conclusion that the doctrine of the Trinity was not part of Christian religion. This may have eased Rabbi Isaac's entry into the theological disputes of the time.

In this fairly wild scene in which many different religious groups were interacting, Rabbi Isaac ben Abraham of Troki, which is a suburb of Vilnius, himself a Karaite and grandson of a medical doctor from the Crimea, came into contact with a wide range of religious ideas. He obviously discussed the differences between his own beliefs and those of some others in the area in person and also studied texts from different groups. Rabbi Isaac seems to have consulted some of the leading anti-trinitarians of the time and to have discussed their arguments with them. One who is mentioned most is Syzmon Budny, a close associate of Faustus Socinus, the leader of the anti-trinitarians who had fled from Italy to Geneva to Poland. It was the burning of Michael Servetus, an early Socinian leader, in Geneva in 1553 that made the anti-trinitarians move east to one area where they were tolerated, namely, Poland and Lithuania.

We do not know how learned Rabbi Isaac was or how many languages he knew; we know some of the people he talked to because he mentions his discussions with them. One of his aims was probably to prevent young Jews from being attracted to some form of anti-trinitarianism or some of the new forms of Protestantism that were emerging.[6] His work is set forth as a defense of the Jewish faith but is, by and large, an attack on Christianity, drawing on all sorts of materials available to him. Unlike any other criticism of Christianity written by a Jewish author up to the end of the sixteenth century, Rabbi Isaac does not appeal to any special Jewish reading of texts but just plunges into an attack on the historical statements made in the Gospels and whether they make any coherent sense or provide any basis for messianic religion. The result is probably the strongest critique of Christianity written by a Jewish thinker in the last four hundred years. The *Chizzuk Emunah* is based almost entirely on examination of passages from the New Testament, the inconsistencies among them, and the contradictions between Christian claims about the

Old Testament and the actual text of the Jewish scriptures. The fact that Rabbi Isaac based his arguments strictly on the same biblical texts that Christians read, rather than appealing to any other sources of authority, such as the Talmud, made his tract especially challenging for Christians.

The rabbi does not seem to have been interested in looking for textual variants that might undermine the credibility of the New Testament. He accepted the Greek text as it was used in the Poland of his day and then sought to show that it was full of inconsistencies, errors, and absurdities. In any event, he argued, the authors of the Gospels had written long after the events they described, and the New Testament was therefore of no historical value, since "they testify about things, that they didn't see with their own eyes."[7]

Rabbi Isaac laid out his objections to Christianity clearly in the first chapter of the *Chizzuk Emunah*. That Jesus was not the Messiah predicted in the Jewish scriptures "is evident:—1st, from his pedigree; 2ndly, from his acts; 3rdly, from the period in which he lived; and 4thly, from the fact that, during his existence, the promises were not fulfilled which are to be realised on the advent of the *expected* Messiah, whereas the fulfilment of the conditions alone can warrant a belief in the identity of the Messiah."[8] The initial attack on the conclusions to be drawn from the genealogy of Joseph at the beginning of Matthew is that Joseph rather than Jesus is from the Davidic line. A couple of earlier Jewish writings against Christianity had challenged Jesus's credentials of coming from the messianic House of David, and the early medieval *Sefer Toldot Yeshu* went further, giving Jesus an illegitimate lineage from a Roman soldier.[9] Rabbi Isaac is not interested in pursuing in what may have actually been the case, just in disputing the New Testament claim that it is basing its story on that of the Old Testament. Rabbi Isaac argued that not only was Joseph not the father if Jesus was born of a virgin, but the inconsistencies between the lineages presented in Matthew and in Luke proved that neither source could be considered valid or reliable. If Joseph was from a Davidic family, and Joseph is not the father of Jesus, then what difference does the whole story make?

Subsequent sections of the *Chizzuk Emunah* argued that Jesus's actions, as reported in the Gospels, had not fulfilled the Biblical prophecies. He had not, for instance, restored the Jewish kingdom, as the Jewish prophets had explicitly said the Messiah would do. He had not meant to abrogate the laws of Moses; those Christians who had done so, abolishing the custom of circumcision and the observance of the Sabbath, had acted "on their own accord and responsibility, for they have no authority whatever for doing so from Jesus and his Apostles."[10] In a passage of his work omitted from the abridged translation that is still the most extensive version of the work available in English, the rabbi asked himself how Christians could believe "their articles of faith, which contradict human reason." The answer, he suggested, could only be that they were still under the influence of their pagan ancestors, who had been able to believe not only that a god might have been born of a virgin, but even that a deity might spring from the head of a virgin.[11]

Even if almost everything that is in Rabbi Isaac's *Chizzuk Emunah* had appeared in one form or another in a previous writing against Christianity, his text packaged the material in a way that was much more suitable for seventeenth- and eighteenth-century readers. Since the rabbi was a Karaite and used no rabbinical arguments, the text was much more accessible to non-Jews and Marranos, the descendants of the Spanish Jews who had been forcibly converted to Christianity but still retained some loyalty to their ancestors' faith. The *Chizzuk Emunah* reads somewhat like a lawyer's brief against Christianity, and the reader can easily follow the points being made and the arguments offered without having to know about Jewish medieval theology and argumentation.

Rabbi Isaac began writing his polemic some time before his death in 1593. His student, Josef Malinowski, finished the table of contents and put the manuscript into circulation in 1594. The history of its impact, which has been going on for the last four centuries, shows the curious ways in which the same text can be used both for and against different religious traditions. Starting out as a polemical curiosity addressed essentially to Jews, it has gone through revival after revival, surfacing in different languages besides its original Hebrew: in Spanish, German, Latin, Yiddish, Ladino, and English, among others. George Bethune English paraphrased many of its arguments in 1813. An abbreviated and much-toned-down English version was published by Moses Mocatta in 1851, and another partial English translation appeared in 1876. In recent decades, Mocatta's abridged version has been reissued several times; it is currently available in two different reprint editions.

Although published versions of the *Chizzuk Emunah* are now easily available, it took nearly a century before Rabbi Isaac's manuscript found its way into print. It did circulate widely in the Jewish world, and the history of the text is complicated by the fact that some who copied it altered the text; one such version, made by a rabbi who deleted passages reflecting the author's Karaite views and inserted material in line with mainstream Jewish traditions, eventually became the basis of the first published version of the work in 1681.[12] From the start, the work inspired strong reactions. Selections from the work were translated into Spanish in 1621 as *Fortificacion de la Ley* by a Sephardic rabbi, Isaac Athias, who was then leading a congregation in Hamburg.[13] The Spanish version seems to have been frequently copied in the western Sephardi diaspora, the network of communities founded by Jews whose ancestors had come from Spain and Portugal after those countries expelled them in the 1490s, but it was never published. There were copies in Amsterdam, London, and other Sephardic centers as well as some of the American colonies.

Other disciples sought to get the work published and brought it to Western Europe, where Hebrew publications were becoming a major business. There is some indication that Hebrew publishers in Amsterdam turned down printing the work, possibly because the author was a Karaite and not a rabbinical Jew. Apparently the leading Dutch Hebrew printer, Menasseh ben Israel, turned it down. We do not know why, but the Jewish community in Amsterdam had pledged not to cause any scandal to their Christian hosts and might have felt that publication of this work would be a violation of the agreement.

Christian thinkers in Western Europe were not totally unprepared to consider a Jewish critique of their religion. Around the same time that Rabbi Isaac was writing the *Chizzuk Emunah*, the French legal theorist Jean Bodin wrote his *Colloquium*. It is a dialogue among seven different religious thinkers in which the Jew, Solomon, wins the argument about which is the best religion. Bodin's *Colloquium* was not published, and no one seems to have known about it until the 1650s, when a copy surfaced in Paris during an inheritance fight among his descendants. Copies were made in Paris; at least one was taken to England, where it was copied again; and other copies made it to Germany. It was occasionally mentioned as being a direct attack on Christianity; critics claimed that Bodin's views reflected the fact that he was of Jewish ancestry. A group of scholars, including Gottfried Leibniz, were preparing a copy for publication in the late seventeenth century, but it did not appear in print until the middle of the nineteenth century and then only in a truncated form. The full text has appeared only fairly recently.[14]

As manuscript copies of the *Chizzuk Emunah* spread through the Jewish world, some Christians learned of its existence and got a sense of its content. A lengthy treatise from 1644 by Johann (Johannes) Müller, head pastor of the St. Petri church in Hamburg, treats mainly the arguments in *Chizzuk Emunah* as well as those of the anti-Christian polemic *Sefer ha-Nizzahon* by Rabbi Lipmann, written some time prior to 1410. Müller speaks of a German refutation that was also circulating at the time, although this may refer to Theodore Hackspan's refutation of Lipmann's polemic.[15] Müller's work was entitled *Judaismus oder Judenthumb, das ist ausfuerhlicher Bericht von des juedischen Wolckes Unglauben, Blindheit und Verstockung* (a second edition appeared in 1707).[16] During the seventeenth and eighteenth centuries, manuscript translations of Rabbi Isaac's work also appeared in French, Dutch, German, and Portuguese. Copies of these versions are in the Ets Haim collection, the library of the Sephardic synagogue in Amsterdam. Nevertheless, curious Christians complained that Jews were reluctant to share copies of the *Chizzuk Emunah* or other anti-Christian works with them.

The tolerant attitude of the Dutch toward the Jews had led to the development of a large Jewish community in Amsterdam after 1600 and made the country a center of Jewish-Christian contacts. Although the Dutch authorities never banned writings by members of the Amsterdam synagogue in the seventeenth century, they had made an implicit agreement with the Jewish community that it would not allow the circulation of works that insulted Christianity or that would cause scandal, a term not defined. In the first decades of the seventeenth century, the Amsterdam authorities took note of a Jewish community that was establishing itself there. Apparently they were originally tolerated because they, like the Dutch, had been victims of the Spanish Inquisition. But the Dutch authorities felt they needed juridical advice as to whether the Jewish community could be legalized and function within the newly established Dutch

Republic. The question was turned over to Hugo Grotius, a leading jurist and a liberal Calvinist, who drew up a fairly elaborate list of restrictions to guard against the Jews taking advantage of the Dutch citizenry. Before Grotius's plan could be discussed, he himself had to flee the bigotry of the orthodox Calvinists and left the country for good.[17] Gradually a way of living with the Jewish community was worked out but never formalized. On the Dutch side, they were most anxious that the Jewish community would take care of any indigent Jewish person and that they would prevent or avoid scandal against Christians, whatever that might mean. By and large, as far as we know, the Jewish community kept their side of the bargain. They could discuss and read criticisms of Christianity as long as they kept the material within the Jewish community, which they seem to have done most of the time. However, on the flyleaf of the critique of Christianity by Orobio de Castro, another Jewish author of the period, is a note indicating that he had not published his work for fear of causing scandal but that he had sent it to the Jesuits in Brussels, who liked it very much.[18]

The Jewish community in Amsterdam was at first mainly made up of Jews from Spain and Portugal but gradually grew to contain a fair number of people from Eastern Europe. The Amsterdam synagogue became a meeting place for Jews and all sorts of Christians. Many Christians who participated were millenarians, who expected the culmination of world history and the return of Jesus on Earth to occur around 1655–56. For them a crucial prelude to this would be the conversion of the Jews, which would take place by divine intervention. The view of the leading English Puritan divine, the very learned and pious Joseph Mede, was that only a token conversion, not a mass change of faith, would be necessary.[19] Christians could help by assisting the Jews, by being friendly with them and by looking for signs of the forthcoming conversion. This would involve taking note of Jewish criticisms of Christianity.

Excitement grew among Calvinist-oriented Christians about the impending events. One finds signs of this in France, Bohemia, Hungary; in many German cities; and especially in the Netherlands and England. It was rumored that a group of Hungarian Jews had converted to Christianity on their own to get ready for the events.[20] Two amazing projects were set forth in England and France to deal with the marvelous future. One is the plan drafted by John Dury and Samuel Hartlib to create a Col-

lege of Jewish studies in London in 1642, and the other is the plan offered
by Isaac La Peyrère, the secretary of the Prince of Condé, to recall the
Jews to France and create a special Jewish Christian church for them,
which would have no beliefs that the Jews might find offensive. La
Peyrère's plan was laid out in his *Du Rappel des Juifs*, of 1643. The
author was himself from an important Calvinist family in Bordeaux, a
family of Portuguese Marranos who had become Protestants.[21] Dury and
Hartlib were very significant figures in the reformulation of the British
state in the Puritan Revolution. Thus I think one has to be willing to consider that these plans could have been meaningful and realistic at the time
they were offered. The Dury-Hartlib plan was endorsed by the Westmin-
ster Assembly of Puritan Divines and was to have a thousand pounds per
annum to support its activities, including three professorships, funds for
students, and funds for translating and publishing texts. There is no sug-
gestion that the professors were supposed to prove that the Christians are
right and the Jews wrong. In fact, one of the three professorships was
offered to Rabbi Menasseh ben Israel of Amsterdam. In Dury's pamphlet
describing the virtues of the plan, he kept stressing that if they were carried out, they could make Christianity sound less offensive to the Jews
and Judaism better known to Christians. Even though money was never
provided, a whole series of activities went on in the Netherlands and later
in England that seemed to be part of the mission of the college. These
involved the editing and publishing of Hebrew religious texts such as the
Mishna in Hebrew, with vocalized dots, and the translation of Hebrew
works into Latin and Spanish.[22]

Another project tied to this millenarian excitement involved providing the funds for an Amsterdam rabbi to make an exact model of
Solomon's temple, which is supposed to be a microcosm of the world.
People could study it regardless of their religious background and pre-
sumably profit from the knowledge. We know that when the model was
completed around 1646, it was displayed outside the rabbi's house next
to the synagogue, and a fee was charged to look at it. This ran into two
problems. Viewers were making so much noise that they interfered with
rituals in the synagogue, and, according to Jewish law, there was not
supposed to be any exchange of money on the Sabbath. Both of these
problems were worked out to satisfy Christians, and the model was on

display for about twenty-five or thirty years. Tourists from all over Europe treated the Amsterdam synagogue as one of the major tourist attractions in Amsterdam. The Queen of England, Henrietta Maria, visited twice in 1642, and scholars came to consult the rabbis. There are four paintings of activities in the synagogue by non-Jewish artists, and many Calvinists visited the synagogue. Menasseh ben Israel said that at least half the people who attended services were not Jews, and the paintings seem to bear him out. We have descriptions by the French scholar Pierre Daniel Huet of being escorted into the synagogue by Menasseh, sitting with him, and causing a disturbance when he put his feet on a sacred object. An Anglican bishop, Thomas Burnet, studied with one of the Amsterdam rabbis, attended services with him, then discussed sermons with him. A leading Dutch millenarian, Peter Serrarius, says he regularly rushed to the synagogue when any strange event occurred to see what the Jews' interpretation was and where they would fit it in the sequence of the events that would precede the coming of the messiah.[23]

An additional major scheme by the English millenarians was to try to have the Jews readmitted to England. This was proposed when a Portuguese explorer claimed to have found a tribe in the Andes Mountains holding a Jewish service on a Friday night. In 1646 the explorer came to Amsterdam and before a notary told Menasseh ben Israel his account. Menasseh wrote this out in French, and it was passed on to John Dury, who used it as a basis to claim that Native Americans might be Jews and that the lost tribes were reappearing just before the end of days. In order to prepare for this, it was necessary to see if all the anticipated pre-millenial events had taken place. Menasseh ben Israel, in his most famous work, *The Hope of Israel,* had argued that the messiah would not come until the Jews were scattered to the four corners of the earth. Now that there were Jews known to be in China, India, and elsewhere, the only corner that seemed to be lacking Jews was England. So the readmission of the Jews to England would have monumental messianic consequences. That this was not taken lightly is evidenced by the English diplomatic preparations and negotiations with Menasseh to get him to come to England and discuss the conditions of readmission with Oliver Cromwell. This became a significant issue in English political life in the latter part of 1655–56.[24]

At the same time, among the same people, Rabbi Isaac's critique of

Christianity was known and did not seem to be too disturbing. We know that the manuscript of Rabbi Isaac's work was known to John Dury by the late 1640s. It was probably known to the chief rabbi, Saul Levi Morteira, in 1656 when he was completing his own attack on Christian beliefs. One puzzling thing about the case of Rabbi Isaac and his book is that there does not seem to have been any move to prevent the circulation of his work. Yet all over Europe, there were violent rejections of deviant points of view. In England, it was not safe to be a Catholic or to be a Christian who worshiped on the Sabbath instead of Sunday; people actually got killed for that. In the tolerant Netherlands, there was no toleration of Catholicism, and there were continuous attacks on liberal forms of Calvinism. One possible explanation might be that the orthodox Calvinists throughout the seventeenth century were treating Jews as a special case, since it was the conversion of the Jews that would be all-important in religious history. There is an interesting example in John Dury's answer to a group in Germany that wrote to him and asked whether it was lawful to be a true and believing follower of the law of Moses and a practicing Christian simultaneously. Dury's answer comes down to yes, but you had better be careful where you do this, and he recommends that it not be tried in Germany but rather in the Netherlands.[25] In the Netherlands, the millenarians may have seen Rabbi Isaac's attack as one of the events to be expected before the coming of the messiah and hence treated it with patience and without animosity.

The middle decades of the seventeenth century was when figures such as Isaac La Peyrère, Thomas Hobbes, and Spinoza started to examine the Old Testament as a historical document and raised questions about its veracity, thereby establishing the modern tradition of biblical criticism. Were they influenced by Rabbi Isaac's work? None of them addressed these issues with regard to the New Testament. In his very detailed analysis in chapter seven of his *Tractatus Theologico-Politicus*, Spinoza examines problems in various books of the Old Testament but does not carry this into the New Testament. This would seem to indicate that La Peyrère, Hobbes, and Spinoza did not know about Rabbi Isaac's attack. It seems likely that the chief rabbi of Amsterdam, Saul Levi Morteira, had carefully studied and used Rabbi Isaac's text in his own polemical attack on Christianity, *Tratado da verdade da lei de Moises*

("Treatise on the Truth of the Law of Moses"). Since his work was completed only in 1660 and was not published at the time, we do not know if Spinoza ever had access to it before he left the Jewish community.[26]

Although some of the millenarians and philosemites of the 1640s and 1650s were familiar with the content of Rabbi Isaac's work, few seem to have had direct contact with it. This situation changed in 1681, with the first publication of the text. In 1665, a professor of jurisprudence and Oriental languages at the German University of Altdorf, Johann Wagenseil, traveled through Western Europe to North Africa. Wagenseil had a strong interest in Jewish religious ideas. In the Moroccan town of Ceuta, Wagenseil encountered Jews "gathered together from the more distant parts of Africa in order to buy and sell merchandise. I immediately came into unbelievably great favor with these people by telling them the history and status of the European Jews," he wrote in the preface to his translation of the *Chizzuk Emunah*. "In return they not only informed me about their own institutions and the history of Africa, but, moreover, one of them . . . gave me this book in manuscript form." Wagenseil had known of the work through Johann Müller's German refutation of it. He justified his decision to put it into print on the grounds that "This Hizzuk Emunah is indeed a bulwark which deserves that we Christians should put forth our efforts to refute it, lest it might further strengthen [the Jews] in their errors, and hinder them in the acknowledgement of truth."[27] Wagenseil published the work, along with other Jewish anti-Christian texts, under the title of *Tela Ignea Satanae* ["Satan's Fiery Darts"], providing the Hebrew and Latin texts as well as his own refutation.[28]

Wagenseil separated his criticism of the rabbi's arguments from any criticism of Jews as such. In contrast to some of the rabid anti-Semitism then current in Germany, Wagenseil insisted these charges were not based on any facts. He debunked some of the more fantastic stories, such as that the Jews extracted blood from children and used it to make matzoh at Passover. He insisted that he only sought to answer the arguments of the Jews, not to attack them as people, although he did preface his Latin version of the *Chizzuk Emunah* with the comment that "this harmful book has corrupted many among the Jews, and they will soon produce more such depraved books unless we put a clamp on them in a befitting manner, or unless my keen arguments defeat the Jewish polemicists."[29] His hope was that better understanding between Christians and Jews would eventually lead to the conversion of the latter, and he mentioned the work of seventeenth-century figures like the French writer Isaac La Peyrère and Rabbi Menassah ben Israel, who had promoted closer contacts between the followers of the two religions.[30]

Wagenseil's published Latin edition of the *Chizzuk Emunah,* issued in 1681, made Rabbi Isaac's ideas available to Christian readers throughout Europe and opened a new era in the story of his impact. This printed version of the text shows up in various libraries at the end of the seventeenth century, as far afield as Ireland, Sweden, Germany, and soon, America. There is little evidence that readers found Wagenseil's refutation of Rabbi Isaac very interesting. It was actually dropped in later editions. A number of other Christian theologians, however, felt compelled to answer the anti-Christian arguments that Wagenseil's Latin translation had put into circulation.[31] Among other things, defenders of Christian orthodoxy noted with alarm that Socinian anti-trinitarians were borrowing some of the rabbi's arguments.[32]

In England, a prominent theological writer, the bishop of Bath and Wells, Richard Kidder, mentions having a copy of Wagenseil's edition of the *Chizzuk Emunah* in a work that he published in 1699 titled *A Demonstration of the Messias. In which the Truth of the Christian Religion is defended, especially against The Jews.* In this book, he writes:

> I have taken all possible Care to inform my self what it is that the Jews have to object against Christianity. To that Purpose I have read over their several printed Nizachons, and R. Isaac's Book, which he calls Chizuck Emunah, which are Books filled with Objections against Christianity, and treat of the Matter, *ex professo.*[33]

Kidder was interested in Jewish attacks on Christianity and had in his possession one entitled *Porta Veritatis* that Rabbi Menasseh ben Israel had sold to Ralph Cudworth, Regius professor of Hebrew at Cambridge University, in 1655, as well as a couple of other manuscripts. Although Kidder made use of Wagenseil's publication, he opposed the publication of Jewish anti-Christian works, "lest by that means it should be printed, without an answer, to the prejudice of Christianity." He thought that they should either be burnt or else kept in restricted libraries, where only qualified experts could see them.[34] In addition to Kidder's work, a refutation of three chapters from Rabbi Isaac's work was written by a Huguenot pastor, Jacques Gousset of Dordrecht, and published in 1688 under the title *Controversiam adversus Judaeos ternio*. When Gousset died in 1704, he left behind an expanded and completed refutation of Rabbi Isaac's arguments, which Arnold Borst edited and published in 1712 in Amsterdam under the title *Jesu Christi Evangeliique veritas salutifera, demonstrata in confutatione libri Chizzuk-Emunah a R. Isaaco scripti*.[35]

The Wagenseil edition of the *Chizzuk Emunah* seems to have been widely available and discussed by many people who were less directly concerned to refute it during the seventeenth and into the eighteenth century, including the philosopher Pierre Bayle, the Huguenot polemicist Pierre Jurieu, the English deist Anthony Collins, Voltaire, and the historian of the Jews Jacques Basnage, the last being the only one who seems to be sufficiently outraged to suggest that it should be banned. Another leading intellectual figure who read it was Bishop Pierre Daniel Huet, who had it in his private library, and whose library became part of the French royal library in the eighteenth century. His copy shows that he marked it and made some notes.[36] In the article "Weile" in his *Dictionnaire historique et critique*, Bayle mentions Rabbi Isaac and his book, along with the names Abarbanel and Lipmann, author of the *Nizachon*, without giving any details to indicate whether or not he had read the book and what he thought of it. Bayle mentions, however, a Portuguese Jew who was converted by Weile's critique of the Jewish arguments.[37]

Signs of a particular interest in the rabbi's work appear in the antagonistic comments of the leading authority on the history of the Jews at the time, Jacques Basnage of Rotterdam, and in the approval of the rabbi's arguments by the English deist theologian, Anthony Collins. Basnage, a millenarian, seems to have been convinced that the millenarian climax of world history would occur in 1716; God would bring about the end of history by effecting the conversion of Jews. In the meantime, Basnage, like many Calvinist millenarian predecessors, advocated a very philo-Semitic approach to the Jews as a way of encouraging them to play their necessary role at the end of history.

This new stage of Jewish-Christian interchange was augmented by the sudden availability of a collection of Jewish anti-Christian texts, including

Rabbi Isaac's, that were auctioned off in The Hague in 1715. Most of the material was written by Spanish and Portuguese Jews in Amsterdam, but the collection also included some copies of the *Chizzuk Emunah*. For at least two or three decades, Christian scholars had heard of the existence of these Jewish anti-Christian texts, but had been unable to obtain any copies. Suddenly in 1715, the library of M. Sarraz, the secretary of the Elector of Saxony, was put up for auction. The catalogue proclaimed that one of the great features of the collection was the numerous anti-Christian manuscripts it contained. Sarraz was the son-in-law of Jacques Basnage. The latter quickly rummaged through the anti-Christian materials and summarized them in his last edition of his history of the Jews in 1716.[38] Although he was normally in favor of tolerance for the Jews, Basnage was shocked by the vehemence of Rabbi Isaac's polemic. "His book is one of the most dangerous ever written against Christianity," Basnage wrote. "The author goes through the entire Gospel, and highlights all the places in the Sacred History that give him the possibility of raising problems. He follows these up strongly, and at the same time refutes Christian responses. He reasons more judiciously than the rabbis normally do." Wagenseil's ineffective critique of the *Chizzuk Emunah* left Basnage unsatisfied. "This learned man should have followed the author step by step, and refuted him as convincingly as he did Lipman[n]," he wrote.[39]

After the sale of the Sarraz collection, the Reverend Anthony Collins, who had been trying to obtain some of this material, suddenly received copies of several Jewish polemics against Christianity, including the Spanish manuscript version of the *Chizzuk Emunah*, and used them in the deist polemics he wrote at the end of his life, questioning the grounds of Christianity.[40] A young French writer, Voltaire, came to London in 1724. He was very eager to meet Collins and discuss their heretical ideas together. Unfortunately, the English prelate was ill and unable to meet Voltaire. His close friend, the Reverend Samuel Clarke, who was Newton's handpicked successor as professor of mathematics at Cambridge, was able to make Voltaire aware of the new material. Both Collins and Voltaire thus had access to Rabbi Isaac's arguments in both Spanish and Latin. Collins included a brief summary of the rabbi's critique of Christianity in the last editions of his work. This text was reprinted many times in the rest of the eighteenth century.

Voltaire, whose own library, now in Saint Petersburg, contains Wagenseil's edition of the *Chizzuk Emunah* and a Spanish manuscript version, used the work to discredit both Christianity and Judaism. As an opponent of the Church, he appreciated the fact that Rabbi Isaac "has brought together all the objections that unbelievers have fastened on ever since. . . . In fact, the most dedicated unbelievers have hardly said anything that is not in this *Fortification of the Faith* of Rabbi Isaac."[41] In his *Philosophical Dictionary*, he devoted more space to Rabbi Isaac than to any other Jewish critic of Christianity, although he professed shock at the "horrible profanations" found in his writings, and he made critical comments about his work in several other places.[42] Voltaire alerted some of his French associates to the rabbi's discussion, as a result of which the work is cited by people like Baron d'Holbach.[43]

Not all the attacks on biblical religion made during the eighteenth century were derived from sources such as the *Chizzuk Emunah*. By the middle of the eighteenth century, someone like David Hume could dismiss the Old Testament as being a barbarous book written by barbarous people in barbarous times. Hume asks his reader

> To lay his hand upon his heart, and after a serious consideration declare, whether he thinks that the falsehood of such a book, supported by such a testimony, would be more extraordinary and miraculous than all the miracles it relates; which is, however, necessary to make it be received, according to the measures of probability above established.[44]

Hume was not interested in historical details that might throw light on biblical passages. Instead, he relegated the whole text to some sort of uncivilized fantasy that needed no further discussion. In contrast, Rabbi Isaac treats the problem of the truth or falsity of the historical claims in the New Testament as something that requires the most careful examination in terms of precise translation of the language, understanding the circumstances, motives, and actions of various people in the story or history.

The truth or falsity of the Bible still mattered intensely to many eighteenth-century thinkers, however. In England, Rabbi Isaac was cited in the debates about the merits of Christianity between Joseph Priestley and David Levi toward the end of the century. Priestley, a scientist and Unitarian minister from Birmingham, was willing to abandon some traditional Christian beliefs, such as the claim that Jesus was the son of God, but he also made a strong effort to get the Jews to accept a diluted form of Christianity. His "Letter to the Jews," which cited the "celebrated treatise intitled the *Bulwark of the Faith*,"[45] was answered by David Levi, the only Anglo-Jewish theologian of the period, whose arguments also showed familiarity with that work.[46]

Meanwhile, in eighteenth-century Germany, other writers continued to respond to Rabbi Isaac's views. In 1715, a Christian pastor, Christian Gottlieb Unger, collated the printed text with a reliable manuscript copy and correctly established the identity of its author, which had remained uncertain up to that time.[47] In his *Bibliothecae Hebraeae*, Johann Christoph Wolf translated parts of the work into German. He also noted that there were significant differences between the various manuscripts of it in circulation and thus laid the basis for a critical study of the text.[48] Another German writer excited by Rabbi Isaac's views was a schoolteacher in Hamburg, Hermann Samuel Reimarus (1694–1768). Reimarus was worrying about conflicts in the accounts of the life of Jesus in the four Gospels. He had read the Latin-Hebrew edition of the rabbi's text, and it soon became clear to him that the Gospels were just human accounts and could be mistaken, and a completely new approach to the New Testament was now needed. It was no longer to be examined as a historical account, but in terms of the context and motivations of its authors. In a manuscript that he wrote in the 1730s or 1740s, Reimarus summarized Rabbi Isaac's arguments and concluded that "this Jew is the most thorough and strongest opponent of Christianity."[49] Reimarus came into contact with Gotthold Ephraim Lessing, the famous German Enlightenment author and the curator of the great Herzog August Library in Wolfenbüttel. They apparently exchanged views and ideas about the status of the New Testament. After Reimarus died, his children found his manuscript, which they turned over to Lessing, who published parts of it anonymously as *Apologie oder Schutzschrift für die vernünftigen Verehrer Gottes* (1774–78). This became the beginning of modern higher criticism of the New Testament, which was developed in the nineteenth century by figures such as David Friedrich Strauss. Thus the quest for the historical Jesus began in Germany when Reimarus tried to resolve the questions that arose from Rabbi Isaac's attacks on the New Testament.

We will return yet again to the German reception of the *Chizzuk Emunah*, but first some words are needed on the author whose text, the first American English use of Rabbi Isaac's ideas, is reproduced in this volume. George Bethune English graduated from Harvard in 1807. He first studied law but then entered Harvard's Divinity School and was "approbated" as a minister by the Boston Association of the Unitarian Church in 1811. He obtained a position as an assistant librarian at Harvard, where he came across the text of Rabbi Isaac's work. As one of his critics wrote, "The effect of this discovery upon his own mind was a firm conviction that the Christian system was not only without foundation, but was a mean and despicable system, hostile to the best interests of individuals and of society, and loaded with the monstrous guilt of oppressing and destroying millions of innocent people."[50] Startled by the points raised by the rabbi, Bethune English tried to find some knowledgeable person, acquainted with Hebrew, with whom to discuss them. Bethune English then wrote his small book, published in 1813. It apparently caused a great stir when it came out. "You seem not to have heard of the book which engages all the attention here at the present:—Mr. English's apology for leaving his profession," one Unitarian reader, Henry Ware Jr., wrote to his father. "You will have heard of it, however, before you receive this—for it will pass like wild-fire through the country; and like that, too, it will flash, and crackle, and sparkle, and dazzle, and amaze for a moment."[51]

In this case, the use to which the rabbi's arguments were put took place in the context of a dispute between the Unitarians and the Congregationalists in Massachusetts. At the time, the Unitarians were declaring their independence from orthodox Christianity, but still wanted to be counted as Christian. Among other things, they were still involved in missionary work to convert heathens, especially in Asia.

A prize student at the Harvard Divinity School and former classmate of Bethune English, Edward Everett was enlisted to write the official answer to Bethune English's work. He composed a five-hundred-page reply, which was supervised by the leaders of the Unitarian Church in Boston. As the controversy about his work spread, Bethune English wrote to Rabbi Gershom Seixas, a leading figure in the small American Jewish community and, at that time, one of the trustees of Columbia University. Seixas was wary of endorsing Bethune English's anti-Christian position.

He judged the young man to be "a strict disciple of the late Dr. Priestley" and told his daughter that "I mean not to be concerned in the business." Nevertheless, he met with Bethune English in 1814 and later wrote to his daughter that the author had told him "that he had gained more knowledge of yr. Father, in the short conversation he had with him, than from all the Books which he has read."[52]

Bethune English was forced to give up his duties in the Unitarian Church. He answered his critics and stressed, both in the original book and in the answers, that Christianity had done grave misdeeds to its opponents: first and continuously to the Jews and second to every other group with whom it came into contact. He felt that Christianity should stop persecuting and make some sort of retribution for all the damage it had caused over the many centuries. His own religious views are difficult to define with precision. In a defense of his work published in 1813, he seemed to take a deist position, writing that "Whether the Old Testament contains a revelation from God, or not, its moral precepts are, as far as I know, unexceptionable; there is not, I believe, any thing extravagant or impracticable in them, they are such as promote the good order of society. Its religion is in fact merely *Theism* garnished, and guarded by a splendid ritual, and gorgeous ceremonies; the belief of it can produce no oppression and wretchedness to any portion of mankind, and for these reasons I for one will never attempt to weaken its credit, whatever may be my own opinion with regard to its supernatural claims."[53]

Although *The Grounds of Christianity Examined* drew heavily on the *Chizzuk Emunah* and even offered readers some lengthy quotations from it, apparently the first time any of Rabbi Isaac's arguments had been translated into English, Bethune English had also borrowed from other sources. His assertion that Christianity was a dualistic faith similar to Zoroastrianism, for example, and his discussion of the late-eighteenth-century Shaker sect were not taken from Rabbi Isaac's work. In a later explanation of his position, written after he had lived in the Middle East for some time, Bethune English made a stronger statement of faith in the Old Testament: "What I have learned and seen in Europe, Asia and Africa, while it has confirmed my reasons for rejecting the New Testament, has rooted in my mind the conviction that the ancient Bible does contain a Revelation from the God of Nature, as firmly as my belief in the first proposition of Euclid." He was convinced, he wrote, "that this world was made and is governed by just such a Being as the Jehovah of the Old Testament; while the palpable fulfilment of predictions contained in that book, and which is so strikingly manifest in the Old World, leaves in my mind no doubt whatever, of the ultimate fulfilment of all that it promises, and all that it threatens."[54] English later lived in Egypt, and it was rumored that he had become a Muslim, but Samuel Knapp, author of the most extended account of English's life, says that English "constantly denied" this charge. Knapp had no doubt that English's true sympathies lay with the Jews. "It was truly an intellectual feast to hear him read the Old Testament in the original, and translate and commentate as he went along. He threw into the shade other translations and commentaries by the minuteness of his knowledge of the Hebrew language, as well as of the habits and manners of the Jewish nation in every age of their history. When on this subject, his whole air and character seemed to change, and he grew as enthusiastic as a Rabinical master, chaunting the pages of prophecy."[55]

It does not appear that Bethune English's critique of Christianity won many supporters. According to Knapp's biographical sketch, written after Bethune English's death, the ex-minister joined the Marine Corps and was sent to the Middle East, where he exchanged his American commission for a position in the Egyptian army. He peppered his new employers with imaginative suggestions, including a modernized version of the "chariot armed with scythes, after the manner of the ancients." Bethune English's war machine "was to be propelled with horses, under bullet-proof cover, in the rear." In other words, the first American disciple of Rabbi Isaac also invented what could be considered a prototype of the armored tank. Alas, Knapp reports, "in trying the machine it was dashed against a stone house in Grand Cairo, and destroyed, but he constantly maintained, that if he could have commanded an American stage driver, it would have gone well, and would have been a most destructive engine of war."[56] Bethune English subsequently published an account of the Egyptian campaign along the Upper Nile in which he had participated.[57] During the 1820s, the US government employed him as a secret agent in the Ottoman Empire. President John Quincy Adams apparently liked him, "notwithstanding his eccentricities, approaching to insanity." He died in

Washington, DC, in 1828.[58] Everett, his first opponent, went on to an illustrious career as an educator and statesman. He became the president of Harvard, a cabinet member, a senator, and a great orator who gave the two-hour-long address at Gettysburg that overshadowed Abraham Lincoln's brief words in 1863. In his later years, however, Everett never returned to the subject of his dispute with Bethune English.

Bethune English's critique of Christianity, inspired by his reading of Rabbi Isaac, was reprinted in 1839 in an edition whose title page said that it was "for the subscribers." We do not know who organized this reprinting, which is identical in content to the original 1813 edition but far more common in American libraries, or why they decided to revive the work. English-speaking readers still did not have access to a direct translation of the *Chizzuk Emunah* for some years afterward. A toned-down and truncated edition of *Chizzuk Emunah*, translated by Moses Mocatta and titled *Faith Strengthened*, appeared in London in 1851, with the strange news on the cover that it was "printed, but not published," an indication that Jews were still fearful of being identified with such an outspoken critique of the Christian scriptures. Instructions stated that it was for Jewish students only. If non-Jews came across it, they were to return it to the Jewish community immediately. Mocatta's translation is still being issued in various forms, into the present century.[59] To date, no more accurate or complete English translation has been undertaken.

Rabbi Isaac's arguments continued to circulate around the globe in the nineteenth century. A Hebrew edition was produced in Calcutta in 1836, but the Malabar Jews on the east coast of India already had their own edition, which they presented to Christian missionaries upon their arrival.[60] Several Ladino editions were also produced in the 1830s. The arguments in the *Chizzuk Emunah* reappeared in America in the 1870s, being set forth by a recent arrival from Jamaica, Frederic de Sola, who was being annoyed by Christians trying to convert him. He put out a truncated version of the text to defend himself and other Jews in his situation.[61]

In the meantime, Isaac of Troki's influence went in several directions in nineteenth-century Germany. First, with the emancipation of the Jews, people could examine aspects of Jewish history that had been overlooked earlier. Among those trying to find a rationale for giving up orthodoxy was Abraham Geiger, who is usually credited with being the founder of

Reform Judaism in Germany and who was interested in exploring various forms of Jewish belief. His studies brought him to examine the Karaites and the contribution of Rabbi Isaac ben Abraham of Troki. As part of the opposition to orthodoxy, he tried to show the value of some of the Karaite contributions, and of the rabbi's criticisms of Christianity.[62] Geiger's contemporary, Heinrich Graetz, observed that Isaac of Troki's work was the "only book by a Karaite author worth reading." He also noted the use that rationalist critics of Christianity had made of the rabbi's arguments.[63]

Geiger was opposed by David Deutsch, a rabbi credited with reviving orthodoxy in Germany, who also noted Rabbi Isaac's text and made it key to understanding both Judaism and Christianity. He edited a new translation into German, as well as a much revised Hebrew text based on the study of many manuscripts. Deutsch's edition was first published privately in 1865, but in 1873, when the unification of Germany had guaranteed Jews full citizenship throughout the country, Deutsch published a second edition that circulated much more widely and remains the only modern version of the full text of the *Chizzuk Emunah* available in any Western language. Deutsch's translation is nearly twice as long as the abridged Mocatta text that remains the standard English version. Whereas Mocatta concentrated on Rabbi Isaac's defense of Jewish interpretations of the Old Testament and omitted some of the work's more stinging condemnations of Christianity, such as Rabbi Isaac's comparison of Christian beliefs to those of the ancient pagans, the fuller version of the work in Deutsch's edition makes clear how direct and outspoken Rabbi Isaac was in his criticism of the New Testament.

In his introduction, Deutsch made it clear that his motivation for publishing a German translation of the entire text of the *Chizzuk Emunah* was to counter the pressures on Jews from Christian missionaries. It upset him that "from the Jewish side, no defense has been forthcoming." He recognized that an increasing number of Jews no longer knew Hebrew and were therefore unable to read the various editions of the work in that language. He also recognized that parts of the book would be offensive to Christians. "I would gladly have toned down many of the author's expressions," he wrote, but "this would have contradicted the duty of a translator." In any event, Christians already knew what Rabbi Isaac had to say, thanks to the availability of Wagenseil's Latin translation.[64]

Whereas nineteenth-century Jews used the *Chizzuk Emunah* to defend themselves against Christian conversion attempts, Christian evangelists continued to study it with an eye toward overcoming Jewish objections to their faith. A Protestant scholar of early Jewish and Christian materials, Hermann Strack of Berlin, who trained many of the leading missionaries to the Jews active at the end of the nineteenth century, proposed to publish a thorough refutation of Rabbi Isaac in the 1880s, but the project, perhaps meant as a response to Deutsch's German translation, was never carried out. Several decades later, however, an English writer, A. Lukyn Williams, took up the task. Strack contributed a preface to Lukyn Williams' *Christian Evidences for Jewish People*, saying that "It will prove useful to Christian readers who may be at a loss how to answer the objections raised in the *Chizzuk Emunah*."[65] Christian evangelists continue to republish Lukyn Williams' work; the most recent edition appeared in 1998, with a cover blurb billing it as "the foremost response to Isaac of Troki published to date." Christian missionary groups such as the Jews for Jesus continue to regard Rabbi Isaac as a dangerous opponent and to refute his arguments.[66]

While Christians continue to concern themselves with Rabbi Isaac's work, modern Jews have also helped keep it alive. In the past few decades, three different reissues of the 1851 Mocatta English text have appeared, put out to counteract conversionist activity. The well-known Jewish publishing house Ktav issued an American edition in 1970, with an introduction by Trude Weiss-Rosmarin, and an English-language publisher in Jerusalem reissued the work in 1999, with an introduction calling it "the most solid and comprehensive defense of the Jewish faith against the challenge of Christian dogma."[67]

Even in the twentieth century, Rabbi Isaac's arguments have also continued to serve secularists who reject all versions of revealed religion. One of the last discoveries about the rabbi's influence that Richard and Jeremy Popkin shared before Richard's death was the realization that Richard's wife, Juliet, Jeremy's mother, had an ancestor who was also a reader of the *Chizzuk Emunah*. Juliet Popkin's paternal grandfather, Abraham Greenstone, had been part of the great East European Jewish migration to America at the end of the nineteenth century. An advocate of pacifism and socialism, he worked diligently to write a book refuting belief in God, which he finally published at his own expense in 1930, under the title *Sound Reason versus Blind Faith*. Reading Greenstone's chapter-and-verse critique of the Gospels leaves little doubt that Rabbi Isaac was one of his inspirations.[68]

Thus, for over four hundred years, this text by a heretical Jewish author has appeared, and reappeared, and reappeared, and has been used as ammunition by Christians, anti-trinitarians, rationalists, and Jews. George Bethune English's *The Grounds of Christianity Examined*, the first work in English to give extensive publicity to Rabbi Isaac's arguments, has gone largely unnoticed. This new edition of Bethune English's tract documents an important episode in American debates about the truth of Christianity and provides important evidence of the way in which Rabbi Isaac's *Chizzuk Emunah* helped fuel disputes in the New World. One can hope that this republication of Bethune English's work will spur interest in the history of American skepticism about biblical revelation and in the continuing impact of the anti-Christian polemic first written in Lithuania in 1593.

NOTES

1. George Bethune English, *The Grounds of Christianity Examined, by Comparing the New Testament with the Old*, "Reprinted for the subscribers," (N.p., 1839). This edition appears to be identical to the original 1813 edition, printed in Boston. There was another reprint edition in 1852. See pp. 55 in this volume.

2. Samuel Cary, *Review of a Book Entitled 'The Grounds of Christianity Examined, by Comparing the New Testament with the Old,' by George Bethune English, A.M.* (Boston: Isaiah Thomas, Jr., 1813), p. 26.

3. See p. 65 in this volume.

4. English, *Grounds*, pp. 57–58.

5. For a short discussion of the religious atmosphere in sixteenth-century Lithuania, see M. Waysblum, "Isaac of Troki and Christian Controversy in the XVI Century," *Journal of Jewish Studies* 3 (1952): 62–77.

6. Friedrich Niewöhner, "Der Karäer Isaak von Troki und seine Widerlegung der Antitrinitarier 1585," in Mihály Balálz and Gizella Keserü, eds., *György Enyedi and Central European Unitarianism in the 16–17th Centuries* (Budapest: Balassi Kiadó, 2000), pp. 253–57.

7. Isaac of Troki, *Befestigung im Glauben von Rabbi Jizchak, Sohn Abrahams*, 2nd ed., ed. David Deutsch (Sohrau and Breslau: Commissionsverlag von H. Skutsch, 1873 [orig. 1865]), p. 284.

8. Isaac of Troki, *Faith Strengthened*, trans. Moses Mocatta (New York: Ktav, 1970 [orig. 1851]), p. 5.

9. See Jean-Pierre Osier, *L'Evangile du ghetto* (Paris: Berg International, 1984).

10. Isaac of Troki, *Faith Strengthened*, p. 89.

11. Isaac of Troki, *Befestigung im Glauben*, p. 29.

12. Abraham Geiger, *Isaak Troki. Ein Apologet des Judenthums am Ende des sechsehnten Jahrhunderts* (Breslau: J. U. Kern, 1853), p. 30; Julius K. Gutmann, "A Study of Isaac ben Abraham's *Hizzuk Emunah*," thesis, Hebrew Union College, 1935, pp. 23–24.

13. M. Kayserling, ed., *Biblioteca espanola-portugueza-judaica: Dictionnaire bibliographique des auteurs juifs, de leurs ouvrages espagnols et portugais et des oeuvres sur et contre les juifs et le judaisme* (Nieuwkoop: B. de Graaf, 1961; reprint of 1890 original), pp. 14–15.

14. Richard H. Popkin, "The Dispersion of Bodin's Dialogues in England, Holland and Germany," *Journal of the History of Ideas* 49 (1988): 157–160.

15. Theodoricus Hackspan, *Tractatus de usu librorum Rabbinicorum: Prodromus Apologiae pro Christianis adversus Lipmannum triumphantem.*

16. Johann Müller, *Judaismus oder Judenthumb, das ist ausfürhlicher Bericht von des jüdischen Wolckes Unglauben, Blindheit und Verstockung*, 2nd ed. (Hamburg: Härtel, 1707).

17. Jonathan Israel, *European Jewry in the Age of Mercantilism*, rev. ed. (Oxford: Clarendon Press, 1989), p. 64.

18. Yosef Kaplan, *From Christianity to Judaism: The Story of Isaac Orobio de Castro* (New York: Littman Library, 1989), p. 187.

19. David Katz, *Philosemitism and the Readmission of the Jews to England, 1603–1655* (Oxford: Clarendon Press, 1992), pp. 52–54.

20. This story may have been based on a pamphlet published in England in 1655 titled *A Narrative of the Proceedings of a Great Councel [sic] of Jews, Assembled in the Plain of Ageda in Hungaria, about 30 Leagues Distant from Buda, to Examine the Scriptures concerning Chirst; on the 12th of October 1650* (London: Richard Moon, 1655), which reported the proceedings of an imaginary Jewish council that the author suggested might be "a preparative and hopeful sign of the Jews' Conversion." See Richard H. Popkin, "The Fictional Jewish Council of 1650: A Great English Pipedream," *Jewish History* 5, no. 2 (Fall 1991): 7–22.

21. Richard H. Popkin, *Isaac La Peyrère (1596–1676): His Life, Work and Influence* (Leiden: Brill, 1987), pp. 95–96.

22. Richard H. Popkin, "The First College for Jewish Studies," *Revue des Etudes Juives* 143 (1984): 351–64, and Richard H. Popkin, "Hartlib, Dury, and the Jews," in *Samuel Hartlib and Universal Reformation: Studies in Intellectual Communication*, ed. Mark Greengrass, Michael Leslie, and Timothy Raylor (Cambridge: Cambridge University Press, 1994), pp. 118–36.

23. A. Lewis Shane, "Jacob Judah Leon of Amsterdam (1602–1675) and His Models of the Temple of Solomon and the Tabernacle," *Acta Quatuor Coronati* (AQC), pp. 146–49; Richard H. Popkin, "Another Spinoza," *Journal of the History of Philosophy* 34 (1996): 133–34.

24. See Richard H. Popkin, "The Lost Tribes, the Caraites and the English Millenarians," *Journal for Jewish Studies* 37 (1986): 213–27.

25. The full text of Dury's discussion appears in Richard H. Popkin, "Can One Be a True Christian and a Faithful Follower of the Law of Moses? The Answer of John Dury," in *Secret Conversions to Judaism in Early Modern Europe*, ed. Martin Mulsow and Richard H. Popkin (Leiden: Brill, 2004), pp. 33–50.

26. On Saul Levi Morteira, see Richard H. Popkin, "Jewish Anti-Christian Arguments as a Source of Irreligion from the Seventeenth to the Early Nineteenth Century," in *Atheism from the Reformation to the Enlightenment*, ed. Michael Hunter and David Wootton (Oxford: Clarendon Press, 1992), pp. 168–71.

27. Cited in Gutmann, "Study," pp. 24–25.

28. Johann Christoph Wagenseil, *Tela Ignea Satanae sive arcani & horribiles judaeorum adversus Christum Deum & christianam religionem libri* (Altdorf, 1681). Some manuscripts of the translation apparently circulated without Wagenseil's refutation, and it is to one of these that Edward Everett refers during the dispute with Bethune English.

29. Cited in Gutmann, "Study," p. 25.

30. Some scholars, such as Hans Joachim Schoeps, have regarded Wagenseil as relatively sympathetic to the Jews, while others, including Frank Manuel, have counted him among the ancestors of anti-Semitism. See Schoeps, *Philosemitismus im Barock. Religions und Geistesgeschichtliche Untersuchungen* (Tübingen: J. C. B. Mohr, 1952), pp. 12, 67, 165; and Manuel, *The Broken Staff: Judaism through Christian Eyes* (Cambridge, MA: Harvard University Press, 1992), pp. 150–51. Richard Popkin died before being able to consult Peter Blastenbrei, *Johann Christoph Wagenseil und seine Stellung zum Judentum* (Erlangen: Harald Fischer Verlag, 2004), whose author gives a more extended discussion of Wagenseil's attitude toward Judaism than any earlier scholar. Blastenbrei shows that Wagenseil

had extensive contacts with Jews, that he argued for the right of Jews to publish their own religious works, that he thoroughly refuted ritual-murder accusations, and that he opposed efforts to expel the Jews from German communities. Acccording to Blastenbrei, Wagenseil recognized that Jews would not accept Christian arguments for the divinity of Jesus or the doctrine of the trinity. Late in his life, he did adopt millenarian views and came to believe that Jews would be converted in connection with the Second Coming. See also Paul Gerhard Ariug, *'Wage du, zu irren und zu traumen': Juden and Christen unterwegs. Theologiscke Biographien, biographische theologie in christlich-jüdischen Dialog der Barockzeit* (Leipzig: Verlag Wissenschaft und Politik, 1992).

31. Among the early responses to the book were B. H. Gebhardi, *Centum Loca Novi Testamenti, quae R. Isaac ben Abraham, in suo Chizzuk Emunah, i.e. Munimine Fidei depravaverat, vindicata* (1699), and Jacobus Gousset, *Jesu Christi Veritas Salutifera, demonstrata in confutatione Libri Chizzouk Emounah, a R. Isaco scripti* (1712).

32. Martin Mulsow, *Moderne aus dem Untergrund. Radikale Frühaufklärung in Deutschland 1680–1720* (Hamburg: Felix Meiner Verlag, 2002), pp. 49–50.

33. Richard Kidder, *A Demonstration of the Messias. In which the Truth of the Christian Religion is defended, especially against The Jews. Part II. By the Right Reverend Father in God, Richard Lord Bishop of Bath and Wells* (London: printed by J. H. for W. Rogers at the Sun, and M. Wotton at the Three Daggers in Fleetstreet, 1699).

34. Mulsow, *Moderne aus dem Untergrund*, p. 51.

35. Jacques Gousset, *Jesu Christi Evangeliique veritas salutifera, demonstrata in confutatione libri Chizzuk-Emunah a R. Isaaco scripti*, ed. Arnold Borst (Amsterdam, 1712); see A. Fürst, *Christen und Juden: Licht- und Schattenbilder aus Kirche und Synagoge* (Strauburg: Strauburger Druckerei und Verlagsanstalt, 1892), pp. 109–14.

36. Richard Popkin had studied Bishop Huet extensively, but we have been unable to find a precise reference for this claim in the notes he left for this essay when he died.

37. Pierre Bayle, "Weile, Frideric Ragstat de," in Pierre Bayle, *Dictionnaire historique et critique*, 5th ed. (Amsterdam: P. Brunel et al., 1740), 4: 492.

38. Richard H. Popkin, "Jacques Basnage's *Histoire des Juifs* and the Biblioteca Sarraziana," *Studia Rosenthaliana* 21 (1987): 154–62.

39. Jacques Basnage, *Histoire des Juifs, depuis Jésus Christ jusqu'à present*, 9 vols. (1716 ed.), 9: 937.

40. Anthony Collins, *A Discourse on the Grounds and Reasons of Christianity* (London, 1724), pp. 82–83.

41. Voltaire, *Mélanges*, 3: 344, cited in David Deutsch, *Befestigung im Glauben*, pp. vi–vii.

42. Voltaire, *Philosophical Dictionary* (London: W. Dugdale, 1843), 2: 367. On Voltaire's attitude toward the *Chizzuk Emunah*, see Joshua Szechtman, "Voltaire on Isaac Troki's *Hizzuk Emunah*," *Jewish Quarterly Review* 48 (July 1957): 53–57.

43. Richard Popkin did not provide a citation for this assertion.

44. David Hume, *Enquiries Concerning the Human Understanding and Concerning the Principles of Morals*, ed. L. A. Selby-Bigge, Sect. X, Part II (Oxford: Clarendon Press, 1951), p. 130.

45. Joseph Priestley, *Letters to the Jews; Inviting Them to an Amicable Discussion of the Evidences of Christianity* (New York: J. Harrisson, 1794 [orig. 1786]), p. 34.

46. On David Levi, see Richard H. Popkin, "David Levi, Anglo-Jewish Theologian," *Jewish Quarterly Review* 87 (July–October 1996): 79–101.

47. Geiger, *Isaak Troki*, p. 32.

48. Johann Christoph Wolf, *Bibliothecae Hebraeae* (Hamburg, 1733).

49. Hermann Samuel Reimarus, *Apologie oder Schutzschrift für die vernünftigen Verehrer Gottes*, ed. Gerhard Alexander (Frankfurt, 1972), 2: 268.

50. Cary, *Review of Book Entitled 'The Grounds of Christianity Examined,'* p. 16.

51. Henry Ware Jr., to Henry Ware Sr., October 20, 1813, cited in Paul Revere Frothingham, *Edward Everett: Orator and Statesman* (Boston and New York: Houghton Mifflin, 1925), p. 29.

52. Seixas letters in David da Sola Poole, *Portraits Etched in Stone* (New York: Columbia University Press, 1952), pp. 367–68. I am grateful to Professor Jonathan Sarna for providing me with this reference (—*JDP*).

53. George Bethune English, *A Letter Respectfully Addressed to the Reverend Mr. Channing, relative to His Two Sermons on Infidelity* (Boston: Printed for the author, 1813), p. 26.

54. George Bethune English, *Five Pebbles from the Brook, Being a Reply to 'A Defence of Christianity' Written by Edward Everett* (Philadelphia: Printed for the author, 1824), p. v.

55. Samuel L. Knapp, *American Biography*, pt. VI of *The Treasury of Knowledge* (New York: Conner and Cooke, 1833), 6: 96. Knapp, like English, came from Massachusetts. He pursued various careers but was best known for his pioneering history of American literature. The *Dictionary of American Biography*'s entry on him comments that "as a biographer he is ornate, laudatory, and patriotic, and wholly untrustworthy." George Harvey Genzmer, "Samuel L. Knapp," *Dictionary of American Biography* (New York: Charles Scribner's

Sons, 1933), 10: 452.

56. Knapp, *American Biography*, 6: 94.

57. George Bethune English, *A Narrative of the Expedition to Dongola and Sennaar, under the Command of His Excellence Ismael Pasha, undertaken by order of His Highness Mehemmed Ali Pasha, Viceroy of Egypt*, "first American edition" (Boston: Wells and Lilly, 1823).

58. W. L. W——t, Jr., "English, George Bethune," *Dictionary of American Biography*, 3: 165.

59. Isaac Troki, *Faith Strengthened*, trans. Moses Mocatta (New York: Ktav, 1970). According to David Deutsch, who translated the entire text into German in 1865, Mocatta had had only a handful of copies of his work printed, to give out to trusted friends. *Befestigung im Glauben*, p. 438.

60. Waysblum, "Isaak of Troki," p. 62.

61. Frederic de Sola Mendes, *Defence, Not Defiance. A Hebrew's Reply to the Missionaries* (New York: Office of the Independent Hebrew, 1876). De Sola Mendes, the son of a rabbi, was born in Jamaica in 1850. He studied in England and Germany and was ordained as a rabbi in 1873. He moved to the United States to take a rabbinical post in New York in 1874 and was an important figure in American Jewish life for the next several decades.

62. Geiger, *Isaak Troki*, passim.

63. Heinrich Graetz, *History of the Jews*, vol. IV (Philadelphia: The Jewish Publication Society of America, 1894), 4: 648–49.

64. David Deutsch, "Vorrede des Herausgebers und Uebersetzers," in *Befestigung im Glauben*, p. iii.

65. Hermann L. Strack, "Preface," in A. Lukyn Williams, *Christian Evidences for Jewish People*, 2 vols. (Eugene, OR: Wipf and Stock, 1998 [orig. 1911]), 1: xii.

66. See, for example, Rich Robinson, "When Opposition Knocks," (orig. pub. 1 July 1992).

67. Trude Weiss-Rosmarin, introduction to Isaac of Troki, *Faith Strengthened* (New York: Ktav, 1970), pp. v–xiv; Zeev Peter Breier, introduction to Isaac of Troki, *Faith Strengthened* (Jerusalem: Kest-Lebovitz Jewish Heritage and Roots Libary, 1999), p. ix.

68. Abraham Greenstone, *Sound Reason versus Blind Faith* (Bronx, NY: A. Greenstone, 1930).

THE GROUNDS OF CHRISTIANITY EXAMINED

by Comparing the New Testament with the Old.

By George Bethune English, A. M.

"First understand—then judge."
"Bring forth the people blind, although they have eyes;
"And deaf, although they have ears.
"Let them produce their witnesses, that they may be justified;
"Or let them hear in their turn, and say, THIS IS TRUE."

ISAIAH

TO
THE INTELLIGENT AND THE CANDID,
WHO ARE
WILLING TO LISTEN TO EVERY OPINION
THAT IS SUPPORTED BY REASON;
NOT AVERSE TO BRINGING THEIR OWN OPINIONS
TO THE TEST OF EXAMINATION;

THIS BOOK
IS RESPECTFULLY DEDICATED
BY
THE AUTHOR.

CONTENTS

43

PREFACE

The celebrated Dr. Price, in his valuable "Observations on the Importance of the American Revolution," addressed to the people of the United States, observes, that "It is a common opinion, that there are some Doctrines so sacred, and others of so bad a tendency, that no Public Discussion of them ought to be allowed." Were this a right opinion, *all the persecution that has ever been practised* would be *justified*. For if it is a part of the duty of civil magistrates to prevent the discussion of such Doctrines, they must, in doing this, act on *their own judgments* of the *nature* and *tendency* of Doctrines; and, consequently, they must have a right to prevent the discussion of all Doctrines, which they *think* to be too sacred for discussion, or too dangerous in their tendency; and this right they must exercise in the only way in which civil power is capable of exercising it; "by inflicting penalties upon all who oppose sacred Doctrines, or who maintain pernicious opinions." In *Mahometan* countries, therefore, magistrates would have a right to silence, and punish all who oppose the divine mission of *Mahomet*, a doctrine there reckoned of the most sacred nature. The like is true of the doctrines of *transubstantiation*, worship of the Virgin Mary, &c. &c. in *Popish* countries; and of the doctrines of the *Trinity, Satisfaction*, etc. in *Protestant* countries. All such laws are *right*, if the opinion I have mentioned is right. But in reality, civil power has nothing to do in such matters, and civil governors go miserably out of their proper province, whenever they take upon them the care of truth, or the support of any doctrinal points. They are not judges of truth, and if they pretend to decide about it, they will decide wrong. This, all the countries under heaven think of the application of civil power to doctrinal points in every country, *but their own*. It is indeed, superstition, idolatry, and nonsense, that civil power at present supports almost everywhere, under the idea of supporting sacred truth, and opposing dangerous error. Would not therefore its perfect neutrality be the greatest blessing?—Would not the interest of truth gain unspeakably, were all the Rulers of States to aim at nothing but keeping the peace; or did they consider themselves bound to take care, not of the *future*, but the *present* interest of man; not of their *souls*, and of their *faith*, but of their *persons* and *property*; not of any *ecclesiastical*, but *secular* matters only?

'All the experience of *past time* proves, that the consequence of allowing civil power to judge of the nature and tendency of Doctrines, must be making it a hindrance to the progress of truth, and an enemy to the improvement of the world.'

'I would extend these observations to all points of faith, however sacred they may be deemed. Nothing *reasonable* can suffer by discussion. All Doctrines, *really* sacred, must be *clear*, and incapable of being opposed with success.'

'That *immoral tendency* of Doctrines which has been urged as a reason against allowing the public discussion of them, may be either *avowed* and *direct*; or only a *consequence* with which they *are charged*. If it is *avowed* and *direct*, such doctrines *certainly will not spread*; the principles rooted in human nature will *resist them*, and the advocates of them will be soon *disgraced*. If, on the contrary, it is only a *consequence* with which a Doctrine is *charged*, it should be considered how apt all parties are to charge the doctrines they *oppose* with bad tendencies. It is well known, that *Calvinists*, and *Arminians*, *Trinitarians* and *Socinians*, *Fatalists* and *Free-Willers*, are continually exclaiming against one another's opinions, as dangerous and licentious. Even Christianity itself could not, at its first introduction, escape this accusation. The professors of it were considered as *Atheists*, because they opposed Pagan Idolatry; and their religion was, on this account, reckoned a destructive and pernicious enthusiasm. If, therefore, the Rulers of a State are to prohibit the propagation of all doctrines, in which *they apprehend* immoral tendencies, an opening will be made, as I have before observed, for *every species of persecution*. There will be no doctrine, however *true*, or *important*, the avowal of which will not, in *some country or other*, be subjected to civil penalties."[1]

These observations bear the stamp of good sense, and their truth has been abundantly confirmed by experience. And it is the peculiar honor of the United States, that in conformity with the principles of these observations, perfect freedom of opinion, and of speech are here *established by law*, and are the *birthright* of every citizen thereof. *Our* country is the *only one* which has not been guilty of the folly of establishing the ascendency of one set of religious opinions, and persecuting, or tolerating all others; and which does not permit any man to harass his neighbour because he thinks differently from himself. In consequence of these excellent institutions, difference of religious sentiment makes here no breach in private friend-ship, and works no danger to the public security. This is as it should be; for, in matters of opinion, especially with regard to so important a thing as *Religion*, it is every man's *natural right*, and duty, to think for himself; and to judge upon such evidence as he can procure, after he has used his best endeavours to get information. Human decisions are of no weight in this matter, for another man has no more right to determine what *my* opin-ions shall be, than I have to determine what *another* man's opinions shall be. It is amazing that one man can *dare* to presume he has such a right over another; and that any man can be so weak, and credulous, as to imagine, that another has such a right over *him*.

As it is every man's *natural right*, and *duty* to think and judge for himself in matters of opinion; so he should be allowed freely to bring for-ward, and defend his opinions, and to endeavour, when he judges proper, to convince others also of their truth.

For unless all men are allowed freely to profess their opinions, the means of information, with respect to opinions, must in a great measure be wanting; and just inquiries into their truth be almost impracticable; and, by consequence, our natural *right*, and *duty* to think, and judge for ourselves, must be rendered almost nugatory, or be subverted, for want of materials whereon to employ our minds. A man by himself, without com-munication with other minds, can make no great progress in knowledge; and besides, an individual is *indisposed* to use his own strength, when an undisturbed laziness, ignorance, and prejudice give him full satisfaction as to the truth of his opinions.—But if there be a *free profession*, or com-munication of sentiments, every man will have an opportunity of acquainting himself with all that can be known from others. And many for their own satisfaction will make enquiries, and in order to ascertain the truth of opinions, will desire to know all that can be said on any question.

If such liberty of professing, and teaching, be not allowed, error, if authorized, will keep its ground; and truth, if dormant, will never be brought to light; or, if authorized, will be supported on a false, and absurd foundation, and such as would equally support error; and, if received on the ground of *authority*, will not be in the least meritorious to its professors.

Besides, not to *encourage* capable and honest men to profess, and defend their opinions when different from ours, is to *distrust* the truth of our own opinions, and to *fear* the light. Such conduct must, in a country of sense, and learning, increase the number of unbelievers, already so greatly complained of: who, if they see matters of opinion not allowed to be professed, and impartially debated, think, justly perhaps, that they have *foul play*, and therefore reject many things as false, and ill grounded, which otherwise they might perhaps receive as truths.

The grand principle of men considered as having relation to the Deity, and under an obligation to be religious, is, that they ought to consult their reason, and seek every where for the best instruction; and of *Christians*, and *Protestants*, the duty, and *professed* principle is, to consult reason, and the Scripture, as the rule of their faith and practice.

But how can these, which are practical principles, be duly put in practice, unless all be at liberty, at all times, and in all points, to consider, and debate with others, (as well as with themselves,) what reason and Scripture say; and to profess, and act openly, according to what they are convinced they say?—How can we become better informed with regard to religion, than by using the best means of information? which consist in consulting reason, and Scripture, and calling in the aid of others. And of what use is it to consult reason, and Scripture *at all*, as any means of information, if we are not, upon conviction, to follow their dictates?

No man has any reason to apprehend any ill consequences to *truth*, (for which alone he ought to have any concern) from *free enquiry* and *debate*. For *truth* is not a thing to dread examination, but when *fairly* proposed to an unbiased understanding, is like light to the eye; it *must* distinguish itself from *error*, as *light* does distinguish itself from *darkness*. For, while free debate is allowed, truth is in no danger, for it will never want a *professor* thereof, nor an *advocate* to offer some plea in its behalf. And it can never be wholly banished, but where human decisions, backed by human power, carry all before them.

We ought to examine the *foundations* of opinions, not only that we may attain the discovery of *truth*; but we ought to do so on this account, because that it is our *duty*; and the way to recommend ourselves to *the favour of God*. For opinions, how true soever, when the effect of *education*, or *tradition*, or *interest*, or *passion*, can *never* recommend a man to God. For those ways have no merit in them, and are the worst a man can possibly take to obtain *truth*; and therefore, though they may be objects of *forgiveness*, they can never be of *reward* from Him.

Having premised these observations in order to persuade and dispose the reader to be candid, I will now declare the *motives* which induced me to submit to the consideration of the intelligent, the contents of this volume. The author has spared, he thinks, no pains to arrive at certain Truth in matters of *Religion*; the sense of which is what distinguishes man from the brute; and in this most important subject that can employ the human understanding, he has been particularly desirous to become acquainted with the Grounds and Doctrines of the *Christian Religion*; and nothing but the difficulties, which he in this volume lays before the public, stagger his faith in it.

It may perhaps add to the interest the Reader may take in this work, to inform him, that the Author *was* a believer in the Religion of the New Testament, after what he conceived to be a sufficient examination of its evidence for a divine origin. He had terminated an examination of the controversy with the Deists to his own satisfaction; i. e., he felt convinced that their objections were not insurmountable, when he turned his attention to the consideration of the ancient, and obscure controversy between the Christians and the Jews. His curiosity was deeply interested to examine a subject, in truth, so little known, and to ascertain the causes, and the reasons, which had prevented a people more *interested in the truth* of Christianity *than any other* from believing it: and he sat down to the subject without any suspicion that the examination would not terminate in convincing him still more *in favour* of what were then his opinions. After a long, thorough, and startling examination of their Books, together with all the answers to them he could obtain from a Library amply furnished in this respect, he was finally, very reluctantly, compelled to feel persuaded, by proofs he could neither refute nor evade, that how easily soever Christians might answer the Deists, so called, the Jews were clearly too hard for them. Because they set the Old and New Testaments in opposition, and reduce Christians to this fatal dilemma.—Either the Old Testament contains a Revelation from God, or it does not. If it does, then the New Testament cannot be from God, because it is palpably, and importantly repugnant to the Old Testament in Doctrine, and some other things. Now Jews and Christians, each of them, admit the Old Testament as containing a divine Revelation; consequently the Jews *cannot*, and Christians *ought not*, to receive and allow any thing as a Revelation from God which *flatly contradicts* a *former*, by them *acknowledged*, Revelation: *because* it cannot be supposed that God will *contradict himself*. On the other hand—if the Old Testament be *not* from God, still the New Testament must go down, because it asserts that the Old Testament *is* a Revelation from God, and builds upon it as a foundation. And if the foundation fail, how can the house stand? The Author pledges himself to the Reader, to prove that they establish this dilemma completely. And he cannot help thinking, that there is reason to believe, that if both sides of this strangely neglected controversy had been made public in times past, and become known, that the consequences would have been long ago fatal *at least* to the New Testament.

But though he believes that the New Testament cannot stand a close examination, when its pretensions are tested by the Old Testament, yet he is not prepared to affirm, that the Old Testament itself is invulnerable. In fact, so much can be said, and such a strong case can be made out of both sides of the question relating to its supernatural claims, that though he shall always respect the Old Testament as the venerable mother of the doctrine of the Unity of God, and the source from whence arose Christianity and Mahometanism, and as undoubtedly the most ancient, and curious monument of antiquity we possess in the shape of a Book; yet, with regard to its supernatural claims, he has not as yet been able to come to a decision satisfactory to himself. Whether however the Old Testament be of divine authority or not, the argument he carries on is just as strong in one case as the other; since it is *believed to be* of divine authority by both Jews and Christians; and the reasoning in the volume sets out with taking for granted this, which is acknowledged on both sides of the controversy, that is the subject of the Book.*

The Author has been earnestly dissuaded from making public the contents of this volume on account of apprehended mischievous consequences. He thought, however, that the age of *pious frauds* ought to be

---

*There is nothing which can more readily induce a man of feeling, and benevolence, to *hope* that the supernatural claims of the Old Testament *may* be true, than the promises contained in its Prophecies. The splendid descriptions contained in the Old Testament of the renovation of the earth, and its restoration to a paradisiacal state; and the promises it holds out of the happiness of the human race upon it, "when the earth is to be all Paradise, far more blessed than that of Eden, and far happier days," are prospects, however remote, or *problematical*, so delightful to the mind grieved with the misery and sufferings of the present state of things, that the good man will certainly wish that it *might be* so. The Philosopher, while he assents that such things *may* happen, (because an eternity is to come; because there is no repugnance nor impossibility in the nature of things to prevent; and because the attributes of God seem to require that something like them should take place some time or other) yet must feel sorry, that the ancient Book which holds out such splendid prospects should not be attended with demonstrative evidence of its divine authority.

It is certainly a great pity that the Old Testament is a subject that admits of such a strong case being made out of either side of the question with regard to its supernatural claims. A very great deal indeed (besides what is about to be mentioned) can be alleged in favour of its claims to a Divine Origin. The vast antiquity of the Book itself—the correct state in which it has been preserved, and handed down, through a series of so many ages—the interesting nature of its contents—the venerable simplicity of its style—the solemn sublimity of its poetry—the manifest and unrivalled excellence of its moral precepts (from whence was derived all *that is practicable* in the morality of the New Testament and the Koran)—the foresight and sagacity displayed in its political and ceremonial arrangements, in order to keep the Hebrews *distinct* from other nations, that they might for ages continue to answer the avowed and grand purpose of giving them their law, viz. "that they might be to all nations the witnesses of the unity of God,—that sublime and peculiar distinction of their religious creed,—the fact that the only nations on the globe which profess to believe in the Unity of God *derived* that belief from the *posterity* of ABRAHAM, viz. from Moses, Jesus Christ, and Mahomet; and the equally certain fact, that Christianity and Mahometanism, the only established Religions, besides the Mosaic, that have the least claims to rationality, were derived from the Old Testament and were founded by *descendants* from that Patriarch,—the singular, and perfectly unique character, and history of the Hebrew nation,—that it has subsisted from times of such immense antiquity, and has survived so many horrible catastrophes; and that it still subsists one and the same, wherever scattered, or however oppressed. Add to this the numerous prophecies of their sacred books, with regard to some of which it certainly *looks* as if they had been fulfilled.—All these things are so singular, unparalleled, and astonishing, that I should not think much of that man's understanding, nor of his *knowledge of the subject*, who could dogmatically *decide*, that all these circumstances can *be entirely* and *easily* accounted for, by referring them to the *sagacity* of their Lawgiver.

On the other hand, however.—when we are almost disposed to credit the supernatural claims of the Old Testament; when we read of the speaking of Balaam's ass; Joshua's stopping the sun; Jonah's living in the belly of a great fish, &c.; the man of sound judgment would, I should think, be apt to hesitate, and then perhaps settle into persevering doubt.

Since however, neither reason, nor, to do it justice, the Old Testament itself, intimates such scepticism to be criminal in a *Gentile*, we may, without uneasiness, to use the words of Josephus, say "of these things let every one think as he pleases."

past, and their *principle* discarded, at least in *Protestant* countries. Deception and error are always, sooner or later, discovered; and truth, in the long run, both in politics and religion, will never be ultimately harmful. If what the Book states is *true*, it ought to be *known*, if it is *erroneous*, it can, and will be *refuted*.

The Author therefore makes it public, for these reasons, because he thinks, that the matter contained in the Book, is true and important—because he wished, and found it *necessary* to justify himself from contemptible misrepresentations uttered behind his back; and to give to those who know him, good and sufficient reasons for past conduct, of which, those to whom he is known cannot be ignorant; and finally, he thought it right, and proper, and *humane*, to give to the world a work which contained the reasons for the unbelief of the countrymen of Jesus Christ; who for almost eighteen hundred years have been made the unresisting victims of, as the reader will find, groundless misrepresentation, and the most amazing cruelty; because they refused to believe what it was *impossible* that they should believe, on account of reasons their persecutors *did not know*, and *refused* to be informed of.

If the arguments and statements contained in this volume should be *found to be correct*, he believes that every honest and candid man, after his first surprise that they should not have been made known before, will feel for the victims of a mistake so singular, and so ancient as the one which is the subject of the following pages; and will think with the author, that it is time, high time, that the truth should be known, and justice be done to them.*

---

*"Do you know (says Rousseau) of many Christians who have taken the pains to examine with care what the Jews have to say against them. If some persons have seen any thing of the kind, it is in the books of *Christians*. A fine way truly *to get instructed in the arguments of their adversaries!* But what can they do? If any one should dare to publish among us Books in which he openly favours their opinions, we punish the Author, the Editor, the Bookseller. This *policy is convenient*, and sure always to be in the right. *There it a pleasure in refuting people who dare not open their lips.*" Emilius. [The passage Bethune English refers to is in Jean-Jacques Rousseau, *Emile*, book 4, p. 1077, cited from http://projects.ilt.columbia.edu/pedagogies/rousseau/em_eng_bk4.html, but he was using a different translation.] In the same work he says, that "he will never be convinced that the Jews have not something strong to say, till they shall be permitted to speak for themselves without fear and without restraint." It was this hint of Rousseau's which first excited the Author's curiosity with regard to the subject of this Book. [Present-day scholarship usually rates Rousseau as more sympathetic to the Jews than most of the other leading French philosophers of the Enlightenment. See Robert Badinter, *Libres et égaux. L'emancipation des juifs 1789–1791* (Paris: Fayard, 1989), pp. 53–54.]

There is not in existence a more singular instance of the mischievous mistakes arising from taking things *for granted* which require *proof*, than the case before the reader. The world has all along been in total error with regard to the reasons and the motives which have prevented the Hebrew nation from receiving the System of the New Testament. They have been successfully accused of incorrigible blindness and obstinacy; and while volumes upon volumes have been written against them, and the arguments therein contained supported and enforced by the power of the Inquisition, and the oppressions of all Christendom, these unfortunate people have not been *willingly* suffered to offer to the world one word in their own defence.—They have not been *allowed*, after hearing with patience, both arguments, and 'railing accusations' in abundance, *to answer in their turn*; but have been compelled, through the fear of confiscation, persecution, and death, to leave misapprehensions unexplained, and misrepresentations unrefuted.

Is it then to be wondered at, that mankind have considered their adversaries as in the right, and that deserted by reason, and even *their own Scriptures*, they were supported in their opinion only by a blind and pertinacious obstinacy, more worthy of wonder, than of curiosity? Alas! the world did not consider, that nothing was more *easy* than to *confute* people, whose tongues were *frozen by the terror of the Inquisition!!* But, thanks to the good sense of this enlightened age, those times are past and gone. There is now one happy country where freedom of speech is allowed, where every harmless religious opinion is protected by law, and where every opinion is listened to that is supported by reason. The time, I trust, is now come, when the substantial arguments of this oppressed, and, in this respect, certainly calumniated people may be produced, and their reasons set forth, without the fear of harm, and with the hope of a hearing from the intelligent and candid. They, we believe, will be fully convinced, that their adversaries have for so long a time triumphed over them without measure, only because they have been suffered to do so *without contradiction*.

The reader is assured, that, notwithstanding the subject, he will find nothing in this volume but what is considered by the author to be fair and liberal argument; and such, no *honest* man ought to decline looking in the face. He has endeavoured to discuss the important subject of the Book in the most inoffensive manner; for he has no wish, and claims no right, to wound the feelings of those who differ from him in opinion.—There is not, nor ought there to be, a word of *reproach* in it against the moral character of *Jesus Christ*, or the *twelve* Apostles; and the utmost the author attempts to prove, is, that their system was *founded*, not upon fraud and imposture, but upon a *mistake.* After the deaths of Christ and his Apostles, it was indeed aided and supported by very bad means; but its *first* founders, the author believes, were guilty of no other crime than that of being mistaken; a very common one indeed.[2]

He hopes, therefore, that such a discussion as the one now laid before the public, will be *fairly* met, and *fairly* answered, if answered at all; and that recourse will not be had to dishonest and ungentlemanly misrepresentations, and calling names, in order to prevent people from examining things they have a *right* to know, and in order to *blind* and *frighten* the Public—the Jury to which he appeals. It is infallibly true, that the knowledge of truth is, and must be, beneficial to mankind; and that, in the long run, it never was, and never can be harmful. It is equally certain that God would never give a Revelation so slightly founded as to be endangered by any *sophistry of man.* If the Christian system be from God, it will certainly stand, no human power can overthrow it. And therefore no *sincere* Christian who *believes* the New Testament, ought to be *afraid* to meet, half way, the objections of any one who offers them with fairness, and expresses them in decent language; and no *sensible* Christian ought to shut his ears against his neighbour, who respectfully asks "a reason for the faith that is in him."

The Author has been told indeed, that '*supposing the Christian System to be unfounded*, yet that it is reasonable to believe, that the Supreme Being would view any attempts to disturb it with displeasure, on account of its moral effects.' But is not this something like absurdity? Can God have made it *necessary*, that Morals should be founded on *Delusion*, in order that they might be *supported*? Can the God of TRUTH be displeased to have men convinced that they have been mistaken, or imposed upon by Revelations pretended to be from Him, which if in fact *not* from him, must be the offspring either of error or falsehood? And if the Christian System be in truth not from God, can we suppose, that in his eyes its Doctrines with regard to *Him* are atoned for by a few good moral precepts? Can we suppose that that Supreme and awful Being can feel Himself *honoured* in having his creatures made to believe, that He was once nine months in the womb of a woman; that God, the Great and Holy, went through all the impurities of Infancy; that he lived a mendicant in a corner of the Earth, and was finally scourged, and hanged on a Gibbet by his own creatures? If these things be *in truth* all *mistakes*, can we suppose, that God is *pleased* in having them believed of Him? On the contrary, can they, together with the Doctrine of the Trinity, I would respectfully ask, be possibly looked upon by Him (if they *are not true*) otherwise, than as so many—what I forbear to mention. But this is not all. The Reader is requested to consider, that the Christian System is built upon the prostrate necks of the whole Hebrew nation. It is a tree which flourished in a soil watered by their tears; its leaves grew green in an atmosphere filled with their cries, and groans; and its roots have been moistened and fattened with their blood. The ruin, reproach, and sufferings of that People are considered, by its advocates, as the most striking proofs of the Divine authority of the New Testament. And for almost eighteen hundred years the System contained in that Book has been the cause of miseries, and afflictions, to that nation, the most horrible, and unparalleled in the history of man.

Now, if that system be *indeed* Divine, all this may be very well, and as it should be. But, if perchance, it *should turn out* to be *a mistake*, if it be in *truth* not from God, will not then that system be justly chargeable with all those shocking cruelties, which, *on account of it*, have been inflicted on that people?[3]

If that system be *verily*, and *indeed*, founded on a mistake, no language—no indignation can do justice to its guilt in this respect. All its good moral effects are a mere drop of pure water in that *Ocean* of Jewish and Gentile blood it has caused to be shed, by embittering men's minds with groundless prejudices. And if it be not divine, if it be *plainly*, and *demonstrably proved* to have originated in error, who is the man, that after considering what has been suggested, will have the heart to come forward, and coolly say, "that it is better, that a whole nation of men should continue, as heretofore, to be unjustly hated, reproached, cursed, and plundered, and massacred on account of it, *rather* than that the received religious System should be demonstrated to be founded on mistake?" No! if it be *in fact* founded on mistake, every man of honour, honesty, and *humanity*, will say without hesitation—"Let the Delusion (if it is one) be done away! which must be supported at the expense, of Truth, of Justice, and the happiness and respectability of a whole nation, *who are men like ourselves*, and more unfortunate than any others in having already suffered but too much affliction and misery on account of it." No! though the moral effects ascribed to this System of Religion were as good, as great, and *ten times greater*, than they ever have been, or can be, yet, if it *is* a Delusion, it would be absolutely *wicked* to support it, since it is erected upon the sufferings, wretchedness, and oppression, of a people who compose *millions* of the Great Family of Mankind.

It is remarkable that the ablest modern advocates for the Truth, and divine authority of the Gospel, as if they knew of no certain demonstrative proof which could be adduced in a case of so much importance, seem to content themselves, and expect their readers should be satisfied, with an accumulation, of *probable* arguments in its favour. And it has even been said, that the case admits of *no other kind of proof*. If it be so, the Author requests all, so persuaded, to consider for a moment, whether it could be reconciled to any ideas of wisdom in an *earthly* Potentate, if he should send an Ambassador to a foreign state to mediate a negociation of the greatest importance, without furnishing him with *certain, indubitable*, credentials of the *truth* and *authenticity* of *his mission*? And to consider further, whether it be just or seemly, to attribute to the Omniscient, Omnipotent Deity, a degree of weakness and folly which was never yet imputed to any of his human Creatures? for unless men are hardy enough to pass so gross an affront upon the tremendous Majesty of Heaven, the *improbability* that God should delegate the Mediator of a most important Covenant to be proposed to all mankind, without enabling him to give them *clear*, and, in reason, *indisputable* proof of the divine authority of his mission, must ever infinitely *outweigh* the aggregate sum of all the *probabilities*, which can be accumulated in the opposite scale of the balance.[4] And to conclude, I presume it will not be denied, that the authenticity and celestial origin of any thing pretending to be a Divine Revelation, before it has any claims upon our faith, ought to be made clear beyond all *reasonable* doubt; otherwise, it can have no just claims to a right to influence our conduct.

As for the opinions and the arguments contained in this volume, I have but trembling hopes that they will meet with favour, merely because the author is sincere, and wishes to do right. Conscious that I make a perilous attempt, in daring to defend myself by attacking ancient error, supported by multitudes, with no other seconds besides Truth and Reason, it would be bootless for me to ask indulgence for them on account of my good intentions; and as they can derive no credit from the authority of the writer, I am sensible they must fall by their own weakness, or stand by their own strength. I must leave them therefore to their fate; and I can cheerfully do it, without fear for the issue, if the Reader will only be candid, and will comply with my earnest request—"first to understand, and then judge."

Before I conclude these prefatory remarks, I would observe, that as the contents of this volume will be perfectly novel to nine hundred and ninety-nine out of a thousand, it is but justice to the public, and to myself, to *avow*, that I do not claim to have originated *all* the arguments advanced in this Book.—A very considerable portion of them were selected and derived from ancient and curious Jewish Tracts, translated from Chaldee into Latin, very little known even in Europe, and not at all known *there* to any, but the curious and inquisitive. And I reasonably hope, that discerning men will be much more disposed to weigh with candour the arguments herein offered, when they consider, that they are, in many instances, the reasonings of learned, ancient, and venerable men, who, in times when the inquisition was in vigour, suffered under the most bloody oppression, and whose writings were cautiously preserved, and secretly handed down to the seventeenth century in *Manuscript*, as the printing of them would assuredly have brought all concerned to the stake.[5] Some few other arguments were derived from other authors, and were taken from works not so much known as I hope they will be.

Finally, I commit my work to the discretion of the good sense of the reader, believing that if he is not convinced, he will, at least, be interested; and hoping that he will discover from the complexion of the Book (what my own heart bears witness to) that the Author is a sincere inquirer after truth, and perfectly willing to be convinced that he is in an error, by any one who can *remove* the difficulties, and *refute* the arguments, now laid by him before the public, with deference and respect.

THE GROUNDS OF CHRISTIANITY EXAMINED, BY COMPARING THE NEW TESTAMENT WITH THE OLD

CHAPTER I.

CHRISTIANITY is founded on *Judaism*, and the New Testament upon the *Old*; and Jesus of Nazareth is the person said in the New Testament to be promised in the Old, under the character and name of *the Messiah* of the Jews, and who, *as such only*, claims the obedience, and submission of the World. Accordingly it is the Design of the Authors of the New, to prove Christianity from the Old Testament; which is said Jo. 5: 39, to contain the words of Eternal Life: and it represents Jesus and his Apostles, as fulfilling by their Mission, Doctrines, and Works, the *Predictions of the Prophets and the Law:* which *last*, is said to prophesy of, or to typify Christianity.

Matthew, for example, proves several parts of Christianity from the Old Testament, either by asserting them to be things foretold therein as to come to pass under the Gospel Dispensation; or to be founded on the notions of the Old Testament.

Thus he proves Mary's being with child by the Holy Spirit, and the Angel's telling her "*she shall bring forth a Son, and call his name Jesus,*" and the other circumstances attending his miraculous birth; Jesus's birth at Bethlehem; his Flight into Egypt; the slaughter of the Infants; Jesus dwelling at Nazareth and at Capernaum, in the borders of Zabulon, and Napthali; his casting out Devils, and healing the sick; his eating with Pub-

licans and sinners: his speaking in Parables that the Jews might not understand him; his sending his Disciples to fetch an ass and a colt; the Children's crying in the Temple; the Resurrection of Jesus from the Dead;
Jesus's being betrayed by Judas, and Judas's returning back the thirty
Pieces of Silver, and the Priest's buying the Potters' Field with them; and
his hanging himself, &c. &c. All these events, and many more are said to
be *fulfillments* of the Prophecies of the Old Testament, see Mat. 1, 2, and
4 chapters, and ch. 8, v. 16, 17, and ch. 9; 11, 13, and ch. 13; 13, ch. 21;
2–7, 15, 16, ch. 22; 31, 32, ch. 26; 54, 56, ch. 27; 5–10.

Jesus himself is represented as proving the Truth of Christianity thus. He
joining himself to two of his Disciples, (Luke 28: 15–22) after his resurrection, who knew him not, and complaining of their mistake about his person,
whom they now took not to be the Messiah, because he had been condemned to Death, and crucified; he observing their disbelief of his resurrection, which had been reported to them by "*certain women* of their acquaintance," upon the credit of the affirmation of angels, said unto them "O Fools,
and slow of heart to believe all that the Prophets have spoken. Ought not
Christ (i. e. the Messiah) to have suffered these things, and to enter into his
Glory? and beginning at Moses, and all the Prophets he expounded unto
them in all the Scriptures the things concerning himself."

Again he discoursed to all his Disciples, putting them in mind, that
before his Death, he told them (Luke 24–44, 46, 47,) that "all things must
be fulfilled which were written in the law of Moses, and in the Prophets,
and in the Psalms concerning him;" adding, "thus it is written, and thus it
behoveth Christ (i. e. the Messiah) to suffer, and to rise from the dead the
third day; and that repentance, and remission of sins should be preached
in his name, beginning at Jerusalem."

When the People of several Nations, Acts 2: 12, were amazed at the Apostles speaking in their several tongues, and when many mocked the Apostles,
saying they were full of new wine, Peter makes a speech in public, wherein,
after saying they were not drunk, because it was but the third hour of the day,
he endeavours to show them, that this was spoken of by the Prophet Joel, and
he concludes with proving the resurrection of Jesus from the Book of Psalms.

Peter and John tell the people assembled at the Temple, "that God had
showed *by the mouth of all His Prophets*, that Christ should suffer."—
Acts 3: 18.

Peter to justify his preaching to the Gentiles, concludes his Discourses with saying, Acts 10, 43—"To Jesus gave *all the Prophets witness* that through his name whosoever (i. e. Jew or Gentile) believeth in him, shall receive remission of sins."

Paul also endeavours to prove to the Jews in the Synagogue of Antioch, (Ib. v. 13,) that the History of Jesus was contained in the Old Testament, and that he, and Barnabas were commanded in the Old Testament to preach the gospel to the Gentiles.

On the occasion of a dispute among the Christians whether the Gentile Converts were to be circumcised after the Law of Moses, and to observe the Law, we find, that after much disputing, the point was settled by James by quotation from Amos.

The Bereans are highly extolled (Acts 17: 11,) *for searching the Scriptures*, i. e. the Old Testament *daily*, in order to find out whether the things preached to them by the Apostles, *were so, or no*; who if they had not proved *these things*, i. e. Christianity from the Old Testament, ought, according to their own principles, to have been rejected by the Bereans, as teachers of false Doctrine.

Paul, when accused before Agrippa by the Jews, said (Acts 26: 6,)— "I stand, and am judged for the hope of the promise made of God unto our Fathers"—i. e. for teaching Christianity, or the true Doctrine of the Old Testament, and to this accusation he pleads guilty, by declaring in the fullest manner, that he taught *nothing* but the Doctrines of the Old Testament. Having, therefore, says he, obtained help of God, I continue unto this day, witnessing both to small and great, saying *none other things than those which the Prophets and Moses did say should come*, that the Christ should *suffer*, and that *he should be the first who should rise from the Dead*, and should show light unto the people and unto the Gentiles."

The author of the first Epistle to the Cor., says, 15 ch. v. 4, that "Jesus rose again from the dead the third day according to the Scriptures,"—that is according to the Old Testament; and he is supposed to ground this on the history of the Prophet Jonas, who was three days and three nights in the fish's belly, though the cases do not seem to be parallel, for Jesus being buried on Friday evening, and rising on Sunday morning, was in the tomb but *one day* and *two nights*.

But most singular is the argument of the Apostle Paul (in his Epistle

to the Galatians) to prove Christianity from the Old Testament. "Tell me,"
says he (Gal. 4. 21,) "ye that desire to be under the Law, do ye not hear
the Law? For it is written, that Abraham had two Sons, the one by a bond-
maid, the other by a free-woman. But he who was of the bond-woman,
was born after the flesh; but he who was of the free-woman, was by
promise. Which things are *an Allegory*. For these are the two Covenants,
the one from Mount Sinai which gendereth to bondage, which is Agar.
But this Agar is Mount Sinai in Arabia, and answereth to Jerusalem that
now is, and is in bondage with her Children. But Jerusalem which is
above is free, which is the Mother of us all. For it is written (Isaiah 54–1,)
'Rejoice thou Barren that bearest not, break forth, and cry thou that tra-
vailest not, for the desolate hath many more children than she which hath
an husband.' Now we Brethren, as Isaac was, are children of the Promise.
But as then he that was born after the flesh persecuted him that was born
after the spirit, even so it is now. But what saith the Scripture (Gen. 21, v.
10, 12,) cast out the bondwoman and her son, for the son of the bond-
woman shall not be heir with the Son of the free-woman. So then
Brethren we are not the children of the bond-woman, but of the free.
Stand fast therefore in the Liberty wherewith Christ hath made us free,
and be not entangled again with the yoke of bondage."

In fine, the Author of these Epistles reasons in the same singular
manner from the Old Testament throughout; which is, according to him,
(2 Tim. iii. 15,) "able to make men wise unto Salvation;" asserting himself and others to be ministers, of the New Testament, as being ministers,
not of "*the letter*" but of "*the Spirit*," (2 Cor. iii. 6.) That is, of the Old
Testament, *spiritually understood*; and endeavouring to prove, especially
in the Epistle to the Hebrews, that Christianity was *veiled* and *contained*
in the Old Testament, and was *implied* in the Jewish History and Law,
both which he considers as *Types* and *Shadows* of Christianity.

CHAPTER II.

How Christianity depends on the Old Testament, or what proofs are to be
met with therein in behalf of Christianity, are the subjects of almost all the
numerous Books written by Divines, and other Apologists for Chris-

tianity; but the chief, and principal, of these proofs may be justly supposed to be urged in the New Testament itself, by the Authors thereof; who relate the History of the first preaching of the Gospel, and profess themselves to be Apostles of Jesus, or companions of the Apostles.

Some of these proofs, as a specimen, have been already adduced. And if they are *valid proofs*, then is Christianity *strongly* and *invincibly* established on its true foundations.

It is established upon its *true foundations*, because Jesus and his Apostles did, as we have seen, ground Christianity on those proofs; and it is strongly, and invincibly established on those foundations; because a proof drawn from an *inspired* Book is perfectly conclusive. And Prophecies delivered in an inspired Book, are, *when fulfilled*, such as may be justly deemed *sure*, and *demonstrative* proof; and which Peter (2 Peter i. 19,) prefers as an *argument for the truth of Christianity*, to that miraculous attestation (whereof he and two other Apostles are said to have been witnesses,) given by God himself to the Mission of Jesus of Nazareth.— His argument appears to be as follows: "Laying this foundation, that Prophecy proceeds from the Holy Spirit, it is a stronger argument than *a miracle*, which depends upon external evidence, and testimony." And this opinion of Peter is corroborated by the words of Jesus himself, who, in Mat. xxiv. 23, 24. Mark xiii. 21, 22. affirms, that *miracles wrought in confirmation of a pretender's being the Messiah* are *not* to be considered *as proof of his being so*: "though they show great signs and wonders, believe it not," is his command to his Disciples.

Besides, Prophecies fulfilled seem the most proper of all arguments to evince the truth of a New Revelation, which is designed to be universally promulgated to men. For a man who has the Old Testament put into his hands, which contains *Prophecies*, and the New Testament afterwards, which is said to contain their *completions*, and is once satisfied, as he may be with the greatest ease, that the Old Testament existed before the New, may have a *complete internal, Divine demonstration* of the Truth of Christianity, without long, and laborious enquiries. Whereas, arguments of another nature, such, for instance, as relate to the *authority* and *genuineness* of the Books, and the *Persons*, and *Characters* of *Authors*, and *witnesses*, require more application and understanding than fall to the share of the bulk of mankind; or else are very precarious in themselves, since we know that in the first centuries there were numberless forged Gospels, and Apocryphal writings imposed upon the credulous as apostolic, and authentic; and there were in the Apostles' times, as many, and as great Heresies, and Schisms as, perhaps, have been since in any age of the Church. So that, setting aside the before mentioned internal proofs from *prophecy*, (which were the Apostles' proofs, and in their nature sufficient of themselves) we should have no *certain* proof at all for the Religion of the New Testament.

ON THE OTHER HAND, if the proofs for Christianity from the Old Testament are *not valid*, if the arguments founded on that Book be *not* conclusive, and the Prophecies cited from thence be *not fulfilled*, then has Christianity *no just foundation*; for the foundation on which *Jesus* and *his Apostles* built it, is then *invalid* and *false*. Nor can *miracles* said to have been wrought by Jesus and his Apostles in behalf of Christianity, avail anything in the case. For miracles can never render a foundation *valid*, which is in itself invalid; can never make a *false* inference *true*; can never make a prophecy *fulfilled*, which is *not* fulfilled; and can never designate a *Messiah*, or *Jesus for* the Messiah, if both are not *marked out* in the Old Testament, no more than they could prove the *Earth* to be the *Sun*, or a *mouse* a *lion*.

Besides, Miracles *said to have been* wrought, may be often justly deemed false reports, when attributed to persons who claim an authority from the Old Testament, which they impertinently allege to support their pretensions. God can never be supposed *often* to permit miracles to be done for the confirmation of a *false* or *pretended* mission; and if, at any time, he *does* permit miracles to be done in confirmation of a pretended mission, we have express directions from the Old Testament (acknowledged by Christians to be of Divine authority, Deut. xiii. 1, 2,) *not to regard* such miracles; but to continue firm to the antecedent Revelation given by *Himself*, and contained in the Old Testament, notwithstanding any "signs or wonders," which, under the circumstance of attesting *something contrary* to an antecedent Revelation, we are forewarned of, as being *no test of truth*. No *New* Revelation, however supported by miracles, ought ever to be received as coming from God, unless it *confirms*, or at least does *not contradict*, the preceding standing Revelation, *acknowledged* to be from God.

Accordingly, we find from the New Testament, that all the recorded miracles of Jesus could not make the Jews believe him to be the *Messiah* when they thought that he did not *answer the description* of that character given by the Prophets; on the *contrary*, they procured him to be crucified for pretending to be, what to them he appeared plainly not to be.

Nor had his miracles alone any effect on his own brethren and kindred, who seem (Mark vi. 4, Jo. vii. 5,) to have been more incredulous in him than other Jews. Nor had they the effect they are supposed to have been fitted to produce, among his immediate followers and Disciples; some of whom did not believe in him, but deserted him, and particularly had *no faith* in him, when he spake of his *sufferings*; and thought that he could not be their Messiah when they saw him suffer, notwithstanding his miracles, and his declaration to them that he was the Messiah. And so rooted were the Jews in the notion of the Messiah's being a *temporal Prince*, a conquering Pacificator and Deliverer, even after the death of Jesus, and the progress of Christianity grounded on the belief of his being the Messiah, that they have in all times of distress particularly in the apostolic era, in great numbers followed impostors giving themselves out as the Messiah, with force, and arms, as the way to restore the kingdom of Israel. So that the Jews, who it seems, mistook in this most important matter, and after the most egregious manner, the meaning of their own Books, might, till they were set right in their interpretation of the Old Testament, and were *convinced from thence* that Jesus was the Messiah, might I say, as justly reject Jesus asserting his mission, and Doctrines with *miracles*, as they might reject any other person, who in virtue of miracles, would lead them into Idolatry, or any other breach of their law.

In fine, the *miracles* said to have been wrought by Jesus, are, according to the Old Testament, the gospel scheme, and *the words of Jesus himself*, no *absolute proof* of his being the *Messiah*, or of *the truth of Christianity*; and Jesus laid no great stress upon them as proving doctrines, for he *forewarned* his disciples, that "signs and wonders" would be performed, so great and stupendous, as to deceive, if possible, the very elect, and bids them *not to give any heed to them*.*

---

*There are a great many persons who conceive that Christianity is sufficiently proved to be true, if the miracles of Jesus are true; even without any regard to the *prophecies*, so often appealed to by him. But supposing the miracles to be true; yet no miracles can prove that which is *false in itself* to be true. If therefore Jesus be not foretold as the Messiah in the Old Testament, no miracles can prove Jesus to be the Messiah foretold, nay it is a stronger argument to prove Jesus to be a false pretender, that he appealed to prophecies *as relating to him*, when in fact they had no relation whatever to (continued from p. 67) him; and by that means imposed upon the ignorant; than it would be that he came from God, merely because he worked miracles; for "*False Christs and false prophets* may *arise, and* may *show such great* SIGNS AND WONDERS *as to deceive, if it were possible, the very elect.*" Mat. xxiv. 24. Yet no Christian would allow it to be argued *from thence*, that those *false* Christs were *true* ones; nor would any one conclude, that a man came from God, (notwithstanding any miracles he might do) if he appealed to Scripture for that *which is no where in it*. In fine, if *miracles* would prove the Messiahship of *Jesus*, so also they would prove the Messiahship of the *false Christs*, and false prophets spoken of above. Nay more, they would demonstrate the Divine mission of *Antichrist himself*; who, according to the epistle to the Thessalonians, (3 Thes. ch. ii. 8, 9, 10.) and the Revelations, ch. xiii. 13, 14, was to perform "great signs and wonders," equal to any wrought by *Jesus*; for the *same* Greek words are used to express the wonderful works, or "great signs and wonders" of *Antichrist*, which are elsewhere used to express the miracles, or "great signs and wonders" of *Jesus himself*.

It is a striking circumstance, that the earliest apologists for Christianity laid little stress upon the miracles of its founder.

Justin Martyr, in his apology, is very shy of appealing to the miracles of Jesus in confirmation of his pretensions; he lays no stress upon them, but relies entirely upon the *prophecies* he quotes as in his favour. Jerome, in his comment on the eighty-first Psalm, assures us, "that the performance of miracles was no extraordinary thing; and that it was no more than what Appollonius and Apulius, and innumerable imposters had done before."

Lactantius saw so little force in the miracles of Christ *exclusive* of the prophecies, that he does not hesitate to affirm their utter inability to support the Christian religion *by themselves*. [Lactan. Div. Inst. L. v. c. 3.]

Celsus observing upon the words of Jesus, that "false prophets, and false Christs shall arise, and show great signs and wonders:" sneeringly observes, "A fine thing truly! that miracles done by *him* should prove *him* to be a God, and when done by *others* should demonstrate *them* to be false prophets and impostors."

Tertullian, on the words of Jesus, here referred to by Celsus, says as follows: "Christ foretelling, that many impostors should come and perform many wonders, shews, that our faith cannot *without great temerity* be founded on miracles, since they were so early wrought by false Christians themselves." [Tertul. in Marc. L. ii. s. 3.]

Indeed miracles in the two first centuries were allowed very little weight in proving *doctrines*. Since the Christians did not *deny*, that the heathens performed miracles in behalf of their gods, and that the heretics performed them as well as the orthodox. This accounts for the perfect indifference of the heathens to the miracles said to have been performed by the founders of Christianity. Hierocles speaks with great contempt of what he calls "the little tricks of Jesus." And Origen, in his reply to Celsus, waives the consideration of the Christian miracles, "for (says he) the very mention of these things sets you Heathens upon the broad grin." Indeed, that they laughed very heartily at what in the eighteenth century is read with a grave face, is evident from the few fragments of their works written against Christianity which have escaped the *burning zeal* of the fathers, and the Christian emperors; who piously sought for, and burned up these mischievous volumes to prevent their doing mischief to posterity. This conduct of theirs is very suspicious, Why burn writings they could so triumphantly refute, if they were refutable? They should have remembered the just reflection of *Arnobius*, their own apologist, against the heathens, who were for abolishing at once such writings as promoted Christianity—"Inter cipere scripta et publicatam velle submergere lectionem, non est Deos defendere, sed *veritatis testificationem timere*." [Arnob. contra Gentes. Liber iii.] ["For when you would carry off writings, and suppress a book given forth to the public, you are not defending the gods, but dreading the evidence of the truth."—*Ed.*]

CHAPTER III.

HAVING shewn from the *New Testament*, and proved from *the nature of the case*, that the whole credit and authority of the Christian religion, rests and depends upon Jesus' being the Messiah of the Jews; and having stated the principles which ought to govern the decision of this question, and established the fact, that the pretensions of any claiming to be considered as *this Messiah*, must be tested *solely* by the *coincidence* of the character, and circumstances of *the pretender* with the *descriptions* given by the *prophets*, as the *means* by which he may be known to be so. It is proper, in order that we may be enabled to form a correct opinion, to lay before the reader those passages of the Old Testament which contain the promise of the appearing, and express the characteristics of this 'hope of Israel,' this beneficent Saviour, and august monarch, in whose time a suffering world, was, according to the Hebrew prophets, to become the abode of happy beings.

Leaving out for the present the consideration of *the Shiloh* mentioned in Gen. xlix. the first prophecy we meet with, supposed to relate to this great character, is contained in Num. xxiv. 17, 19. "There shall come a star out of Jacob, and a sceptre shall rise out of Israel, and shall smite the corners of Moab, and destroy the children of Seth." Geddes interprets the latter clause—"shall destroy the sons of Sedition;" but it probably means, according to the common interpretation, that this monarch was to govern the whole race of men, i. e. the children of *Seth*, for Noah, according to the Old Testament, was descended from him, and of the posterity of Noah, was the whole earth overspread. And in verse 19, it is added, "out of Jacob shall come he that shall have *dominion*."*

God says to David, 2 Sam. vii. 12. "And when thy days shall be fulfilled, and thou shall sleep with thy fathers, I will set up thy seed after

---

*Before going into the consideration of the following prophecies, the author would warn the reader *to bear in mind*, that whether these prophecies *ever will be* fulfilled is a question of *no import in the world* to the question under consideration, which is—whether they *have been* fulfilled eighteen hundred years ago, in the person of *Jesus Christ*, who is asserted by Christians to be the person foretold in these prophecies, and to have fulfilled their predictions. This question can be easily decided, and only, we think, by appealing to past history, and to the scenes passing around us, and comparing them with these predictions.

thee, which shall proceed out of thy bowels; and I will establish his kingdom. He shall build a house for my name, and I will establish the throne of his kingdom for ever. I will be his Father, and he shall be my Son. If he commit iniquity, I will chasten him with the rod of a man, and with the stripes of the children of men, but my mercy shall not depart from him, as I took it from Saul, whom I put away before thee, and thy house, and thy kingdom shall be established before me, and thy throne shall be established for ever." Mention is made of this promise in several of the Psalms, but it certainly suggests no idea of such a person as *Jesus of Nazareth*, but only that of a temporal prince of the posterity of David. It implies, that his family would never entirely fail, for though it might be severely punished, it would recover its lustre again. And connecting this promise with that of the glory of the nation in general, foretold in the books of Moses, it might be inferred by the Hebrews who believed them to be of Divine authority, that after long and great calamities (the consequences of their sins,) the people of Israel would be restored to their country, and attain the most distinguished felicity under a prince of the family of David. This is the subject of numberless prophecies throughout the Old Testament.

Passing over all those prophecies in which *the national glory* is spoken of, *without* any mention of *a prince* or *head*, I shall recite, and remark upon the most eminent of those in which mention is made of any *particular person*, under whom, or by means of whom, the Israelitish nation, it is said, would enjoy the transcendent prosperity elsewhere foretold.

The second Psalm is, no doubt, well known to my reader, and supposing it to refer to the *Messiah*, it is evident, that it describes him enthroned upon mount Zion, the favorite of God, and the resistless conqueror of his enemies.

The next prophecy of this distinguished individual is recorded in Isaiah ix. 6. "Unto us a child is born, unto us a son is given, and the government shall be upon his shoulder: and the Wonderful, the Counsellor, the mighty God, the everlasting Father *shall call his name*, the Prince of Peace." (For thus it is pointed to be read in the original Hebrew, and this is the meaning of the passage, and not as in the absurd translation of this verse in the English version.) "Of the increase of his government there shall be no end, upon the throne of David, and his kingdom, to order it, and to establish it with judgment, and with justice from henceforth and for ever: the zeal of the Lord of Hosts will do this." Here again we have a mighty Monarch, sitting upon *the throne of David*, upon *earth*; and not a *spiritual* king placed by idolatrous superstition *in heaven*, upon the throne of "the mighty God, the everlasting Father."

The next passage which comes under notice, is in the eleventh chapter of Isaiah, in which a person is mentioned, under whom Israel, and the whole earth was to enjoy great prosperity and felicity. He is described as an upright prince, endued with the spirit of God, under whose reign there would be *universal peace*, which was to take place after the return of the Israelites from their dispersed state, when the whole nation would be united and happy.

"There shall spring forth a rod from the trunk of Jesse, and a scion from his roots shall become fruitful, and the spirit of the Lord shall rest upon him; the spirit of wisdom, and understanding; the spirit of counsel and strength; the spirit of knowledge, and the fear of the Lord; and he shall be quick of discernment in the fear of the Lord; so that not according to the sight of his eyes shall he judge, nor according to the hearing of the ears shall he reprove; but with righteousness shall he judge the poor, and with equity shall he work conviction on the meek of the earth. And he shall smite the earth with the blast of his mouth; and with the breath of his lips shall he slay the wicked one; and righteousness shall be the girdle of his loins, and faithfulness the cincture of his reins. Then shall the wolf take up his abode with the lamb; and the leopard shall lie down with the kid; and the calf, and the young lion, and the fatling shall come together, and a little child shall lead them. And the heifer, and the she bear shall feed together. Together shall their young ones lie down. And the lion shall eat straw like the ox. And the suckling shall play upon the hole of the asp; and upon the den of the basilisk shall the new weaned child lay his hand. They shall not hurt, nor destroy in my holy mountain. For the earth shall be full of the knowledge of the Lord, as the waters cover the depth of the sea. And it shall come to pass in that day, the root of Jesse which standeth for an ensign to the people, unto him shall the nations repair, and his resting place shall be glorious."

As the scion here spoken of is said to spring from *the root* of Jesse, it looks as if it were intended to intimate, that the *tree itself* would be cut down, or that the power of David's family would be *for some time extinct*; but that it would revive in 'the latter days.'

The same Prince is again mentioned, chap, xxxii. 1, 3, where the people are described to be both virtuous, and flourishing, and to continue to be so.

"Behold a King shall reign in righteousness, and Princes shall rule with equity; and the man shall be a covert from the storm, as a refuge from the flood, as canals of waters in a dry place, as the shadow of a great rock in a land of fainting with heat; and him the eyes of those that see shall regard, and the ears of them that hear shall harken—till the spirit from on high be poured out upon us, and the wilderness become a fruitful field, and the fruitful field be esteemed a forest; and judgment shall dwell in the wilderness, and in the fruitful field shall reside righteousness, and the work of righteousness shall be peace, and the effect of righteousness *perpetual quiet*, and *security*. And my people shall dwell in a peaceful mansion, and in habitations secure, and in resting places undisturbed."

The same prophet chap. lxii. 1, speaks of a person under the title of *"God's Servant,"* of a meek disposition, raised up by God to enlighten the world, even the Gentile part of it; to bring prisoners out of their confinement, and to open their eyes; alluding probably, to the custom too common in the East, of sealing up the eyes, by sewing or fastening together the eyelids of persons, and then imprisoning them for life. It is *doubted* however whether the Prophet meant, or had in view, in this passage, the *Messiah* or *his own nation*.

"Behold my servant whom I will uphold, mine elect in whom my soul delighteth; I will make my spirit rest upon him, and he shall publish judgment to the nations. He shall not cry aloud, nor raise a clamour, nor cause his voice to be heard in the public places. The bruised reed shall he not break, and the dimly burning flax he shall not quench. He shall publish judgment so as to establish it perfectly. His force shall not be abated, nor broken, until he has firmly seated judgment in the Earth, and the distant nations shall earnestly wait for his Law.

"Thus saith the Lord, even Jehovah, who created the Heavens, and stretched them out; who spread abroad the Earth, and the produce thereof, who giveth breath to the people upon it, and spirit to them that tread thereon. I, the Lord, have called thee for a righteous purpose, and I will take hold of thy hand, and I will preserve thee: and I will give thee for a covenant to the people, for a light to the nations; to open the eyes of the blind, to bring the captive out of confinement, and from the dungeon, those that dwell in darkness. I am Jehovah, that is my name, and my glory will I not give to another, nor my praise to the graven images. The former predictions, lo! they are come to pass, and new events I now declare. Before they spring forth, behold I make them known unto you." See also chap. xlix. 1, 12, and chap. liv. 3, 5.

In the 3rd chapter of Hosea, verses 4 and 5; it is said by the Prophet, that "the sons of Israel shall abide many days without a King, and without a Prince, and without sacrifice, and without a statue, and without an Ephod, and without Teraphim. Afterward shall the sons of Israel return, and shall seek the Lord their God, and David their King, and shall fear the Lord, and his goodness in the latter days."

Micah ch. v. 2, speaks of the Messiah thus, "And thou Bethlehem Ephratah, art thou too little to be among the leaders of Judah? Out of thee shall come forth unto me, him who is to be ruler in Israel; and his goings forth have been from of old, from the days of hidden ages. Therefore will he (God) deliver them up, *until* the time *when she that bringeth forth, hath brought forth*, and *until* the residue of their brethren shall return together, with the Sons of Israel. And he shall stand and feed his flock, in the strength of the Lord, in the majesty of the name of the Lord his God, and they shall abide, for now shall he be great unto the ends of the earth, and he shall be Peace."

Jeremiah also speaks of the restoration of the Israelites, under a Prince of the family of David, chap. xxiii. 5, 8.

"Behold the days are coming, saith the Lord, that I will raise up unto David a righteous branch, and a King shall reign, and act wisely, and shall execute justice, and judgment in the Earth. *In his days* Judah shall be saved, and Israel shall dwell in security, and this is the name by which Jehovah shall call him, OUR RIGHTEOUSNESS." (Heb.) The same is mentioned chap. xxx. 8. 9. "And it shall be in that day, saith the Lord of Hosts, I will break his yoke from off his neck, and his bands will I burst asunder, and strangers shall no more exact service of him; but they shall serve the Lord their God, and David their King, whom I will raise up for (or to) them.—The voice of joy, and the voice of mirth, the voice of the Bridegroom, and the voice of the Bride, the voice of them that say, Praise ye the Lord of Hosts, for the Lord is gracious, for his mercy endureth forever, of them that bring praise to the house of the Lord. Thus saith the Lord of Hosts, yet again shall there be in this place that is desolate (Jerusalem and Palestine,) without man and beast, and in all the cities thereof, an habitation of shepherds folding sheep, in the cities of the hill country, and in the cities of the plain, and in the cities of the south, and in the land of Benjamin, and in the environs of Jerusalem.—Behold the days come, saith the Lord, that I will perform the good thing which I have spoken concerning the house of Israel, and concerning the house of Judah. *In those days, and at that time,* (He that readeth, let him *observe.*) I will *cause to grow up of the line of David* a branch of righteousness, and he shall execute judgment and justice in the earth. *In those days* Judah shall be saved, and Jerusalem shall dwell securely, and this is he whom Jehovah shall call— "OUR RIGHTEOUSNESS," (Heb.) Surely thus saith the Lord, there shall not be a failure in the line of David, of one to sit upon the throne of the house of Israel, neither shall there be a failure in the line of the Priests, the Levites, of one to offer before me burnt offerings, and to perform sacrifice continually." See ch. xxxiii. 14. In this place, the *perpetuity of the tribe of Levi*, as well as that of *the house of David*, is foretold. See also Jer. ch. xxx. 9.

Contemporary with Jeremiah was *Ezechiel.* He likewise describes this happy state of the Israelites under a king of the *name of David*, chap. xxxiv. 22.

"Therefore will I save my flock, and they shall no more be a prey: and I will judge between cattle, and cattle, and will set up one Shepherd over them, and he shall feed them, even my servant David. He shall feed them, and he shall be their Shepherd, and I, the Lord, will be their God, and my servant David a Prince among them. I, the Lord, have spoken it, and I will make with them a covenant of Peace, and will cause the evil beasts to cease out of the land; and they shall dwell safely in the wilderness, and sleep in the woods and I will make them, and the places round about my hill, a blessing. And I will cause the shower to come down in the season. There shall be showers of blessing; and the tree of the field shall yield her fruit; and the earth shall yield her increase; and they shall be safe in their land; and shall know that I am the Lord."

In another passage, this Prophet says, that the two nations, Israel and Judah, shall have one King, and that this King shall be named David, who shall reign forever, chap. xxxvii. 21, 28. "Say unto them, thus saith the Lord God, behold I will take the children of Israel from among the Heathen whither they be gone, and will gather them on every side, and bring them into their own land. And I will make them one nation in the land, upon the mountains of Israel, and one King shall be King to them all, and they shall be no more two nations, neither shall they be divided into two kingdoms any more at all. Neither shall they defile themselves any more with their Idols, nor with their detestable things, nor with any of their transgressions. But I will save them out of all their dwelling places wherein they have sinned, and will cleanse them, so shall they be my people, and I will be their God. And David my servant shall be King over them, and there shall be one shepherd. They shall also *walk in my judgments*, and *observe my statutes* and *do them*. And they shall dwell in the land that I have given unto Jacob my servant, wherein your fathers have dwelt, and they shall dwell therein, even they, and their children, and their children's children *forever*. And *my servant* David shall be *their Prince forever*. Moreover I will make a covenant of peace with them. It shall be *an everlasting covenant* with them, and I will place them, and multiply them, and will set my sanctuary in the midst of them, for evermore. My tabernacle also shall be with them, and I will be their God, and they shall be my people, and the heathen shall know, that I the Lord do sanctify Israel, when my sanctuary shall be in the midst of them *for evermore*."

The natural construction of this seems to be this, "that a descendant of David, called *by that name*, should reign over the Israelites forever."

In the very circumstantial description which Ezechiel gives of the state of the Israelites in their own country, yet expected by the Jews, he speaks of the *Prince*, and the portion assigned him, chap. xlv. 78. And in his description of the temple service, he moreover speaks of *the gate*, by which *the prince* is to enter into it. See chap. xlvi. 1, 2.

The next, and last passage I shall quote, is from the Book of Daniel, who, in the first year of Belshazzar king of Babylon, had a vision of four beasts, representing the four great Empires. At the close of his account of which he speaks of "one like the son of man" being brought into the presence of God, and receiving from the Eternal an everlasting kingdom, chap. vii. 13. "I saw in the night visions, and behold one like the son of man came with the clouds of heaven, and come to the ancient of days; and they brought him near before him. And there was given him dominion, and Glory, and a kingdom, *that all people, nations, and languages should serve him.* His dominion is *an everlasting dominion*, which shall not pass away, and his kingdom that which shall not be destroyed."

I have now gone through the prophecies which are allowed *both by Jews and Christians* to relate to one person whom they call the *Messiah*. It must be evident from all these passages, that the characteristics of this, to both parties, highly interesting personage, as described by the Hebrew prophets, are these:

1. That he was to be a *just, beneficent, wise,* and *mighty monarch*, raised up and upheld, and established by God, to be the means of promoting *universal peace*, and *happiness*. That Israel should be *gathered to him*, and established in their own land; which was to be the seat of dominion, and the centre of union, and of worship to all the people, and nations of the earth; who were to live under the government, and receive, and obey the laws of this beneficent Prince; and enjoy unspeakable felicities *on the earth*, then changed to *an universal paradise*. And for all this happiness, they were to worship and glorify the true God *only*, and glorify Jehovah, and give thanks to Him, "because He is good, and his mercy endureth forever."

2. That this prince was to be of the line of David, and as it should seem, *called* by *that name*, and was to reign on his throne in *Jerusalem*.

3. That according to Micah, Jeremiah, and Ezechiel, (see the quotations) his *manifestation*, and *the restoration* of *Israel* were to be *contemporaneous*. See Hosea, chap. iii. 4, 5. And from Jeremiah xxxiii. 15, and from Micah v. 2, it should seem also, that he *was not to be born*, till the time of that restoration should be *nearly arrived*.

The Prophecies concerning the Messiah of the Jews being now laid before the reader, we have only *to apply* these descriptions to know whether an individual *be* their Messiah or *not*. For, (according to the principles laid down, and established in the preceding chapter) where the foregoing characteristics given by the prophets *do centre* and *agree*, that person *is* the Messiah foretold: But where they are *not found* in any one claiming that character, *miracles are nothing to the purpose*, and nothing is more certain than that he has no right to be considered as such; and could he with a word turn the sun black in the face, in proof of his being the Messiah, he is nevertheless not to be regarded—for, whether such a person *has yet* appeared, can certainly only be known by considering whether the world has *ever yet seen* such a person as this Messiah of the Hebrew Prophets.

CHAPTER IV.

HAD Jesus of Nazareth come into the world, *merely*, as a person sent with a revelation from God, he would have had a right to be attended to, and *tried* upon that ground; and if his doctrines and precepts were consistent with reason, consistent with one another, and with prior revelations, really such, and all tending to the honor of God, and the good of men, his miracles, with these circumstances, ought to have determined men to believe in him.

But since he claimed to be the *Messiah* of the Jews, *foretold* by *their Prophets*, it is requisite, that *that claim* should be made out; and it is *reasonable* in itself, and *just* to him, and *necessary* to all those who will not take their religion upon trust, that he should *be tried*, by examining whether this claim *can* be made out or *not*. The argument from prophecy becomes *necessary* to establish the claim of the Gospel; and as truth is consistent with itself, so *this claim* must be *true*, or it *destroys all others*.

Besides, what notions of common morality must he have, who pretends to come from God, and declares (Jo. v. 37,) "that the Scriptures testify of him," if *in fact* the Scriptures do *not* testify of him? What honesty or sincerity could he have, who could "*begin at Moses* and *all the Prophets*, and expound unto his disciples in all the Scriptures the things concerning himself," if neither Moses nor the Prophets ever spake *a word about him*? The prophets therefore *must decide* this question, and *the foundation* of Christianity must *be laid* upon *them*; or else, to avoid one difficulty, Christians will be forced into such absurdities, as no man can palliate, much less can extricate himself out of.

Furthermore, this claim must he made out to the satisfaction of *the Gentile* as well as *the Jew*. For since *the fundamental article* of Christianity is, that Jesus *is the Christ*; (Jo. xx. 31,) that is to say, that he is *the Messiah* prophesied of in the Old Testament; whoever comes into the world as such, must come as the Messiah of the Jews, *because* no other nation did expect, or pretend to the proof a Messiah. Moreover, whoever comes as this *Messiah of the Jews*, must, at least, pretend to answer the character of their Messiah plainly delivered in the writings of their prophets; and the Jews themselves receiving those writings as divine, were not bound to, neither *could they* consistently with their *duty*, receive *any*, who did *not* answer in *all points* to the description therein given.

Let us now test the character of Jesus of Nazareth, by the description of the Messiah given by the Hebrew Prophets. If his character corresponds in *all respects* with that given by those prophets, he is undoubtedly to be acknowledged *as* the King of Israel foretold: but if they do *not* exactly correspond, if there be the *slightest* incongruity, he *certainly* was *not* this Messiah. For it is evident, that *some* of the characteristic marks given, *may* belong to *many* illustrious individuals, but *the whole* can belong to, and be found in *only one person*.

The first characteristic of the Messiah, the reader will recollect, was, according to the prophets, that he was to be "the Prince of Peace," in whose times righteousness was to flourish, and mankind be made happy. That he was to sit upon the throne of David, judging right; and that to him and their own land was Israel to be gathered, and all nations serve and obey *him*; and worship *one God*, even Jehovah.

But of Jesus we read, that he asserted, that his kingdom was "*not of this world.*" Instead of effecting peace among the nations, he said, "Think not that I am come to send *peace* on earth, I have come to send a *sword*, I have come to put *division* between a son and his father; the mother and the daughter; the daughter-in-law and her mother-in-law." "Think ye (said he to his disciples,) that I have come to put *peace* on earth, I tell you nay, but rather *division*." Again, "I have come to put *fire* on the earth."—These are not the characteristics of the Messiah of the prophets of the Old Testament. For of him Zechariah (ch. ix.) says, that "He shall speak *peace* to the nations;" and of him Isaiah says, ch. ii. "Nation shall not lift up sword against nation, neither shall they learn war any more."—And so far from being the author of *division*, *sword*, and *fire*, according to Malachi, in the times of the Messiah, "the heart of the parents was to be converted to the children, and the heart of the children to their parents."

In the times of the Messiah, wars were to cease, righteousness was to flourish, and mankind be happy. Whether this has yet taken place, the experience of almost nineteen centuries, and the present state of the world, can enable every one to determine for himself.

In the times of the Messiah, Israel was to be gathered, and planted in their own land, in honor and prosperity.—But not many years after the death of Jesus of Nazareth, the Jewish nation underwent the most dreadful calamities; and to this day, so far are they from being gathered, they are scattered to the four quarters of the globe. Instead of being in honor and prosperity, their history, since his time, is one dreadful record of unparalleled sufferings, written in letters of blood, by the hands of Murder, Rapine, and Cruelty.

Again—the true Messiah was, it seems, to be called DAVID, and was to reign at *Jerusalem*, on the throne of David; but the name "*Jesus*" is not the same as "*David*," and Christians have assigned him a *spiritual* kingdom, and a throne *in Heaven!* But was the throne of *David* in *Heaven?* No! it was in *Jerusalem*, and no more in Heaven than that of the *Caesars*.

Lastly, it appears from the prophecies of Hosea, Micah, Jeremiah, Isaiah, and Ezechiel, quoted in the last chapter, that the *manifestation* of their Messiah, was to be *contemporaneous* with the restoration of Israel, and from the quotations adduced from the *three first mentioned* Prophets, it should seem, that *his birth* was *not to take place* many years, before that glorious event. But Jesus of Nazareth was born *almost two thousand years ago*: and the children of Israel yet expect a deliverer. And to conclude, it was foretold by Malachi, and believed by the Jews, then, and ever since, that *Elias the Prophet*, who did not die, but was removed from the earth, should *precede* the coming of the Messiah, and prepare them for his reception. But the Prophet Elias certainly has *not yet* appeared!

Indeed, nothing appears to be more *dissimilar* than the character of *the Messiah*, as given by the Hebrew Prophets, and that of *Jesus of Nazareth*. It seems scarcely credible, that a man, who, though amiable and virtuous, yet lived in a low state, was poor, living upon alms, without wealth, and without power: and who (though by misfortune) died the death of a malefactor, *crucified* between two robbers, (a death exactly parallel with being hanged at the public gallows in the present day,) should ever be taken for that mighty Prince, that universal Potentate, and benefactor of the human race, foretold in the splendid language of the prophets of the Old Testament.

CHAPTER V.

BUT since one would esteem it almost incredible, that the Apostles could persuade men to believe Jesus to be this Messiah, unless they had, at least, some proof to offer to their conviction; let us next consider, and examine the proofs, adduced by the Apostles, and their followers, from the Old Testament for that purpose.

Of the *strength* or *weakness* of the proofs for Christianity out of the Old Testament, we are well qualified to judge, as we have the Old and New Testaments in our hands; the first containing what are offered as *proofs* of Christianity, and the latter the *application* of those proofs, and we should seem to have nothing more to do, but to compare the Old and New Testaments together.

But these proofs taken out of the Old Testament and urged in the New, being sometimes *not to be found* in the Old, nor urged in the New, according to the *literal* and *obvious sense* which they appear to bear in their supposed places in the Old, and therefore *not proofs* according to the rules of interpretation established by reason, and acted upon in interpreting *every other* ancient book: almost all Christian commentators on the Bible, and advocates for the religion of the New Testament, both ancient and modern, have judged them to be applied in a *secondary*, or *typical*, or *mystical*, or *allegorical*, or *enigmatical* sense. That is, in a sense different from the *obvious* and *literal* sense which they bear in the Old Testament.

Thus, for example, Matthew, after having given an account of the conception of Mary, and the birth of Jesus, says (ch. i.) "All this was done that it might be fulfilled which was spoken by the Prophet, saying, "Behold a virgin shall be with Child, and shall bring forth a son, and they shall call his name Immanuel." But the words as they stand in Is. ch. vii. 14. from whence they are taken, do in their *obvious* and *literal* sense relate to *a young woman* in the days of Ahaz, King of Judah, as will appear, considering the context.

When Rezin, King of Syria, and Pekah, King of Israel, were confederates in arms together, against Ahaz, King of Judah, Isaiah the prophet was sent by God, first to comfort Ahaz, and the nation, and then to assure them by a sign, that his enemies should, in a little time, be confounded. But Ahaz refusing a sign at the Prophet's hand, the Prophet said, (see the chapter,) "The Lord shall give you a sign." Behold a virgin, or *"young woman,"* (for the Hebrew word means *both*, as was truly and justly asserted by the Jews in the primitive ages against the Christians, and is now acknowledged, and established beyond dispute by the best Hebrew scholars of this age,) shall conceive, and bear a son, and shall call his name Immanuel. Butter and honey shall he eat, that he may know to refuse the evil, and choose the good. For before the child shall know to refuse the evil, and choose the good, the land which thou abhorrest shall be forsaken of both her kings." And this sign is accordingly given Ahaz by the Prophet, who, ch. viii. v. 2, 18; took two witnesses and went to the said young woman, who in due time conceived, and bare a son, after whose birth the projects of Rezin, and Pekah were it appears soon confounded, according to the prophecy and *sign* given by the Prophet.

And the Prophet himself, puts it beyond dispute, that this is the proper interpretation of the prophecy, by *express words*, as well as by his whole narration; for he says, "Behold I, and *the children* whom the Lord hath given me, are for *signs*, and for wonders in Israel, from the Lord of Hosts, that dwelleth in mount Zion." Is. viii. 19.

This is the plain drift, and design of the prophet, *literally, obviously,* and *primarily* understood; and thus he is understood by one of the most judicious of interpreters, the great Grotius.[6] Indeed, to understand the prophet as having the conception of Mary, and the birth of her son Jesus from a virgin mother literally, and primarily in view, is a very great absurdity, and contrary to the very intent and design of the *sign*, given by the Prophet.

For the sign being given by Isaiah to convince Ahaz that he brought a message from God to him, to assure him that the two kings should not succeed in their attempt against him; how could a virgin's conception and bearing a son *seven hundred years afterwards*, be *a sign* to *Ahaz*, that the Prophet came to *him* with the said message *from God*? And how *useless* was it to Ahaz, as well as *absurd* in *itself* for the Prophet to say, "Before the child born *seven hundred years hence*, shall distinguish between good and evil, the land which thou abhorrest shall be forsaken of both her kings," which would be *a banter* instead of *a sign*.

But a prophecy of the *certain* birth of a *male* child, of a *particular female* within *a short time*, seems a proper sign, as being not only what could not *with certainty* be foretold except by a person inspired; but considered as *soon coming to pass*, it consequently evidences itself to be a divine sign, and answers all the *purposes* of a sign. And such a sign is agreeable to God's conduct on like occasions; witness his conduct to *Gideon*, and *Hezechiah*, (Jud. vi., 2 Kings xx.)

This prophecy therefore not being fulfilled in Jesus, according to the literal, and obvious sense of the words as they stand in Isaiah; it is supposed that this, like the other prophecies cited in the New Testament, is fulfilled in a *secondary*, or *typical*, or *mystical* sense. That is, the said prophecy, which was literally fulfilled by the birth of the son foretold by the Prophet, was *again* fulfilled by the birth of *Jesus*, as being an event of the same kind, and intended to be *secretly* and *mystically* signified, either by the *Prophet*, or by *God*, who directed the Prophet's speech. If the reader desires further satisfaction that the literal, and obvious sense of this prophecy relates to a son to be born in Isaiah's time, and *not* to Jesus, he is referred to the commentator *Grotius* and to *Huetius'* Demonstrat. Evang. in loc. to the ancient Fathers, and to the most respectable of the Modern Christian commentators, who all *allow* and *show*, that the words of Isaiah are not applicable to the birth of *Jesus*, in their *literal* sense, but only in a *mystical*, or *figurative*, or *allegorical* sense.[7]

Again, Matthew gives us another prophecy, which he says *was fulfilled*. He tells us, that Jesus was carried into Egypt; from whence he returned after the death of Herod, (Mat. ii.) "that it might be *fulfilled* which was spoken of the Lord by the Prophet, saying, 'out of Egypt have I called my son.'" Which being word for word in Hosea, (ch. xi. 1.) and no where else to be found in the Old Testament, are supposed to be taken from thence: where, according to their *obvious* sense they are *no prophecy at all!* but relate and refer to a *past action*, viz. to the calling of the children of Israel out of Egypt; which will, I think, be denied by few. This *passage* therefore, or, as it is styled, *prophecy*, of Hosea, is said, by learned men among Christians, to be *mystically*, or *allegorically applied*, in order to render Matthew's application of it just; and they say, all other methods, of some learned men to solve the difficulties arising from Matthew's citation of this passage, have proved unsuccessful.

Again, Matthew says, (ch. ii.) "Jesus came, and dwelt at Nazareth, that it might be *fulfilled*, which was spoken by the Prophet saying, 'he shall be called a Nazarene;'" but as this passage does not occur in the Old Testament *at all*, we are precluded from ascertaining whether it be *literal*, *mystical*, or *allegorical*.

Jesus says of John the Baptist, (Mat. xi. 14.) "This is Elias that was for to come;" wherein he is supposed to refer to these words of Malachi, (ch. iv. 4.) "Behold I will send you Elijah the Prophet, *before the coming* of the *great* and *terrible day* of the Lord," which, according to their literal, and obvious sense, are a prophecy, that Elijah, or Elias, was to come *in person*—(which we know from the New Testament, as well as elsewhere, was the constant expectation of the Jews.) Besides, this Elijah was to come "before the great and terrible day of the Lord," which has not yet arrived; and, therefore, this prophecy of Malachi referred to by the Evangelist, was certainly not *literally*, but only *mystically* fulfilled in John the Baptist.

Again, Jesus, (Mat. xiii.) cites the prophecy of Isaiah, (Is. vi. 9.) "By hearing ye shall hear, and shall not understand:" and he assures us, that it was *fulfilled* in *his time* in those to whom he spake in *parables*, (which, by the way, he did, it is said, in order to *fulfil* a passage of the Psalms,) though it is manifest, that the prophecy of Isaiah, quoted, according to its literal sense, undoubtedly relates to the obstinate Jews, who lived in the time of Isaiah.

In fine, these, and the many other passages cited, *as prophecies*, from the Old Testament, by the authors of the New, do so plainly relate, in their obvious and primary sense, to other matters than those which they are adduced to prove, that it is allowed by the most learned defenders of

Christianity, that to pretend that they prove in a *literal* sense what they are adduced to prove, is to give up, with both hands, the cause of Christianity to the enemies thereof: who can so easily show, in so many undoubted instances, the Old and New Testament to have no manner of connection in that *respect*; but to be in an irreconcilable state.

These proofs from the Prophets being so different from what we should expect, it behooves us to enquire what could induce Jesus, and his Apostles to quote the Old Testament in such a manner?

The Jews shortly answer this question, by saying, that they did so, because they did not understand the meaning of the Books they quoted. But it has been answered by some learned Christians, that Jesus, and the Apostles did not quote in the manner they did through *caprice* or *ignorance*, but according to *certain methods* of *interpretation*, which were in their times, of established authority among the Jews.

These rules of interpretation, which were supposed to be irrecoverably *lost*, were afterwards recovered to the world, by the learned *Surenhusius*, professor of the Hebrew language in the illustrious school of Amsterdam.[8] He made an ample discovery to the world of the rules by which the Apostles *cited* the Old Testament, and *argued* from thence, wherein the whole mystery of the Apostles applying scripture in a *secondary*, or *typical*, or *allegorical* sense, seems to be unfolded. I shall therefore state this matter from Surenhusius.

He (Surenhusius) says "that when he considered the various opinions of the learned about the passages of the Old Testament quoted in the New, he *was filled with grief*, not knowing where to set his foot; and was much concerned, that what had been done with good success upon profane authors, could not be so happily performed upon the sacred."

He tells us, "that having had frequent occasions to converse with the *Jews*, (on account of his application to Hebrew literature from his youth) who insolently reflected upon the New Testament, affirming it to be plainly corrupted, because it seldom, or never agreed with the Old Testament; some of whom were so confident in this opinion, as to say, they would profess the Christian religion, if any one could reconcile the New Testament with the Old. I was *the more* grieved, because, (says this honest and well meaning man) I knew *not* how to apply *a remedy* to *this evil*." But the matter being of great importance, he "discoursed with several learned men about it, and read the books of others, being persuaded, that the authors of the books of the New Testament, had written nothing, but what was suited to the time wherein they lived; and that Christ, and his Apostles, had constantly followed the method of their ancestors. After he had long revolved this hypothesis in his mind, at last he met with a Rabbin, well skilled in the *Talmud*, the *Cabbala*, and the *Allegorical books* of the Jews. This Rabbin had once embraced the Christian religion, but was again relapsed to Judaism on account of the idolatry of the Papists, yet not perfectly disbelieving the integrity of the New Testament. Surenhusius asked him, what he thought of the passages of the Old Testament quoted in the New? Whether they were rightly quoted, or not? and whether the Jews had any just reason to cavil at them? and at the same time, proposed to him, two or three passages, which had very much exercised the most learned Christian commentators.

The Rabbin having admirably explained those passages, to the great surprise of Surenhusius, and confirming his explications by several places of the *Talmud*, and other writings of the Jewish commentators, and allegorical writers, Surenhusius asked him, what would be the best method to write a treatise, in order to vindicate the passages of the Old Testament quoted in the New? The Rabbin answered, that he thought the best way of succeding in such an undertaking, would be to peruse a great part of the *Talmud*, and the *allegorical*, and *literal* commentators; to observe their several ways of quoting, and interpreting Scripture, and to collect as many materials of that kind, as would be sufficient for that purpose."

Surenhusius took the hint immediately: he read such books as were recommended, observed every thing that might be subservient to his design, and made a book upon the subject. And in the third part of that book he gives us the rules so long sought after, viz. the *ten ways* used, he says, by the Jewish doctors in citing Scripture. And here they are.[9]

1. The first rule is—"reading the words of the Hebrew Bible, not according to the points placed under them, but according to other points *substituted* in their stead," as is done by Peter, Acts iii. 3; by Stephen, Acts vii. 43, and by Paul, 1 Cor. xv. 54; 2 Cor. viii. 15, and Heb. iii. 10; ix. 21; xii. 6.
2. The second rule is—"*changing* the letters, whether those letters

be of the same organ, (as the Hebrew grammarians speak,) or not," as is done by *Paul*, Rom. ix. 33; 1 Cor. xi. 9; Heb. viii. 9, and x. 5; and by *Stephen*, Acts vii. 43.

3. The third is—"changing both *letters* and *points*" as is done by *Paul*, Acts xiii. 41, and 2 Cor. viii. 15.
4. The fourth is—"*adding* some letters, and *taking away* others."
5. The fifth is—"*transposing* words and letters."
6. The sixth is—"*dividing* one word into two."
7. The seventh is—"adding other words to those in the text, in order to make the sense more clear, and to *accommodate it* to the subject they are upon."
8. The eighth is—"changing the *order* of words."
9. The ninth is—"changing the *order* of words, and adding *other words*."
10. The tenth is—"changing the order of words, adding words, and *retrenching* words," which, (says he) is a method often used by *Paul*. Of the application of *all these rules* he gives *examples* taken *from the New Testament*.

It is not necessary to make many observations upon these rules, they speak for themselves most *significantly*: for what is there that cannot be proved from the Old Testament, or any other book, yea, from Euclid's Elements! or even an old almanac! by the help of "*altering* words and sentences; *adding*, *retrenching*, and *transposing*, and *cutting words in two*;" as is stated above by a learned and good man, and sincere Christian; who found out, and brought forward these rules, as the *best means* of getting the authors of the New Testament out of a difficulty, which had long shocked, and grieved, their best friends.

CHAPTER VI.

IT may be objected from divers learned authors, who have been very sensible of the difficulties stated in the preceding chapters, and have, therefore, taken other ground than their predecessors, in order to defend themselves the better; I say, it may be objected to what I have advanced, that

Christianity is not, in fact, grounded on the prophetical, or other quotations made from the *Old*, in the *New* Testament; but that those quotations being allegorically applied by the authors of the New Testament, are merely arguments *ad hominem*, to convince *the Jews* of the truth of Christianity, who allowed such a method of arguing to be valid; and are not arguments to the rest of mankind.

To which I answer—That this distinction is the *pure invention* of those who make the objection, and not only, has no foundation in the New Testament, but is utterly subverted by its *express declarations*. For the authors of the books of the New Testament always argue absolutely from the quotations they cite as prophecies, out of the books of the Old Testament. Moses, and the Prophets, are every where represented to be a just foundation for Christianity; and the author of the Epistle to the Romans, expressly says, ch. xvi. 25, 26, "The gospel which was kept secret since the world began, was now *made manifest* by *the Scriptures of the Prophets* (wherein that gospel was secretly contained) to *all nations*:" by the means of the preachers of the gospel, who gave the *secret* or *spiritual* sense of those Scriptures. For, to the ancient Jews, according to them, the gospel was preached by the types of their law, and therefore must have been considered as truly contained in it.

Besides, the authors of the books of the New Testament were convinced, *long before the publication* of them, that the gospel was to be preached to *the Gentiles* as well as *the Jews*, to *both* of whom, therefore, they reasoned allegorically in their *books*, as Peter and others did in their *sermons*, though with greater success on Gentiles, than on Jews: and as Paul did before Felix, when he said he took his *heresy*, or Christianity, from the law, and the Prophets, Acts xxiv., as also he did before Agrippa. It should therefore seem strange, that books written to all the world, by men equally concerned to convert *Gentiles* as well as *Jews*, and that discourses made *expressly* to *Gentiles* as well as to Jews, should be designed to be pertinent *only* to Jews, much less to a very *few* Jews! Indeed I am ashamed at being thus long engaged in showing what must be self-evident; and did I not fear being further tedious to my reader, I would undertake to bring together passages from the New Testament, where the meaning and intention, of the writers, are *obvious*, in such abundance, as would immediately, and entirely, put the hypothesis of our opponents out of countenance.

These quotations from the Old Testament are certainly urged, and spoken of as *direct* proofs, as *absolute* proofs *in themselves*; and not as mere proofs *ad hominem* to *the Jews*. For if these prophecies are only urged by the Apostles as proofs to *the Jews*, and intended only as proofs founded on the *mistaken* meanings of the Old Testament of *some* Jews of their time, what sense is there in *appealing* upon *all occasions*, to *the Prophets*, and recommending the reading, and search of the Old Testament, for the *trial*, and *proof* of what was preached? For that was to proceed on weakness itself, *knowing* it to be so. Certainly nothing but *a real persuasion*, that the prophecies of the Old Testament were really fulfilled in Jesus, could make them everywhere *inculcate*, and *appeal* to the fulfilling of prophecy. In order to support their hypothesis, Christians have been forced to seek evidence to prove that the phrase, "*this was done that it might be fulfilled*," so frequent in the New Testament, meant no such thing, but was only a habit the Jews had got of introducing by such phrases a handsome *quotation* or *allusion* from the Old Testament. But this evasion must be given up on two accounts: 1, Because most of the European biblical critics of the present day, (the learned annotator on Michaelis' Introduction to the New Testament, Dr. Marsh, among others) frankly acknowledge it not to be tenable;[10] and 2, Because it can be proved not to be so from the New Testament itself. For example, when John represents (Jo. xix. 28,) Jesus upon the cross saying, "I *thirst*, that the Scripture *might be fulfilled*," doth he not plainly represent Jesus *as fulfilling* a prophecy which foretold that the Messiah should *thirst*, or say, "I *thirst*" upon the cross? Nay, does he not suppose him to *say so, in order to fulfil*, or that *he might* fulfil a prophecy? Is it not also suitable to the character of Jesus, who founded his *Messiahship* on the *prophecies* in the Old Testament, and could not but have the accomplishment of those prophecies constantly in view to fulfil, and to intend to fulfil them? And is it not unsuitable in John, in describing his master dying upon the cross, to represent him, as *saying* things, whereby he only *gave occasion* to observe, that he fulfilled, i. e. *accommodated a phrase!* not a prophecy!

Besides, they who set up this *accommodating principle* of accommodation, do, in some cases, take the term *fulfilled* in its proper sense, and do allow it (when convenient) to relate to a prophecy *really fulfilled*. But I would ask them, what rule they have to know when the Apostles mean a prophecy *fulfilled*, and when a phrase *accommodated*, since they are acknowledged to use the strong expression of *fulfilling* in the latter case, no less than in the former?

In a word, unless it be granted, that the citations were intended by the Authors of the New Testament, to be adduced, and applied as prophecies *fulfilled*; if you do suppose them not intended to be adduced, and applied *as prophecies*; then the whole affair of Jesus being *foretold* as the *Messiah* is reduced to *an accommodation of phrases*! And it will assuredly follow, that the citations of Jesus and his Apostles out of the Old Testament, are like, and no better than the work of the Empress *Eudoxia*, who wrote the History of Jesus in verses *put together*, and borrowed out HOMER! or that of *Proba Falconia*, who did the same, in verses, and words taken out of—VIRGIL!

In fine, one of two things must be allowed, either (which is most probable,) the Authors of the New Testament, conceived their citations to be *indeed* prophecies concerning Jesus, and then they were ignorant and blundered, and therefore were not inspired; or they knowingly used them as means to deceive the simple and credulous, into a belief of their being testimonies sufficient to prove what they themselves *knew* they had no relation to, and then they were *Deceivers*: there is no other alternative, and each horn of the Dilemma, must prove as fatal as the other.

Perhaps it may be said, "It is to no purpose for you to object to the *quotations*, or the *arguments* of Jesus, and his Apostles, for God was with them, confirming their Doctrine by signs following. They had from God the power of working miracles, and consequently, their interpretations of Scripture, however strange they may appear to your minds, must be *infallible*, they being men inspired."

To this argument it can be justly answered, first, that the question, whether Jesus be the Messiah, entirely depends, as proved before, upon his answering the characteristics given of that personage by the Jewish Prophets; and all *the miracles in the world*, could never, from the nature of the case, prove him to be so, unless his character does *entirely agree* with the archetype laid down by *them*, as has been already abundantly proved.

Secondly, That whether *these miracles* were *really* performed, or *not*, depends entirely upon the *credibility* of the Authors themselves who have *thus quoted!* which, as shall be shown hereafter, may be disputed: and thirdly, it could be retorted upon *Protestants*, that this same argument is the same in principle with the often refuted Popish argumentation. The Papists pretend to derive all their new invented and absurd Doctrines, and Practices, from the Scriptures by their *interpretations* of them; But yet, when their interpretations are attacked from Scripture, they immediately fly from thence to the *miracles* wrought in their Church, and to the visions of their holy men and saints, for the establishment of their *interpretations*, by which they support those very doctrines and practices; and particularly, they endeavour to prove thus the doctrine of *Transubstantiation*, from the numerous miracles affirmed to have been wrought in its behalf, which reasoning Protestant Christians assert, to be an argument *absurd* and *inconclusive*, therefore they should not use it themselves.

We allow, that if these interpretations of the sense of the Old Testament, had been in existence *before* the Christian Era, it might be something. But we beg leave to remind them, that it is certain, that these interpretations were not published till *after* the events to which they are referred took place, which is a circumstance of *obvious significancy*.

In fine, to this argument, I would answer as in Cicero—[de Natura, Deor. Ed. Dav. p. 209.] Cotta did to Balbus, "*rumoribus* mecum pugnas, ego autem a te *rationes* require." ["You meet me with rumors, whereas I ask you for arguments."]

CHAPTER VII.

BUT it may be asked, how was it possible, that wise and good men could have been led to embrace the Religion of the New Testament, if there were not in the Old Testament, some prophecies which might be conceived by them to supply, at least, *plausible* arguments to prove that Jesus of Nazareth was the Messiah? Are there no other passages in the Prophets, *besides* those quoted in the New Testament, and are there not a few passages quoted in the New Testament, which appear more to the purpose than those we have been considering? To this I candidly answer, that there are, and this chapter will be devoted to the consideration of them.

Two of these prophecies, one from Genesis, and the other from

Daniel, are thought by the advocates of Christianity (because they conceive them to point out, and to limit the time of the coming of the Messiah,) to be stronger in their favour than *any* of those quoted in the New Testament. If so, it is a very singular circumstance, that the inspired authors of the New Testament did not make use of *them*, instead of others not so much to the purpose. This circumstance, of itself, should teach us to examine the prophecies in question with *caution*, and also with *candour*; since many worthy and religious men have thought them sufficient to prove, that Jesus was indeed the Messiah. These prophecies I shall reserve last for consideration, and shall now begin with the others usually adduced, taking them up pretty much in the order in which they stand in the Old Testament.

The first passage is taken from Deut. xviii. 15, "The Lord thy God will raise up unto thee a Prophet from the midst of thee, like unto me, unto him ye shall hearken. According to all that thou desiredst of the Lord thy God in Horeb, in the day of the Assembly, saying, Let me not hear again the voice of the Lord my God, neither let me see this great Fire any more, that I die not. And the Lord said unto me, they have well spoken that which they have spoken. I will raise them up a Prophet from among their Brethren, like unto thee, and I will put my word into his mouth, and he shall speak unto them all that I command him. And it shall come to pass, that whoever will not hearken unto my words which he shall speak in my name, I will require it of him."

This passage is pertinaciously, and *solely* applied to Jesus, by many Christian writers, because it is so applied by Peter, in the 2 ch. of Acts, in his sermon to the Jews, just after he had received the full inspiration of the Holy Spirit, and, of course, must be considered as *infallible*. Nevertheless, these words of Moses are supposed by many learned men, both Jews and Christians, to be spoken of *Joshua*, whom Moses himself afterwards, at the command and appointment of God, declared to be his successor, and who was endowed with the spirit which was upon Moses: See Deut. xxxi. 33; xxxiv. 17: and to whom the Jews then promised to hearken, and pay obedience as they had done before to Moses. But others understand them to be a promise of *a succession of Prophets*, to whom the Jews might, upon all occasions, have recourse. And one, or the other, of these seems to be the certain meaning of the place; from this consideration, that from the context it appears Moses was giving the Jews directions of *immediate* use: and therefore, in promising a Prophet to them *to whom they should hearken*, he seems to intend an *immediate* Prophet, who might be of use to the Jews, and answer their common exigencies, and not a Prophet *two thousand years to come*.

But I take the words to promise a *succession of Prophets*, and for that sense wherein Grotius, and Le Clerc[11] and most of the Jews take them. I shall give my reasons for this, and show that they do not *necessarily* refer to Jesus Christ.

Moses, in the verses preceding this prophecy in the same chapter, Deut. xviii. 9–14, tells the Israelites from God, that "when they came into Canaan, they should not learn to do after the abominations of the people thereof; and particularly, that there should not be found among them any one that useth *Divination*, or an observer of times, &c., or a consulter with familiar spirits, &c. For all, says he, that do these things, are an abomination to the Lord; and because of these abominations the Lord thy God doth drive these people out from before thee. For these nations which thou shalt possess hearkened unto observers of times, and unto diviners. But as for thee, the Lord thy God hath not suffered thee to do so." Then follow the words about the Prophet, "The Lord thy God will raise up unto thee a Prophet from the midst of thee of thy Brethren like unto me, unto him ye shall hearken." All which is as much as to say, "When you come into Canaan, do not hearken to a Diviner, &c., as the Canaanites do, for the Lord will give you a Prophet of your own Brethren, inspired like me, to guide, and instruct you, to whom ye shall hearken." Or rather, "Do not hearken to Diviners, &c., but to Prophets who shall be raised up among you."

Now, that the words cited must relate to a succession of Prophets, to begin upon the Israelites taking possession of the land of Canaan, is manifest, because the raising up of a Prophet to whom they were to hearken, is *the reason given* why they should *not hearken* to a Diviner, &c., when they came into that land; which reason could have no force unless they were to have, 1st—an immediate Prophet in Canaan. (For what sense is there, or would there be in saying, "Don't hearken to such Diviners as are in Canaan, when you *come there*; for you shall have a Prophet of your own, to whom ye shall hearken, *two thousand years after you come there?*")

2dly. As the context shows that the Prophet to be raised up, was an immediate Prophet, so it also shows, that the *singular number here stands for the plural*, according to the frequent custom of the Hebrew language, as is shewn by Le Clerc and Stillingfleet, in loco.[12] For *one single Prophet* to be raised up immediately, who might soon die, could not be a reason why Jews of *succeeding* generations should not hearken to Diviners, in Canaan.

Finally, the words of God by Moses, which follow the promise of a Prophet, evidently shew that by that promise, *Prophets* were intended, in laying down *a rule* for the test, or trial of the Prophets before mentioned, in such a manner, as implies, that *that rule* was to be applied to *all Prophets pretending to come from him*. See the words in Deut. xviii., 19–22.

I shall conclude this explication, by adducing in confirmation of it, the paraphrase of the words given in the Targum of Jonathan. "The nations you are about to possess (says the Jewish Paraphrast) hearken to Jugglers and Diviners: But you shall not be like them; for *your Priests* shall enquire by Urim and Thummim, and the Lord your God shall give you a true Prophet."[13] And this explication is the one adopted by Origen.—[Contra Celsum, p. 28.]

As to the difficulty that is raised against this explication from the words at the end of Deuteronomy, "That there arose not a Prophet since in Israel like unto Moses, whom the Lord knew face to face; in all the signs and wonders which the Lord sent him to do," &c. it is nothing at all. For every one perceives, that the word "like," may be, and frequently *is* used in Scripture, and in common language, to signify similarity in *some*, though not in *every* particular; and every Prophet, who speaks by God's direction, is a Prophet "*like* unto Moses," who did *the same*; though he be *not* like, or *equal* to him "*in doing signs and wonders*;" which is all that is affirmed in the last chapter of Deuteronomy.

And finally, there is nothing to *limit* this prophecy to Jesus of Nazareth, if we *allowed*, (what we reject,) the Christian interpretation; since God might to-morrow, if such were his will, raise up a Prophet like unto Moses in *every respect*, which Jesus certainly was *not*; therefore, it cannot be applied, and *restrained* to the purpose for which it is quoted by Peter.

There is in the same Sermon, in the 2 ch. of Acts, another passage

quoted by Peter from the Psalms, and applied by him to prove the resurrection of Jesus, and on which he lays very great stress, which after all
seems to be nothing to the purpose. Peter says, "him, (i. e. Jesus) God had
raised up, having loosed the pains (or bands) of death, because it was not
possible that he should be holden of it." And why? "For, (because) David
speaketh concerning him, 'I foresaw the Lord always before my face, for
he is on my right hand, that I should not be moved. Therefore did my
Heart rejoice, and my tongue was glad; moreover also my flesh shall rest
in hope. Because thou wilt not leave my soul in Hades, (the place of
departed Spirits,) nor suffer thy *Holy one* to see *corruption*, thou hast
made known to me the ways of life, thou shalt make me full of joy with
thy countenance.'" Men and Brethren, let me freely speak unto you of the
Patriarch David, that he is both dead, and buried, and his sepulchre is with
us unto this day. Therefore being a Prophet, and knowing that God had
sworn with an oath to him, that of the fruit of his loins, according to the
flesh, he would raise up Christ to sit upon his Throne. He, seeing this
before, *spake of the resurrection of Christ*, that *his* soul was not left in
Hades, neither did *his* flesh see corruption.

How imposing is this argument! How plausible it appears! And yet it
is irrelevant, as Dr. Priestley frankly confesses, who tries to save the
credit of the Apostle by the *convenient* principle of accommodation! The
whole force of Peter's reasoning depends upon the word "*corruption*."—
David *did* see corruption, therefore he could not mean *himself*, but "being
a Prophet, &c." he meant *Jesus Christ*. Now the whole of Peter's argument is grounded upon two mistakes, for 1st, the Hebrew word translated
"*corruption*," here signifies "destruction, perdition," and in the next
place, instead of being "thy Holy one," in the singular, it is in the Hebrew
"thy Saints," in general. The passage is quoted from the 16th Psalm: and
I will give a literal translation of it from the Original, which will make the
propriety, or impropriety of Peter's quotation perfectly obvious. The contents, and import of the Psalm, according to the English version, are as
follows:—"David, in distrust of his merits, and hatred of Idolatry, fleeth
to God for perservation. He showeth the hope of his calling, of the resurrection, and of life everlasting."—And the passage in question, according
to the original, reads thus. "I have set the Lord always before me: because
he is on my right hand, I shall not be moved: therefore my heart is glad,

and my glory (i. e. tongue) rejoiceth: my flesh also shall rest in hope. For thou wilt not leave my soul in Hades, neither wilt thou suffer *thy Saints* to see *destruction*. Thou wilt show me the path of Life; in thy presence is fulness of joy, and at thy right hand are pleasures for evermore." That is— "Because I have ever trusted in thee, and experienced thy constant protection, therefore I will not fear death; because thou wilt not forever leave my soul in the place of departed spirits, nor suffer thy saints to *perish from existence*. Thou wilt raise me from the dead, and make me happy forever in thy presence."

In the 4 ch. of the Acts, the Apostles are represented as praying to God, and referring in their Prayer to the 2d Psalm "why did the Heathen rage, &c." as being a prophecy of the opposition of the Jews to Jesus: with how much justice may be seen from these circumstances:

1. That "*the Nations*" as it is in the original, did *not* assemble together to crucify Jesus, as this was done by a few soldiers. 2ndly, The "*Kings of the Earth*" had no hand in it, for they knew nothing about it. And 3dly, Those who were concerned did, by no means, "form *vain designs*," since they effected their cruel purpose. And lastly, from that time to the present; God has not set Jesus as his King upon the "holy hill of Sion," (as the Psalm imports,) nor given him "the Nations for his inheritance, nor the uttermost parts of the Earth for a possession."

The next prophecy usually adduced to prove that Jesus is the Messiah, is the passage quoted from Micah, v. 2, in the second chapter of Mat. "But thou Bethlehem Ephratah, though thou be little among the chiefs of Judah, yet out of thee shall he come forth unto me, that is to be ruler in Israel, whose goings forth have been from of old, from the days of hidden ages." This passage probably refers to the Messiah, but by no means signifies that this Messiah was *to be born* in Bethlehem, as asserted by Matthew; but only, that he was to be *derived* from Bethlehem, the City of Jesse, the father of David, of famous memory, whose family was venerable for its antiquity, "being of the days of hidden ages." And this interpretation is known and acknowledged by Hebrew scholars. But, in order to cut short the dispute, we will permit the passage to be interpreted as signifying that Bethlehem was to be *the birth place* of the Messiah. What then? Will a man's *being born* in Bethlehem be sufficient to make him to be the Messiah foretold by the Hebrew

Prophets? Surely it has been made plain in the beginning of this work, that many more characteristic marks than this *must meet in one person*, in order to constitute him the Messiah described by them!

In Zechariah, ix. 9, it is written, "Rejoice greatly, O Daughter of Sion. Shout O Daughter of Jerusalem! Behold thy king cometh unto thee, the righteous one, and *saved*, or preserved (ac. to the Heb.) lowly, and riding upon an ass, and upon a colt, the foal of an ass." This has been applied by the Evangelists to Jesus, who rode upon an ass into Jerusalem.

But, in the first place, it is to be observed, that there seems to have been a blunder in this transaction; for according to the *Hebrew Idiom* of the passage quoted above, the personage there spoken of was to ride upon "an *ass' colt*;" whereas the Apostles, in order to be sure of fulfilling the prophecy, represent Jesus as riding up an *ass, and the colt too!* "They spread their garments upon *them*, and set him upon *them*." See the Evangelists in loc. In the next place, a man may ride into Jerusalem upon an ass, without being thus necessarily demonstrated to be the *Messiah*. And unless, as said before, every tittle of the marks given by the Prophets to designate their Messiah, be found in *Jesus*, and in *any other* claiming to be that Messiah, his being born in Bethlehem, and riding upon an ass into Jerusalem, will by no means prove him to be so. Besides, those who will take the trouble to look at the context in Zechariah, will find, that the event spoken of in the quotation, is spoken of *as contemporaneous* with the *restoration of Israel*, and the establishment of peace and happiness, which seems to cut up by the roots, the interpretation of Evangelists. And to conclude the argument, Jesus being born in Bethlehem, and riding into Jerusalem, allowing it to be true, would not, we think, frustrate these prophecies of a *future* fulfilment: for no one can disprove, that, if so be the will of God, such a person as the Messiah is described to be, *might* be born in Bethlehem *to-morrow*, and ride in triumph into Jerusalem twenty years afterwards.

The next passage which has been offered as a prophecy of Jesus, is to be found in the 12th ch. of Zech. v. 10, and *part of it* has been *misquoted* by John. "And I will pour upon the House of David, and upon the inhabitants of Jerusalem, the spirit of grace, and supplications, and they shall look *on me*, whom they have *pierced*," So it stands in the English version, but before I state what it *ought* to be, I would observe, that before the

Evangelist, (who, in his account of the crucifixion, applies this passage as referring to Jesus's being *pierced* with a spear,) could make this passage fit his purpose, he had to substitute the word "*him*" for "*me*" as it is in the Hebrew, confirmed by, I believe, *all* the versions, ancient and modern, without exception. Yet, with this change, it will by no means answer his purpose; for the Hebrew word here translated "*pierced*," in this place signifies "*blasphemed*" or "*insulted*" as it is understood by Grotius, who confirms this rendering from the Hebrew of Levit. xxiv. 11, where, in this passage, "the Israelitish woman's son blasphemed the name of the Lord." The Hebrew word translated "*blasphemed*" is from the same root with the Hebrew word translated "*pierced*" in the passage in Zechariah quoted above. So that the passage ought to be translated thus: "I will pour upon the House of David, and upon the inhabitants of Jerusalem, the spirit of grace, and supplications, and they shall look towards me whom they have *blasphemed*." (To "*look towards God*" is a phrase frequently met with, and well understood.) Now to enable us to understand more perfectly this passage, let us consider the context, where we shall find, that it states, that there was to be a war in Judea, and *a siege of Jerusalem*, and then *a deliverance of the Jews*, by the *destruction of all the nations* that should come up at that time, against Jerusalem. *Immediately after* which matters, follows the prophecy under consideration, "I will pour upon the House of David, &c."—Now, from these things thus laid down together, I crave leave to argue in the words of Dr. Sykes, (Essay, &c. p. 268.)[14] "Did *any one circumstance* of all this happen to the Jews about the time of the death of Jesus? or rather was not every thing the *reverse* of what Zechariah says; and instead of all nations being *destroyed* that came about *Jerusalem*, Jerusalem *itself* was destroyed: instead of a spirit of grace and supplications, the Jews have had their hearts *hardened* against the Christ; instead of *mourning* for him whom they have *pierced*, they curse him and his followers, even until this day."

But it is tiresome thus to waste time in proving that *orts and ends* of verses, disjointed from their connection, and even the words quoted, some of them *changed*, and some *transposed*, (though even done according to the rules given by the venerable *Surenhusius*,) prove nothing. We must, therefore, devote the remainder of this long chapter to the consideration of the three famous prophecies, on which Christians have not hesitated, with triumphing confidence, to rest the issue of their cause. These are the prophecy of Shiloh, Gen. xlix.; the 53d chap. Isaiah; and Daniel's prophecy of the *"Seventy Weeks."* I will consider them in order, and thus wind up the chapter.

I have somewhere read in a Catechism, the following question and answer:—Q. "How can you *confound* the Jews, and prove from prophecy, that the Messiah is already come?" A. From these two prophecies, "The sceptre shall not depart from Judah," &c, Gen. xlix.; and this, "Seventy weeks are determined upon thy people," &c. Dan. ix. 24.

But notwithstanding these overwhelming proofs, the stubborn Jews refuse to be confounded! on the contrary, they in fact laugh at Christians, for being so easily imposed upon.

The prophecy concerning *Shiloh*, the Jews acknowledge, refers to their Messiah; but they do not *allow* that it *defines*, or *limits* the time of his coming. And that it in fact does *not*, will be perfectly evident to all who will look at the place in the *Hebrew Bible*, which they will find pointed to read, *not*,—"The Sceptre shall not depart from Judah, and a lawgiver from between his feet *until* Shiloh come, &c." But thus, "The Sceptre shall not depart from Judah, nor a lawgiver from between his feet *for ever, for* Shiloh *shall* come, and to him shall the gathering of the people be." So that the prophecy does not intimate that the Messiah should come *before* the Sceptre be departed from Judah; but that it should not depart *for ever*, but shall be restored when Shiloh comes. This is the plain and obvious sense of the prophecy; and moreover, is the only one that is consistent with *historical fact.* For in truth the Sceptre *had* departed from Judah *several hundred years* before Jesus of Nazareth was born. For, from the time of the Babylonish captivity, '*Judah*' has never been free, but in subjection to the Persians, the Syrians, the Romans, and all the world.

If my readers desire further satisfaction with regard to this interpreta- tion of this famous prophecy: I refer them to the dispute upon this subject between the celebrated *Rittangelius*, and a learned Jew, (preserved in Wagenseil's "Tela Ignea,")[15] where he will find Rittangelius first amicably *inviting* the Hebrew to discuss the point, who does so most ably, and respectfully towards his Christian antagonist; and unanswerably estab- lishes the interpretation above stated, by the Laws of the *Hebrew lan-*

guage, by the ancient interpretation of the *Targum*, by venerable tradition, and by *appealing to history*. Rittangelius *begins* his defence by shuffling, and *ends* by getting in a passion, and calling names; which, his opponent who is cool, because confident of being able to establish his argument, answers by notifying to Rittangelius his compassion, and contempt.

The next prophecy proposed to be considered, is the celebrated prophecy of Isaiah consisting of part of the 52nd and the whole of the 53rd ch. It is the only prophecy which *Paley* thinks worth bringing forward, in his elaborate defence.[16] And it must be confessed, that if this prophecy relates to *the Messiah*, it is by far the most plausible of any that are brought forward, in favour of Jesus Christ. It merits therefore a thorough discussion, and I shall endeavour that it shall be a candid one. This prophecy is quoted by Jesus himself in Luke xxii. 39., and by Philip, when he converted the Eunuch, (Acts viii.) for "beginning at this prophecy, he preached unto him Jesus."

It will not be necessary to cite the passage at length, it being one perfectly familiar to every Christian. I will then, before I consider it, first premise, that since it has been heretofore abundantly made evident, that the Messiah of the Old Testament was not to *suffer* and *die*, but to *live* and *reign*, it is according to the rules of sound criticism, and I think sound Theology too, to interpret this solitary passage, so that it may not contradict very many others of a directly contrary import. Now if this passage can relate *only* to the Messiah, it will throw into utter confusion the whole scheme of the Prophetical Scriptures. But if it can be made to appear, that it does not *necessarily* relate to *him*; if it can consistently with the context, be *otherwise* applied, the whole difficulty vanishes. Now the Authors of the New Testament have applied this prophecy to the *Messiah*, and to *Jesus* as the Messiah; and for doing so, they have been accused of misapplication of it from the *earliest times*; since we know from *Origen*, that the Jews of his time derided the Christians for relying upon this prophecy; alleging that it related to their own nation, and was a prophecy of *their suffering* and *persecuted state*, and of their *ultimate emancipation* and *happiness*. And this interpretation of the prophecy, the learned *Vitringa* in his commentary upon Is. in loc. allows to be the most respectable he had met with among the Jews, and according to him "*to be by no means despised.*"[17]

In order that the fitness, or unfitness of this application of the prophecy may be made apparent, and evident, we will now lay before the reader this famous prophecy, part by part, each part accompanied by the Jewish interpretation.

Isaiah lii. 13, "Behold my servant shall prosper, he shall be exalted, and extolled, and be very high." Interpretation—My *servant Israel*, though he be in great affliction for a time, yet hereafter shall be released from captivity, and be honoured and raised to elevation very high among the nations of the earth. (That the Jewish nation is spoken of in the *singular* number, and under the title of *God's servant* frequently in the Old Testament, is well known, and will be here made certain by a few examples. Isaiah xli. (the chapter preceding the prophecy) "But thou *Israel my servant*, thou *Jacob*, whom I have chosen," presently afterwards, "saying to thee, *thou* art *my servant*." Again, chapter xliv. "Now therefore, hear *Jacob my servant*," and so frequently in the same chapter. See also ch. xlv., and Jer. ch. xxx., and Ps. cxxxvi., and Isaiah throughout, for similar examples.)

"As many were astonished at thee, (his visage was so marred, more than any man, and his form more than the sons of men,")—that is—As many were astonished at thee, on account of thy abject state, and miserable condition, being squalid with misery, and suffering more than any men.

"So shall he sprinkle many nations, the kings shall shut their mouths at him; for that which had not been told them shall they see, and that which they had not heard shall they consider."

Interpretation—As the Gentiles wondered at their abject state, so as to make them a proverb of reproach, so shall they admire at their wonderful change of circumstances, from the depth of degradation to the height of prosperity, and honour. So that they shall lay their hands upon their mouths, which had before time reproached them, when they shall see their felicity to be so far beyond what had been told them, and they shall attentively consider it, and they shall say to each other—"Who hath believed our report, and the arm of the Lord to whom was it revealed? For he *grew up*, (Heb., not "he *shall grow* up" as in the English version) before him as a tender plant, and as a root out of a dry soil, he had no form nor comeliness: and when we saw him, there was no beauty that we should desire him."

The sense is, The Gentiles shall say to each other in wonder, "Who believed what we heard concerning them! And to whom was the interest the Lord took in them made known? For it was a despised people, feeble, and wretched, like a tender plant springing up out of a thirsty soil. Their appearance was abject, and there was nothing attractive in their manners."

"He was despised and rejected of men, a man of sorrows and acquainted with grief, and we hid, as it were our faces from him; he was despised, and we esteemed him not."

That is, They were despised, and held in abhorrence, they were men of sorrow, and familiar with suffering. We looked upon them with dislike, we hid our faces from them, and esteemed them not.

"Surely he hath borne our griefs, and carried our sorrows."

Interpretation—Surely their sufferings are as great as if they had borne the sins of the whole world; or, they are nevertheless the means appointed to remove the sufferings of an afflicted world, for God hath connected universal happiness with their prosperity; and the end of their sufferings is the beginning of our joys.

"Yet did we esteem him *smitten of God*, and afflicted."

Interpretation—Nevertheless we considered them as a *God-abandoned race*, and devoted to wretchedness by him, for having crucified their king.

"But he was wounded for, (or *by*) our transgressions, he was bruised for [or by] our iniquities, the chastisement of our peace was upon him, and through his stripes we are healed."

That is, But instead of being the victims of God's wrath, they were wounded through our cruelty, they were bruised by our iniquitous treatment, we being suffered to do so to chastise them for their sins, and to prove their obedience; and this chastisement is that by which our peace is to be effected; for their chastisement and probation being finished, God will by them impart and diffuse peace and happiness.

"All we like sheep have gone astray, we have turned every one to his own way, and the Lord hath caused to meet upon him the iniquity of us all."

But it is we who have sinned more than they, we have all gone astray in our ignorance, being without the knowledge of God, or of his Law. Yet the Lord hath permitted us to make them the subjects of our oppressive iniquity.

"He was oppressed, [or "exposed to *pecuniary exactions*"] and he was afflicted, yet he opened not his mouth; he was brought as a lamb to the slaughter, and as a sheep before her shearers is dumb, so he opened not his mouth. He was taken from prison and from judgment, and who shall declare his generation, ["into his manner of life, who stoopeth to look?" according to the Hebrew] for he was cut off out of the land of the living; for [or by] the transgression of my people was he stricken. And he made his grave with the wicked: but with the rich were his deaths [or tomb] because he had done no violence, neither was deceit in his mouth."

Interpretation—How passive and unresisting were they when oppressed! they were afflicted, and they complained not; when through false accusations, and mistaken cruelty they were plundered and condemned to die, they went like a lamb to the slaughter, and as a sheep before her shearers is dumb, so they opened not their mouth. They were taken from the dungeon to be slain, they were wantonly massacred, and every man was their foe; and the cause of the sufferers who condescended to examine? for by the thoughtless crimes of my people, they suffered. Yet, notwithstanding their graves were appointed with the wicked, yet they were rich in their deaths: This did God grant them, because they had not done iniquity.

Rabbi Isaac, author of the famous Munimen Fidei,[18] renders the original—"on account of impieties was he given to his sepulchre, and on account of his riches was his death, because he did no violence, neither was deceit in his mouth!"—which he interprets thus. We (the former speakers) raised against them false accusations of impiety, on account of their religion, and refusing to worship our Idols, but their riches were the real cause why we put them to death. Nevertheless they used no violence in opposition to our oppressions, neither would they forsake their religion, and deceitfully assent to ours in hypocrisy.*

"Yet it pleased the Lord to bruise him, he hath put him to grief. When thou shalt make his soul a propitiation for sin, he shall see his seed, he

---

*The person here spoken of by Isaiah is said to *make his grave* with the *wicked*, and be with the *rich* in his *death*. Whereas *Jesus* did exactly the *contrary*. He was with the *wicked* (i. e. the two thieves) *in his death*, and with *the rich* (i. e. Joseph of Aramathea) in *his grave or tomb*. In the *original*, the words *may* be translated that "he shall *avenge* or *recompense* upon the wicked his Grave, and his death upon the rich." Thus do the Targum, and the Arabic version interpret the place: and Ezekiel ix. 10, uses the verb in the verse in *Isaiah* under consideration translated (in the English version.) " He made, &c." In the same sense, given to this place in Isaiah, by the *Targum*, and the *Arabic*, as said above. See the place in Ezekiel, where it is translated—"I *will recompense* their way upon their head." See also Deut. xxi. 8, in the original. The Syriac has it—"The wicked contributed to his burial, and the rich to his death." The Arabic "I will punish the wicked for his burial, and the rich for his death." The Targum, "he will send the wicked into Hell, and the rich who put him to a cruel Death."

shall prolong his days, and the pleasure of the Lord shall prosper in his hands." (This proves that this prophecy cannot refer to any *individual*, but may refer to the *Jewish nation*, because *one individual* cannot be *put to death*, and yet *"see his seed"* and *"prolong his days."*) "After (or on account of) the travail of his soul, seeing he shall be satisfied, by his knowledge shall my righteous servant make many righteous (or show them righteousness,) and he shall bear the burden of their iniquities."

That is, after and for their sufferings, they shall be abundantly rewarded; by their superior knowledge of religious truth, shall they make many wise, "for many nations shall go, and say, come ye and let us ascend to the mount of the Lord, and to *the house of the God of Jacob*, that he may teach us his ways." Mic. 4 ch.

"Wherefore I will give him a portion with the Great, and with the mighty shall be divide the spoil, because he poured out his life unto Death, and was numbered with the transgressors, and himself bare the sin of many, and interceded for the transgressors."

Interpretation—Therefore their reward shall be exceeding great, because for the sake of their duty, they willingly exposed themselves to death, and were accounted as transgressors, and bore the cruel afflictions inflicted by many, and made intercession for them who afflicted them.

Such is the explication given by the Jews of this prophecy. I have made no important alterations of the common English translations; except, that in some passages, I have made it more conformable to the original, by substituting a verb in the *past* tense, instead of leaving it *in the future*, as in the English version. Those Translators have taken certain liberties in this respect to make this prophecy (and several others) more accordant to their own views, which are not supported by the Hebrew: many of these expressions however we have left unaltered, as they are quite harmless. But if any of our readers desire further information with regard to the propriety of this interpretation of this prophecy of Isaiah, we refer him to the *"Munimen Fidei,"* contained in Wagenseil's *"Tela Ignea"* where he will find it amply illustrated and defended.[19] Here, in this work, we shall content ourselves with proving that this prophecy can, by no means, relate to *Jesus Christ*, from these circumstances.—1. Jesus certainly was not exalted, and magnified, and made very great *upon Earth*, which as has been shown, was to be the scene of the exaltation of the Old

Testament Messiah, but was put to a cruel and disgraceful death.—2. He was not *oppressed* by *pecuniary exactions*, as is said of the subject of this prophecy.—3. He was never *taken from prison* to die, for he was never *in one*.—4. He did not "see his seed," nor "prolong his days," since he died childless, and we will not permit the word "seed" to be *spiritualized* on this occasion, for the word seed in the Old Testament, means *nothing else* than *literally 'children,'* which it is not pretended he ever had; and how could he "prolong his days," when he was cut off in his 33rd year.—5. Besides, who were "the *strong* and *mighty*" with whom he divided the spoil? were they the twelve fishermen of Galilee? and what was the spoil divided? In a word, the *literal* application of this prophecy to Jesus, is now *given up* by the most learned Hebrew Scholars, who allow, that the *literal* sense of the original can never be understood of him. See Priestley's notes on the Scriptures, in loco; and the context before and after.

We have now come to the last subject proposed to be considered in this chapter, viz. Daniel's prophecy of the seventy weeks. The "*instar omnium*" of the prophetical proofs of Christianity; and which was for ages held up to the view of "the unbelieving race," as cutting off, beyond doubt, their 'hope of Israel' from ever appearing, since the time so distinctly foretold had elapsed. But such is the instability of human opinions, that it was at length suspected, and at last ascertained by the learned, that "the stubborn Israelites" had some reason for denying that prophecy, any voice in the affair.

During many years, one learned man, after another, had amused himself with destroying the system of his predecessor, and replacing it with his own, not a whit better, but tending to the same end, viz., to make the prophecy of the seventy weeks *tally* and *fit* with the event of *the crucifixion*. At length *Marsham*, a learned Englishman, declared and demonstrated, that his predecessors in this inquiry had been grossly mistaken, for that the prophecy, in all its parts, was totally irrelevant, and irreconcilable with *the time of the crucifixion*.[20] The appearance of his book put all the Theologians of that age in an uproar. But many learned Christians in the last, and present century, now freely acknowledge, that *Daniel* is not on their side, but as much a Jew as his brethren.

This celebrated prophecy literally translated from the original is as follows. Dan. ix. 24, &c. "Seventy weeks are determined upon thy people, and upon thy holy city, to finish the transgression, and to make an end of sins, and to make reconciliation for iniquity, and to bring in everlasting righteousness, and to seal the vision, and prophecy, and to anoint the most Holy, (i. e. the sanctum sanctorum, or Holy of Holies.) Know therefore, and understand, that from the going forth of the word to restore, and build Jerusalem, unto the anointed Prince, shall be seven weeks; and (in) threescore, and two weeks the street shall be built again, and the wall, even in troublous times. And after threescore and two weeks shall the anointed (one) be cut off, and be without a successor: (Heb. "and not, or none to him,") and the City and the Sanctuary shall be destroyed by the people of the Prince that shall come; and the end thereof shall be with a flood, and unto the end of the war desolations are determined. And he shall confirm the covenant with many for one week, and half the week, (i. e. in the midst of the week) he shall cause the sacrifice and the oblation to cease, and for the overspreading of abominations he shall make it desolate, even until the consummation, and that (is) determined be poured upon the desolate."

This is the prophecy on which such stress has been laid, as pointing out the *precise time* of the coming of the Messiah: and I shall fully demonstrate that it hath not the most distant reference to that event. And for the better explanation of the prophecy, it is proper that we attend a little to the context.

*In the preceding chapter of Daniel it is said, that when Daniel was informed of the vision of the two thousand, and three hundred days, he sought for the meaning; but not rightly understanding it, he judged, that that great number was a contradiction to the word of God as delivered by Jeremiah, concerning the redemption at the end of seventy (Jer. xxv. 11, 12, and ch. xxix. 10.) and from thence he concluded, that the captivity was prolonged on account of the sins of the Nation. This doubt arose from his not understanding the prophecy, and therefore the Angel said unto him, "I am now come forth to give thee skill, and understanding." And he proceeds to inform him, that as soon as he began to pray, and God saw his perplexity, the royal command went forth from him, that he should come to Daniel to make him understand the truth of those mat-

*The remainder of this chapter is taken from *Levi*, and *Wagenseil*.

ters, that were to come to pass in future time. And as the angel Gabriel had explained to him the vision from whence his doubt arose, it was incumbent on him to perfect the explanation: and that is what is meant by the expression *"to show"* i. e. as I began the explanation, the commandment was that I should finish it.

Before I proceed to give the Jewish explanation of the prophecy, it is proper to show in what manner the answer of the angel in it agreed to Daniel's question, and also the reason of his using the term weeks, and not years, or times, as in the other visions.

It appears, that Daniel, from the words of Jeremiah, perceived that God would visit all the nations, and punish them for their sins; as may be observed from the following words, "Thus saith the Lord God of Israel unto me. Take the wine cup of his fury at my hand, and cause all the nations to whom I send thee to drink it." Jer. xxv. 15. He then mentions first *Jerusalem*, and afterwards *the Kings of Egypt, Tyre, Sidon*, and *all the Isles* beyond the sea, and many others; and at last *the King of Sheshak or Babylon*.

He also further perceived, that the visitation of each nation would be at the end of *seventy years*, as Isaiah observes of Tyre "and it shall come to pass in that day, that Tyre shall be forgotten *seventy years*." Isaiah xxiii. 15, The same of Babylon. "And it shall come to pass when *seventy years* are accomplished, I will punish the king of Babylon," Jer. xxv. 12, and as it is observed in the next verse, "All that is written in this Book which Jeremiah hath prophesied, against *all the nations*." From whence it appears, that as the visitation of Babylon was to be in *seventy years*, so was that of the other nations to be; for so had the wisdom of God decreed to *wait* according to this number. For which reason, and because the Prophets say that the *restoration* of Israel is to be contemporaneous with the destruction of their enemies, Daniel appears to have judged, that the sins of his nation would be done away by the seventy years of the captivity of Babylon. And therefore the Angel informed him of his error, by telling him, that this was not to be the case with his nation; for that their wickedness was come up before God, and their sin was very grievous; and that therefore their sins would not be atoned for by seventy years, as in the case of the rest of the nations, to whom he allowed seventy years *to see if they would repent*; and if not, then he will punish them. But as for *Israel*, he would not only wait *seventy years*, but *seven times seventy years*; (for thus it is literally, in the Heb. the words translated "seventy weeks," are literally *"seventy sevens,"*) after which, if they had not repented and reformed, their kingdom should be cut off, and they return into captivity, to finish an atonement for their transgressions. Hence the *cause* of Daniel's *question* is evident; and the *propriety* of the Angel's *answer* to the question is manifest; as also the expression of *weeks* or *sevens*.

These seventy weeks are without doubt *four hundred and ninety years*, the time elapsed from the destruction of the first Temple, till the destruction of the second.

This, it seems, was the more necessary for the Angel to inform him of; because Daniel judged, that after their return from Babylon, by means of *that visitation only*, all their sins would be done away. For which reason, the angel showed him that it would not be so, [for the return from Babylon was not *a perfect redemption*, because there was not a *general* collection of *all* that were in captivity, even *all the tribes*, save only a few of Judah and Benjamin, and those not the most respectable. And after their return, they were not free, but were under the dominion of the *Persians*, *Greeks*, and *Romans*. And although they at one time threw off their yoke, and had kings of the *Asmonean* and *Herodian* families, yet was there no king among them of the seed of *David*, neither had they the *Shekinah* nor *the Urim and Thummim*, all which is a manifestation that it was not a perfect redemption, but only a visitation with which God was pleased to visit them; so that they were allowed to build a Temple to the Lord, by *the permission* of *Cyrus*, and *according to the measure given by him*. This was, that they might be the better enabled to do the works of repentance during the time allowed, and thus "make atonement; and thus finish the transgression; and make an end of sins; and make reconciliation for iniquity;" and thus, at the end of the time assigned even *"seventy weeks,"* they would bring in "everlasting righteousness;" i. e. universal virtue and felicity throughout the world, when Jehovah should be known, worshipped, and obeyed by all mankind. But if they did *not* repent, and *amend*, if they did evil, as their fathers, *then* their kingdom was to be *cut off* at the expiration of the seventy weeks; which *in fact took place*.]

After the Angel had thus expressed himself in general terms, he descended to particulars: and laid down *three propositions* (if I may be allowed the term,) or *periods*.

First. "Know therefore, and understand, (that) from the going forth of the word to restore, and build Jerusalem, unto *the anointed Prince*, (shall be) seven weeks."

That is, it shall be *seven weeks* or *forty nine years* from the destruction of the first Temple, to *Cyrus*, "*the anointed Prince*," who shall give leave to build the second. (With regard to the import of the phrase "the going forth of the word," I refer the reader to Levi's Letters to Priestley,[21] and shall here only concern myself with settling the meaning of the expression of "the anointed Prince.") Many Christians have objected to the term Messiah, or *anointed*, being applied, as in our interpretation to *Cyrus* a Heathen Prince; and they apply it themselves to *Jesus of Nazareth*. But that the term or appellation *Messiah can* be applied to *Cyrus* is evident; since we *find it so applied* by God himself in the xlv. ch. of Isaiah. "Thus saith the Lord to his *anointed*, to *Cyrus*." 2. It is a singular fact, that the appellation "*Messiah*" is *never* applied to *the expected deliverer of the Israelites* in the *whole Bible*, except *perhaps*, in the ii. Psalm. It is an appellation indifferently applied to *Kings*, and *Priests*, and *Prophets*; to *all* who were *anointed*, as an induction into their office, and has nothing in it *peculiar* and *exclusive*; but the application of it to the expected Deliverer of Israel, *originated in and from the Targums*. 3. In order to make this prophecy, and this phrase—"*Messiah the Prince*," or "*the anointed Prince*" apply to Jesus of Nazareth, Christians connect, and *join together* this *first* member of the prophecy with the *second*, in open defiance of the original Hebrew; and after all, they can reap no benefit from this manoeuvre; for the term '*Messiah Nagid*' or—'the anointed *Prince*,' can never apply to *Jesus*, in this place, at *any rate*; because he certainly was no '*Prince or Nagid*,' a word which in the Hebrew Bible *always*, *without exception*, denotes *a Prince*, or *Ruler*, one invested with *temporal* authority, or *supreme command*. Now, as it is allowed on all hands, that *Jesus* had no such temporal power, as *a Prince* or *Ruler*, it consequently follows, that he can, by no means, be the "*anointed Prince*" mentioned in the prophecy.

Second Period.—"And (in) threescore and two weeks, the street shall be built again, and the wall, even in troublous times."

Here the Angel gave him to understand, that after the seven weeks before mentioned, there would come a time in which the building would be hindered, (and which was on account of the letter written by Rheum, and Shimshai to Artaxerxes; who, in consequence thereof, made the building to cease—See Ezra, and Nehemiah,) till the second year of Darius, who gave leave to finish the building: which continued till the Destruction by the Romans, *sixty two weeks*, besides the *last week*, at the *beginning* of which, the Romans came, and warred against them, and at length entirely destroyed the cities of Judah, Jerusalem, and the Temple. For, from the time that Cyrus first gave leave to build the Temple, till its completion, was *twenty one* years; and its duration *four hundred and twenty*, in the *whole*, sixty three weeks, or *four hundred and forty one years*. But the Angel made his division at *sixty two* weeks, as he *afterwards* described what was to come to pass in the *last week* (and with reason, for the horrible Jewish war lasted *seven years!*) And by the words—"*in troublous times*" he informed Daniel, that during the building of the Temple, they would have continual trouble, and alarms from their enemies, as is mentioned in Ezra and Nehemiah, where we find, that while some worked, the others held the shield and spear. And even after finishing it, they were almost continually in trouble, and persecuted, as is evident from the Books of Maccabees, and from Josephus.

Third Period.—"And *after* threescore and two weeks, shall *the anointed* be cut off, and have no successor. (Heb. "and not or none to him".) And the city, and the sanctuary shall be destroyed by the people of the Prince that shall come; and the end thereof shall be with a flood, and unto the end of the war, desolations are determined."

That is, and after that period, shall *the High Priest* or ("*the anointed one*") be cut off,—[the High Priest is called "*Messiah*," witness Lev. iv. 3.—"If *the Messiah Priest*, (or *anointed Priest*) doth sin, &c."]—and have no successor; and the City, and the Temple shall be destroyed by Titus and the Romans, and until the end of the war, your country shall be swept with the besom of destruction.

The angel finishes the prophecy with these words, "And he (the Prince that shall come) shall *strengthen* the covenant with many for one week. And in the midst of the week (i. e. the *seventieth* and *last week*,) he shall cause the sacrifice and the oblation to cease."

This prediction was fully accomplished; for 1. *Titus* "the Prince that should come" was continually offering peace to the Jews, and tried to "*strengthen* the covenant;" i. e. their old treaties made with the Romans, and in fact, did bring over many. 2. On account of the distress of the siege, the daily sacrifice did, in fact, cease to be offered in the temple some time before its destruction: and the angel further observes, that all this was to come upon them for their sins, "for the overspreading of abominations it should be made desolate."

This is what appears to be a plain, and fair explication, of this prophecy. But since Christians seeing mention made in it of *a Messiah to be cut off*, have eagerly endeavoured to press it into their service, it remains for me to show, that it is *impossible* to make this prophecy refer to "the cutting off" of *Jesus*.

The difficulty that learned Christians have met with in their attempts to do this, will be easily conceived by any person, when he knows, that more than a dozen different Hypotheses have been framed by them for that purpose. But that they have lost their labour will be obvious from this single observation, that "the *anointed one*, or *Messiah*," who the Prophet says was to be "cut off," was to be cut off "AFTER the threescore and two weeks," i. e. *at the destruction of Jerusalem*, or *within* the *seven years preceding that event!* Now we know from the Evangelists, and from profane History, that *Jesus* was crucified *more than* 40 *years before* the destruction of Jerusalem. In addition to this, nothing need be said, for this circumstance lays flat their interpretation at one stroke.

Those who desire to see a more elaborate discussion of this prophecy, and an ample defence of this interpretation, are referred to "Levi's Letters to Priestley." And those who are desirous of seeing an account of the various, contradictory, perplexed, and multitudinous contrivances by which it has been endeavoured to apply this prophecy to Jesus, are referred to Prideaux, Michaelis, and Blayney.[22]

We have now gone through an examination of the evidence adduced *from the Prophets* of the Old Testament to prove that *Jesus* is *the Messiah* of the Old Testament; and those of our readers who love truth, are, we trust, now made sensible, that the Religion of the New Testament, if *built upon such proofs as these*, is evidently founded on—a *mistake*.

CHAPTER VIII.

Many of our readers have, no doubt, heard from the pulpit many exclamations, and declamations against "the blindness of the Jews," in not recognizing their Messiah in Jesus of Nazareth. The reasons of this "Blindness" are made, I think, by this time, pretty intelligible.

Nevertheless, for the further satisfaction of the reader, I will here set down the principal reasons given by Rabbi Isaac in his "Munimen Fidei," which cause the Jews to deny the Messiahship of Jesus.

"At a certain time, says he, a certain learned man of the wise men of the Christians, said unto me, wherefore are you Jews unwilling to believe Jesus of Nazareth to be the Messiah, when yet your veritable Prophets testified of him, whose words you profess to have faith in."

"I gave him this answer. 'How, I require, could we believe him to be the Messiah, when you can produce no genuine proof from the Prophets in his favour? since all those things adduced by the Evangelists from them to prove Jesus the Messiah, are nothing to the purpose. And we have many and evident reasons, to prove that he was not the Messiah. And of these, I will bring forward a few, arising,—1. From his *Genealogy*. 2. From his *Works*. 3. From *the time* of his appearing. 4. From the prophecies of the things to take place in the time of the Messiah *not having been fulfilled* in his age. And in these things are contained the genuine marks, characteristic of our Messiah."

'1. As to what concerns his Genealogy, it does *not prove* this necessary thing, that Jesus was the son of David. Because he was not begotten by Joseph, as the Gospel of Matthew testifies. For in the first chapter of it, it is written, that Jesus was born of Mary when she was yet a Virgin, and had not been known by Joseph, which things being so, the Genealogy of Joseph has nothing to do with Jesus. The descent and origin of Mary is still less known, but it seems from Luke's calling *Elizabeth* who was of *Levi*, her *cousin*, that Mary was of the tribe of *Levi*, and not of *Judah*, and consequently not of *David*, and if she were, still *Jesus* is not more the Son of David, descents being reckoned from the *males only*. Neither is the Genealogy of Joseph rightly deduced from David, but labours under great difficulties.—Matthew, and Luke also, not only disagree, but *irreconcilably* and *flatly contradict* each other in their Genealogies of Joseph. Now, it cannot be, that the testimony of two witnesses, who directly contradict each other in *the matter to be proved by them*, can be received as true. But the prophets have directed us to expect no Messiah, but one born of the seed of David."

'2. As to the *works* of Jesus, we object to what he said concerning himself. "Do not consider me as come to establish Peace on Earth, for I have come to send a sword, and to separate the Son from the Father, and the Daughter from her Mother, and the Daughter-in-Law from her Mother-in-Law," which words are written Mat. ch. 10. But we find the prophecies concerning the Messiah to attribute to him very different works from these; nay the very opposite. For whereas Jesus testifies concerning himself, that he did not come to establish *Peace* in the Earth, but "*Division*," "*Fire*," and "*Sword*;" Zechariah says, concerning the expected Messiah, ch. 9,—"He shall speak Peace to the nations." Jesus says, he come to send "fire and sword" upon the Earth, but Micah says, ch. 2, that in the times of the true Messiah, "they shall beat their swords into ploughshares, and their spears into pruning hooks. Nation shall not lift up sword against Nation, neither shall they learn war any more." Jesus says, that he come "to put *Division* between the Father, and the Son, &c." But in the time of the true Messiah, Elias the Prophet shall come, of whom Malachi prophesied "that he shall convert the heart of *the Fathers* unto *the children*, and the heart of the children to the Fathers." Jesus says, "that he come to serve others, not to be served by them," Mat. xx. 28. But of the true Messiah it is said, Ps. 72,—"All kings shall bow themselves before him, all nations shall serve him." The same also is said by Zechariah, ch. 9,—"His dominion shall be from one sea to the other, and from the river unto the ends of the Earth." And so Dan., ch. 7,—"All dominions shall serve, and obey him."

'3. As to the *Time*, we object to the Christians, that Jesus did *not come at the time* designated by the Prophets. For the Prophets testify that the coming of the Messiah should be "*in the end of Days*," or in the latter days, (which surely have not yet arrived) as it is in Is. ch. 2. "It shall come to pass *in the latter days*, that the mountain of the Lord's house shall be established in the top of the mountains, and *all nations* shall flow unto it," and it immediately follows concerning the king Messiah, "that he shall judge among the nations, and rebuke many peoples, and they shall beat their swords into ploughshares, and their spears into pruning hooks." See also Hosea, ch. 3, and also Dan. ch. 2, where it is written. "God hath made known unto king Nebuchadnezzer what *shall come to pass in the latter days*," (or, in the end of days.) And this pertains to what follows, viz. to this. 'In the days of those kings (i. e. of the kingdoms that arose *out of the ruins* of the Roman Empire) the God of Heaven will raise up a kingdom, which shall never be destroyed.' Thus you see, that the Prophets predicted, that the kingdom of the Messiah should be after the destruction of the Roman Empire, not *while it was in its vigour*, when *Jesus* came; in '*the latter days*,' and not before.*

4. Besides all these difficulties, neither were the promises made to us by the Prophets, concerning the things to come to pass *at the coming of the Messiah*, fulfilled in the time of Jesus. For examples, take the following:—'1. In the time of the King Messiah there was to be one kingdom only, and one only king upon earth, viz. the King Messiah, see Dan. ch. 2. But, behold, we see with our eyes *many independent kingdoms*, distinct, and distinguished by different Laws and Customs, Religious and Political, which things being so, it follows, that the Messiah is not yet come.'

'2. In the time of the King Messiah there was to be only *one Religion*, and *one Law* throughout the world. For it is written in Isaiah, ch. 52, and 66, that *all nations* shall come at stated times to worship Jehovah at Jerusalem—see also Zechariah, ch. 14, and ch. 8, and indeed throughout the writings of the Prophets.'

'3. In the time of the King Messiah, *Idols* were to be cut off, and utterly to perish from the Earth, as it is said in Zechariah, ch. 13, and so in Is., ch. 2, it is written—"And the glory of Idols shall utterly pass away," and so in Zephaniah, ch. 2.—"The Lord shall be terrible among them, when he shall

---

*The Reader is requested to consider the reasoning in the last paragraph. The prophecy in the second chapter of Daniel is commonly supposed to relate to the four Great Empires, the Babylonian, Persian, Grecian, and Roman. This last it is (according to this interpretation,) foretold should be *divided into many Kingdoms*, and that 'in the latter days of these Kingdoms' (*which art now subsisting*,) God would set up a Kingdom which would never be destroyed, that of the Messiah. Of course, according to this interpretation, the Kingdom of the Messiah was not to be, not only, not *till after* the destruction of the *Roman Empire*, but not till *the latter days* of the Kingdoms which *grew up out of its ruins*; whereas Jesus Christ was born in the time of Augustus, i. e. *precisely* when the *Roman Empire itself* was in the highest of its splendour, and vigour; this is a remarkable, and very striking repugnance, to the claims of the New Testament, and, *if substantiated*, must overset them entirely.

make lean (i. e. bring to nothing) all the Gods of the Earth, and all the countries of the nations shall bow themselves to Him, each out of his place.'"

'4. In the times of the Messiah there shall obtain no more sins, and crimes in the Earth, especially among the children of Israel,' as is affirmed in Deut. 30, Zephaniah, ch. 3, and in Jeremiah, ch. 3, and 50, and so also in Ezekiel, ch. 36 and 37.

'5. In the times of the Messiah there shall be peace between man and beast, and between the Tyger and the tame beast. And the little child shall stroke with impunity the variegated skin of the serpent,' (and as one of our own Poets has beautifully said,—

"And with his forked tongue shall innocently play."—

See in Is., ch. 11, and 65, the original from whence he derived his beautiful Poem.)

'6. In the time of the King Messiah there are to be no calamities, no afflictions, no lamentations throughout the world: But the inhabitants thereof are to lead joyful lives in gratitude to the good God, and in the enjoyment of his bounties,' see Is. 65.

'*Lastly.* In the time of the King Messiah, the glory of God was again to return to Israel, and the spirit of the most High God was to be liberally poured out upon them, and they were to be endowed with the spirit of prophecy, and with wisdom, and knowledge, and understanding, and virtue, and God will no more hide his face from them; but will bless them, and give them a ready heart, and a willing mind to obey his Laws, and enjoy the felicities consequent thereupon. And the *Shechinah* shall inhabit the Temple *forever*, and the Glory of God shall never depart from Israel; but they shall walk amid the splendours of the Glory of Jehovah, and all the Earth shall resound with his praise, as is written in Ezech., ch. 37, and 39, and 43, and in Joel, ch. 2, and in Zech., ch. 2, and in Is., ch. 11, and throughout the *latter part of his prophecies, and in Jer.* 31.'[23]

And now Christian Reader! let me ask you this question, has *any one* of the foregoing prophecies been yet fulfilled, either in the days of *Jesus, or ever since*?—Thou canst not say it! Now, then, hear the conclusion, which in sincerity, and with the hand upon the heart, I am compelled to draw from these precedents. "Since these *distinctive characteristics* predicted by the Hebrew Prophets, as to be found in their Messiah, were *certainly,* and *evidently,* never found in *Jesus,* and since these *conditions* and *circumstances,* and many others besides, which to avoid prolixity have been omitted, most assuredly did not take place in *the time of Jesus,* nor *ever since,* and since they were according to those Prophets, certainly to be expected in the time of *their Messiah,* therefore, from all this it seems to be *demonstrable,* (allowing the Prophets to be true,) that Jesus of Nazareth was *not* this true Messiah." And I would ask the candid Christian, in which link of this chain of proofs he can find a *flaw?* and I would ask him too, as *a moral,* and *honest man,* whether any Jew, in his right mind, *could,* without setting at nought what he conceived to be the word of God,—receive him as the Messiah? The honest, and upright answer, I believe will be, that he could not. And accordingly it is very well known that the Jewish Nation have *never done so.* And this, *their obstinacy* as it is called, will not by this time, I think, appear *unreasonable* to any sensible man; and he will now be able duly to appreciate the justice of that idle cant about "*the carnal Jews;*" and their "*worldly minded*" expectation of a temporal Prince, as their Messiah. Certainly, the Jews had very good reason *from their prophecies* to expect no Messiah, but a Messiah who should sit on the throne of David, and confer liberty, and happiness upon *them,* and spread peace, and happiness *throughout the earth;* and communicate the knowledge of God, and virtue, and the love of their fellow-men to every people. Whether this (carnal or not,) would have been better than a *spiritual* kingdom, and a throne in Heaven; together with the ample list of *Councils, Dogmas, Excommunications, Proscriptions, Theological Quarrels, and Frauds; and an endless detail of Blood and Murder;* I leave to the judgment of those capable of deciding for themselves.

Neither, in fact, is it true, that the Jews were so "carnally minded" as to refuse to receive Jesus as their Messiah, because he was *poor* and *in a low estate.* On the contrary, did they not ask him to come out of his evasions? "How long (said they) dost thou mean to keep us in suspense? If thou be the Messiah *tell us plainly!*" These very men were willing to hazard in his favour, their fortunes, their families, and their lives in his cause, against the whole power of the Roman empire. Nay, so urgent were they, that they were going to make him their king by force, and he concealed himself from the honour. The evasions he used to avoid their pressing questions upon the subject, are known to all who have read the Evangelists: and so timid was he in acknowledging himself as the Messiah, that he did not do so, till Simon Peter told him that he was. And can any candid man, after all this, wonder at, or condemn "the blindness," as it is called, of the Jews? or can he refrain from smiling at the frothy declamations, in which divines load that nation with so much unmerited reproach? These Jews had just reason, we think, to doubt his Messiahship; and they had *a right* to satisfactory, and *unambiguous* proof of his being so: even the proofs *laid down by their Prophets.* And this it must be *now* acknowledged they wanted; and certainly, the wise and learned of the Jewish nation might be allowed to have understood their sacred books upon the subject, *as well*, at least, if not *better*, than the illiterate Apostles, who *manifestly* put *new* interpretations upon them, and those confessedly, not agreeable to the *obvious* and *literal meaning* of those books; but contrary to the sense of the Jewish nation. And for this scepticism they might plead the example of the Apostles themselves, who, *at first*, like other unbelieving Jews, expected a temporal Prince; and did *disbelieve* Jesus to be the Messiah, on account of *his death*, notwithstanding his *miracles.* And they continued in these thoughts, till it seems they came to understand the *spiritual sense* of the Scriptures: which spiritual sense, it is said, they obtained by "the traditionary rules of interpretation in use among the Jews." Yet it is rather *inconsistent* and *singular*, that they should place so much dependence upon these *traditionary rules*, and yet pay so *little regard* to the *traditionary explication of the Scriptures*, with respect to the *temporal kingdom* of *the Messiah.**

---

*The sum of our argument may be expressed thus. God is represented in the Prophecies of the Old Testament as designing to send into the world an eminent Deliverer, descended from David, the peace and prosperity of whose reign should far exceed all that went before him; in whom all the glorious things foretold by the Prophets should receive their entire completion; and who should be distinguished by the character of the Messiah or Christ. This is an article of faith common to Christians and Jews. But that Jesus of Nazareth should be esteemed this Messiah, and that Christians can support that opinion by alleging the prophecies of the Hebrew Scriptures as *belonging to*, and *fulfilled* in *him*, is what we can by no means allow, and that especially on account of these inconsistencies.

1. Because, these prophecies acknowledged on both sides *to point out* the Messiah, could not otherwise *answer the end* of inspiring them *than by an accomplishment* so *plain* and *sensible*, as might sufficiently *distinguish* the person meant by them *to be that Messiah.* But no such accomplishment, we contend, can possibly be discerned in *Jesus*, and consequently he cannot be the person meant by them.

(Continued from page 116)

2. Because several predictions, which Christians apply to Jesus, are wrested to a meaning which quite destroys the historical sense of Scripture, and breaks the connection of the passages from whence they are taken. Thus many shreds and loose sentences are culled out for this purpose, which do not appear to have any relation to Jesus, or to the Messiah either; but to have received their proper and intended completion in some other person, whom the Prophet, as is manifest, had then only in view.

3. Because, in their forced applications of the prophecies, Christians finding themselves hard pressed by the simple and natural construction, forsake the *literal*, and take shelter in *spiritual* and *mystical* senses, fly to Hyperboles, and strained metaphors, and thus expound the true meaning and importance of the prophecies quite away; the intent whereof being to instruct men in so necessary a point of faith as that relating to the Messiah, it is reasonable to think they would be delivered in the most perspicuous and intelligible terms. Since ambiguous expressions (capable of such strange meanings as they pretend) would be too slippery a foundation to build such a point of faith upon; would be of no use, or worse than none; would be unable to teach the clear truth, and apt to ensnare men in dangerous errors by leaving too great a latitude for fanciful interpretations, and introducing darkness and confusion, and contradiction inexplicable.

4. Because, admitting, (as indeed it never was, or can be denied,) that many passages of Scripture, and of prophetical Scripture especially, most be figuratively taken; yet we must always put a wide difference between a sense *not just*, as the words in their first signification import, and a sense *directly the contrary* of what they import. And yet we complain that *this latter* is the sense which Christians labour to obtrude upon the gainsayers. We say, that a kingdom *of* this world and *not of this world*; contempt and *adoration*; *poverty* and *magnificence*; *persecution* and *peace*; *sufferings* and *triumph*; a cross and a throne; the scandalous death of a private man *upon a gibbet*, and the *everlasting dominion* of *a universal monarch*, must be *reconciled*, and mean *the self same thing*, before the prophecies appealed to, can do their cause any service. Granting then, that the *goodness* of God, (according to them,) to have been better than his word, by giving *spiritual blessings*, instead of *temporal*, yet what will become of the *truth of God*, if he act contrary to his word? even when it would be for our advantage; if he mislead people by expressions, which, if they mean any thing at all, must mean what the Jews understand by them?

In short, it seems to me, that if Providence has, in truth, any concern with the predictions of the Old Testament, it could not have taken more effectual care to justify the unbelief, and obstinacy of the Jews, than by ordering matters so, that the life and death of Jesus Christ, should be so exactly, and so *entirely* the *very reverse* of all those ideas under which their Prophets had constantly described, and the Hebrew nation as constantly expected their Messiah, and his coming; and to suppose that the Supreme Being meant to describe, and point out such a person as Jesus Christ by such descriptions of the Messiah as are contained in the Old Testament, is certainly substantially to accuse him of the most unjustifiable prevarication, and mockery of his creatures.

In order that the subject we are examining, and the arguments we make use of, may be clearly understood by the reader, he is requested to bear in mind, that the author reasons all along upon the supposed Divine authority of the Old Testament, which is admitted by both Jews and Christians. Whether the supernatural claims of the Old Testament be just, or not, is of no consequence in the world to the controversy we are considering. For the dispute of the Jew with the *Christian* is one thing, and his dispute with the sceptic is another totally different. For whether such a personage as the Messiah is described to be, *has appeared eighteen hundred years ago*, is quite a different thing from the question, whether such a personage *will appear at all*. The Christian says, that he *has* appeared in the person of *Jesus of Nazareth*. This the Jew *denies*, but looks forward to the future fulfillment of the promises in his Bible. While the Sceptic denies that the Messiah *has come*, or *ever will*.

CHAPTER IX.

I am now about to consider a subject, to which, notwithstanding the harsh-
ness of my language in some of the preceding chapters, I approach with feelings of great respect. Far be it from me to reproach the meek, the compassionate, the amiable Jesus, or to attribute *to him*, the mischiefs occasioned
by his followers. No, I look upon his character with the respect which every
man should pay to *purity of morals*: though mingled with something like the
sentiments which we naturally feel for the *mistaken enthusiast*.* Jesus of

---

(Continued from page 117)

But the subject at present under consideration is the dispute of the Jew with the Christian, who
acknowledges the Old Testament to be a Revelation, upon which a new Revelation, that of the New
Testament is founded, and erected. To him the Jew argues, that if the Old Testament *be* a Divine Revelation, then the New Testament *cannot* be a Revelation, because it contradicts, and is repugnant to
the Old Testament, the more ancient, and acknowledged Revelation. Now God cannot be the author
of two Revelations, one of which is repugnant to the other. One of them is certainly false. And if the
Christian, conscious of the difficulty of reconciling the New with the Old Testament, attempts to support the New, at the expense of the Old Testament, upon which the former is, and was built by the
founders of Christianity; then the Jew would tell him, that he acts as absurdly as would the man who
should expect to make his house the firmer, by undermining, and weakening its foundation.

So that whether the Christian *affirms*, or *denies*, he is ruined either way. For he is reduced to this
fatal dilemma. If the Old Testament contains a Revelation from God, then the New Testament is not
from God, for God cannot contradict himself; and it can be proved abundantly, that the *New* Testament
is contradictory, and repugnant to the *Old*, and to *itself too*. If, on the other hand, the Old Testament
contains *no Revelation* from God, then the New Testament must go down at any rate; because it asserts
that the Old Testament *does* contain a Revelation from God, and builds upon it as a foundation.

---

*There was nothing which gave the author, in writing this Book, so much uneasiness, as the
apprehension of being supposed to entertain disrespectful sentiments of the Founder of the Christian
Religion. I would most earnestly entreat the reader to believe my solemn assurances, that by nothing
that I have said, or shall be under the necessity of saying, do I think, or mean to intimate the slightest
disparagement to the moral character of one, whose *purity of morals*, and *good intentions*, deserve any
thing else but reproach. That he was an enthusiast, I do not doubt; that he was a wilful impostor I never
will believe. And I protest before God, that from the apprehension above-mentioned alone, I would
have confined the contents of this volume to myself, did I not feel compelled to justify myself for
having quitted a profession; and did I not, *above all*, think it *my duty*, to make a well meant attempt,
which I hope will be seconded, to vindicate the unbelief of an unfortunate nation, who, *on that
account*, have for almost eighteen hundred years, been made the victims of rancorous prejudice, the
most infernal cruelties, and the most atrocious wickedness. If the Christian religion be, *in truth*, not
well founded, surely it is the duty of every honest, and every humane man, to endeavour to dispel an
illusion, which certainly has been, notwithstanding any thing that can be said to the contrary, the *bona
fide*, and real cause of unspeakable misery, and of repeated and remorseless plunderings, and mas-
sacres, to an unhappy people; the journal of whose sufferings, *on account of it*, forms the blackest page
in the history of the human race, and the most detestable one in the history of human superstition.

Nazareth appears to have been a man of irreproachable purity, of great piety, and of great mildness of disposition. Though the world has never beheld a character *exactly parallel* with his, yet it has seen many *greatly similar*. Contemplative and melancholy, it is said of him by his followers, "he was often seen to weep, but never to laugh." He retired to solitary places, and there prayed: he went into the wilderness to sustain, and to vanquish the assaults of the devil: In a word, he appears by such means to have persuaded himself, as hundreds have done since, that he was the chosen servant of God, raised up to preach righteousness to the hypocrites and sinners of his day. It is remarkable, that he *never claimed* to be the *Messiah*, till encouraged to assume that character by Peter's declaration. And it is observable, that in assuming that name, he could not assume the characteristics of the august personage to whom it belongs; but infused into the character all that softness, meekness, humility, and passive fortitude, which were so eminently his own. The natural disposition and character of Jesus could not permit him to attempt the character of a princely Messiah, a mighty monarch, the Saviour of an oppressed people, and the benefactor of the human race. He could not do this, but he could act as much of the character as was consistent with his own. He could not indeed bring himself to attempt to be the Saviour of his countrymen from the *Romans*, their *fleshly foes*; but he undertook to save them from the tyranny of their *spiritual* enemies. He could not undertake to set up his kingdom *upon earth*; but he told them that he had a kingdom *in another world*. He could not pretend to give unto his followers the splendid rewards of an earthly monarch: but he promised them instead thereof, *forgiveness of sins*, and *spiritual remuneration*.

In a word, he was not a king fit for the 'carnal Jews,' but he was, from his mildness, and compassionate temper, worthy of their esteem, at least, of their *forbearance*. The only actions of his life which betray any marks of character deserving of serious reprehension, are his treatment of the woman taken in adultery; and his application of the prophecy of Malachi concerning *Elias*, to John the Baptist.

As to his conduct to the woman, it was the conduct of a mild, and merciful man, but not that of one who declared, "that he came to fulfil the law." For God commanded concerning such, "that they should surely be put to death." Now though Jesus was not *her judge*, and had *no right* to pronounce her *sentence*; yet the contrivance by which he deterred the witnesses from testifying against her, was a contrivance, directly calculated, totally to frustrate the ends of justice; and which, if acted upon at this day, in Christian countries, would infallibly prevent the execution of the criminal law: For what testimony would be *sufficient* to *prove* a fact, if the witnesses were required to be "*without sin?*" Instead therefore of saying unto them, "whosoever of you is without sin, let him cast the first stone at her;" he *should* have said, 'Men! who made me a judge, or a divider over you? carry the accused to the proper tribunal.'

As to his conduct about the matter of Elias, it was as follows:—It is said, in the 17th chapter of Matthew, that at his transfiguration, as it is called, Moses and Elias appeared to his disciples on the mount, talking with Jesus. Upon coming down from the mount, the disciples asked Jesus, "how say the Scribes that Elias must come first, (that is, *before* the Messiah.) Jesus answered, Elias truly cometh first, and restoreth all things; but I say unto you, that Elias has *come already*, and they have done unto him what they would;" meaning John the Baptist, who was beheaded by Herod.—(See the parallel place in Mark.) And he says, concerning John, (Mat. xi. 14) "And *if ye will receive it*, this is *Elias which was for to come.*"

Now certainly no one will pretend that *John was* the *Elias* prophesied of by Malachi, as *to come* before "the *great*, and *terrible day of the Lord*" which has *not yet* taken place. And besides, that he was not Elias is testified of, and confirmed by *John himself*, who in the gospel of John, chapter 1, to the question of the Scribes asking him, "if he was *Elias?*" answers, "*I am not.*" It is pretty clear that Jesus was *embarrassed* by the question of the Apostles, "how say the Scribes, that Elias must come *first?*" for his answer is confused; for he allows the truth of the observation of the Scribes, and then refers them to *John*, and *insinuates* that *he* was "the *Elias* to come." However it must be acknowledged, that he does it with an air of hesitation, "*if ye will receive it*," &c.

But are these all the accusations you have to bring against him? may be said by some of my readers. Do you account as nothing, his claiming to *forgive sins?* his speeches wherein he claims to be considered as *an object of religious homage?* if not to be God himself? Do you consider these impieties as nothing? I answer by asking the following questions: What would you think of a man, who, *in our times*, should set up those extraordinary claims? and who should assert, that "eating *his flesh*, and drinking *his blood*" were necessary to secure *eternal life*? Who should say, that "*he* and *God* were *one*?" and should affirm (as Jesus does in the last chapters of John) that "God was *inside of him* and *dwelt in him*;" and that "he who *had seen him*, had *seen God*?"—What should we think of this? Should we consider such a man an object of *wrath*, or of *pity*? Should we not directly, and without hesitation, attribute such extravagancies to hallucination of mind? Yes, certainly! and therefore the Jews were to blame for crucifying Jesus. If Christians had put to death every unfortunate, who, after being frenzied by religious fasting and contemplation, became wild enough to assert, that he was *Christ*, or *God the Father*, or *the Virgin Mary*, or even *the Holy Trinity*, they would have been guilty of more than *fifty murders*; for I have read of at least as many instances of this nature; and believe, that more than two hundred such might be reckoned up from the hospital records of Europe alone. And that the founder of the Christian religion was not *always* in his right mind, I think, will appear plain to every intelligent physician who reads his discourses, especially those in the gospel of John. They are a mixture of something that looks like sublimity strangely disfigured by wild and incoherent words. So unintelligible indeed, that even the profoundest of Christian divines have never been able to fathom all their mysteries. To prove that I do not say these things *rashly*, *wickedly*, or out of any *malignity* towards the character of Jesus, which I really respect and venerate, I will establish my assertions by *examples*. For instance—

—Many instances might be adduced of conduct *directly subversive* of the very design to promote which, he said, that he was sent into the world. For example, he said, that he came to preach glad tidings to the *poor* and *uninformed*; and yet he declares to his disciples, that he spake to this very multitude of poor and ignorant people *in parables*, lest they *might understand him*, and *be converted from their sins*, and God should *heal or pardon them*. In the 26th chapter of Matthew, Jesus says, to his disciples in the garden of Gethsemane these strange words, "Sleep on now, and take your rest—*Arise*! let us *be going*." The commentators endeavour to get rid of the strange contradictoriness of these words, by turning *the command* into the *future*; and rendering the Greek word translated "*now*," thus—"*for the rest of your time*," or "*for the future*." And that he asked them "whether they slept for the future"?! which appears to be just as rational, as to have asked, "*how they do tomorrow*"?!

Jo. viii. 51, "Verily, verily, (said Jesus) I say unto you, if a man keep my saying, *he shall never see death.*" Reader, what dost thou think of this saying? Has believing in the Christian religion, at all prevented men from dying as in aforetime? And should we be at all astonished at what the Jews said to him, when they heard this assertion, "Then said the Jews unto him, Now *we know* that thou hast a demon (i. e. art mad)—Abraham is dead, and the Prophets, and thou sayest if a man keep my saying he shall *never taste of death?*" So said the Jews, and if *in our times* a man was to make a similar assertion, should we not say the same?

Many instances might also be given of *absurd* and *inconsequent reasoning*; but I shall only adduce the following:—He reproaches the Pharisees, Luke xi. 47, 48, for building, and adorning the sepulchres of the Prophets, whom their wicked fathers slew; and says to them, "Your fathers slew them, and ye build their sepulchres;" and he adds, "That thus they *showed* that they *approved* the deeds of their fathers!" Surely this is absurd! Did the *Athenians*, by setting up a statue to *Socrates* after his unjust death, *show* to the world that they "*approved*" the deed of them who slew him? Did it not show the *direct contrary*? And was it not intended as a testimony of their *regret* and *repentence*.

Again, "Upon you (says Jesus to the Jews) shall come *all the righteous blood* that has been *shed upon the earth*, from the blood of *Abel, the righteous*, to the blood of *Zechariah*," &c. Now herein is a marvellous thing! How could a man really sent from God, assert to the Jews, that *of them* should be required the blood of *Abel*, and of *all the righteous slain upon the earth*? Did *the Jews* kill *Abel*? or did *their fathers* kill him? No! he was slain by *Cain*, whose posterity all perished in the deluge: how then could God require of the Jews, who lived four thousand years after the murder, the guilt of it: nay more, "of all the righteous blood that had been shed upon the earth," were they guilty of all that too? If *such* assertions, and *such* reasonings, do not prove what I asserted, what can?

It is said, that Jesus, by giving himself up to suffer death, *proved* the truth of his mission and doctrines, by his readiness to die for them. But this is an argument which will recoil upon those who advance it. Are there no instances upon record of mild, zealous, and amiable men who preached to the savages of America, that they ought to worship the *Virgin Mary*? and did they not cheerfully die by the most excruciating torments to prove it? Yes, certainly! And let any Protestant Christian read the accounts of the *preaching, sufferings, deaths,* aye! and *miracles too,* of the Roman Catholic missionaries in Asia and America; and then let him candidly answer, whether he is willing to rest the issue of his controversy with the *Papists* upon the argument of *martyrdom*? We all know the power of enthusiasm upon a susceptible mind; and we have read of, and perhaps seen its effects in producing martyrdoms among people of all religions, in all parts of the world. Nay, more, such is the power of this principle, that even now, women in India burn themselves alive, on the funeral piles of their husbands, to prove, as they say, their love for them, and their determination to accompany them to the other world; when it is well known, that they burn themselves from the impulse of *vanity,* and the fear of *disgrace,* if they should not do so. Nay more still, so little support does martyrdom yield to *truth,* that there are more martyrdoms in honour of the false, rediculous, and abominable idols of Hindostan, than any where else. You may see men hooked through the ribs, and supported, and whirled round in the air, in honour of their gods, clapping their hands, and testifying pleasure, instead of crying out with pain. You may see in that country, the misguided enthusiastic worshippers of misshapen idols, prostrate their bodies before the enormous wheels of the car of *Seeva,* and piously suffering themselves to be crushed in pieces by the rolling mass. And any man who has been upon the banks of the Ganges, can tell you of the *Yoguis,* and of their self-inflicted torments, compared to which, even the cross is almost a bed of roses. Indeed the argument of martyrdom will support any religion; and it has, in fact, been cheerfully undergone by enthusiasts, and zealots of all religions, in testimony of the firm belief of the sufferers not only in the absurdities of Popery, and Brahmanism, but of every, even the most monstrous system that ever disgraced the human understanding. There have been martyrs for *Atheism itself.*

This argument of martyrdom has been more particularly applied to the Apostles, and first Christians. "How can it be imagined, (say Christian Divines,) that simple men like the Apostles could be induced to leave their employment, and wander up and down, to teach the doctrines, and testify to the facts of the New Testament, and expose themselves to persecution, imprisonment, scourging, and untimely, and violent death: unless they certainly *knew*, that both the *doctrines*, and the *facts* were true? Besides, what honours, what riches, could they expect to get by supporting false doctrine, and false testimony."

To this argument I might reply as in the preceding pages, for I would ask, have we not *seen* simple and honest men quit their employments, and wander up and down to preach doctrines which they not only had no means of *certainly knowing* to be *true*, but which they did not even *understand*? Have we not seen such men submit to deprivations of every kind, and exposed to imprisonment, and the whipping post? And do we not certainly know, that some such have cheerfully suffered a most cruel death?

Is it possible! that any sensible man, after reading the History of the Roman Catholic Missionaries, the Baptists, the Quakers, and the Methodists, can be convinced of the *certain truth* of the Christian religion, or seriously endeavor to convince another of it, by such an argument as the above!

But much more than this can be said upon this topic; for it can be shown, that the Apostles in preaching Christianity, did not suffer near so much, as some well meaning enthusiasts in modern times have suffered, to propagate religious tenets notoriously false, and absurd. And that the Apostles could expect to get neither fame, nor honour, nor riches by their preaching, is doubtful. This is certain, that they could not lose much. For they were confessedly men of the lowest rank in society, and of great poverty; poor fishermen, who could not feel a very great regard for their own dignity or respectability. And it was by no means a small thing for such men to be considered as divine Apostles, and "in exchange for heavenly things," to have the earthly possessions of their converts "laid at their feet." Peter left his nets, his boat, and boorish companions, and after persuading his disciples to receive his words for oracles, go where he would, he found ample hospitality from them. This, at least, was an advantageous change, and though they did not acquire fame or respect from the higher ranks of society, they were at least held in great respect by their followers. Neither *George Fox*, nor *Whitfield*, nor *Westley* [*sic*] were honoured by the nobility, or gentry, or scholars of England; or *Ann Lee*, by the most respectable citizens of the United States. Yet among their disciples, the *Quakers*, the *Methodists*, and the *Shakers*, they were held in the most implicit veneration, and can any man believe, that they did not think themselves thus well paid, for the trouble of making converts?

It is true that the Apostles did not acquire *riches*, for they were conversant only with the poor. But neither had they any to lose by taking up the profession of Apostles and Preachers. At least by preaching the gospel, they obtained food, and clothing, and *contributions*; as is evident from many places in the Epistles, where they write to their converts, "it is written, 'thou shalt not muzzle the ox when he treadeth out the corn;'" and Paul tells them, that they must not think from this place, that God takes care for oxen, "for, (says he,) it was undoubtedly written *for our sakes*." Thus we see that the gospel was by no means altogether unprofitable, and many men daily risk their lives for less gain than the Apostles did.

As to the *dangers*, to which it is said they exposed themselves, they had none to fear, except in Judea, which they quickly quitted, finding the Jews too stubborn, and went to the Greeks. From the Greeks, and likewise from the Romans, they had not much to fear, who were not very difficult or scrupulous in admitting new Gods, and new modes of worship. Besides this, the Romans for a great while seem to have considered the Christians merely as a Jewish sect who differed from the rest of the Jews in matters not worth notice; as is to be gathered from *Tacitus* and *Suetonius*. And if the Apostles did speak against the Pagan Gods, it was no more than what the Roman poets and philosophers did: and the magistrates were not then very severe about it. And it is evident from the Acts of the Apostles, that the Roman praetors considered the accusations against Paul and his companions, as mere trifles. But *in Judea*, where the danger was evident, it was otherwise. When Paul was in peril *there*, on account of his transgressions against the law, after being delivered from the Jews by the Roman garrison at Jerusalem, he pleaded before Festus and Agrippa, that he was falsely accused by the Jews; and he asserted that he had taught *nothing* against the Law of Moses, and his country, but that he only preached about the resurrection of the dead; and that it was for this that the Jews persecuted him; and ended by appealing to Caesar. When yet he *knew* that this was *not* the reason of the hatred of the Jews against him; but that it was because he taught that circumcision, and the Law of Moses *were abolished*, and *no longer binding*: which is evident to any who will read the Acts, and the Epistle to the Galatians. So you see by what manoeuvre he got out of the difficulty: first, by at least equivocating, and then by refusing to be tried by his own countrymen, and appealing to Caesar; thus securing himself a *safe conduct* out of Judea, which was too dangerous for him. Among the Gentiles, their doctrine had a better chance of success, for they taught them marvellous doctrines, such as they had been accustomed to listen to, viz., how the Son of God was born of a virgin, and was cruelly put to death; and that his Divine Father raised him from the dead. The idea of God's having a Son of a woman did not shock them, for all their demi-gods they believed had been so begotten; and a great part of their poems are filled with the exploits and the sufferings of these heroes, who are at length rewarded *by being raised from earth to heaven*, as Jesus is said to have been. These doctrines were not disrelished by the common people, but were rejected by the wise and learned. Accordingly we see that Paul could make nothing of the philosophers of Athens, who derided him, and considered him as telling them a story similar to those of their own mythology, when he preached to them Jesus and the resurrection. And in revenge we see Paul railing against both the stubborn Jews, and the incorrigible philosophers, as being unworthy of knowing "the *hidden* wisdom," which was to the one "a stumbling block," and to the other, "foolishness," and which he thought fit only for "the babes," and "the devout women," with whom he principally dealt.

That the New Testament inculcates an excellent morality, cannot be denied; for its best moral precepts were taken from the Old Testament. And if the Apostles had not preached good morals, how could they have expected to be considered by the Gentiles as messengers from God? For if they had inculcated any immoralities, such as rebellion, murder, adultery, robbery, revenge, their mission would not only have been disbelieved, but they would have undergone capital punishment by the sentence of the judge, which it was their business to avoid. *Mahomet*, throughout the Koran, inculcates all the virtues, and pointedly reprobates vice of all kinds. His morality is merely the precepts of the Old and New Testaments, modified a little, and expressed in Arabic. They are good precepts, and always to be listened to with respect, wherever, and by whomsoever inculcated. But surely that will not prove Islamism to be *from God*, nor that Mahomet *was his Prophet!*

That the Apostles suffered death on account of their preaching the gospel, if allowed to be fact, as said before, *proves nothing*. Many have suffered death for *false* and *absurd* doctrines. But whether any of the Apostles, (besides James who was slain by Herod,) died a *natural*, or a *violent* death, the learned Christians do not *certainly know*. For there is extant no authentic history of the Apostles, besides *the Acts*. There are indeed many fabulous narrations published by the Papists, called *Martyrologies*, stuffed with the most extravagant lies, which no learned man now regards; and who, therefore, will credit what such books say of the Apostles? Peter *is said* in them to have been put to death at Rome by Nero, nevertheless most of the learned men of the Protestants assert, that *Peter never was in Rome*, and as for Paul, no one certainly knows *where*, *when*, or *how* he finished his days. So that if we were even to allow the feeble argument of Martyrdom all the influence, and weight given to it, it would not *apply* to the Apostles; who, we are *sure* derived some benefit by preaching the gospel, and *are not* sure that they came to any harm by it.

I will conclude this long chapter, by laying before my reader some extracts from the book written by *Celsus*, a Heathen philosopher, against Christianity, preserved by *Origen* in his work against Celsus. That the entire work of Celsus is lost, is to be regretted; as he appears to have been a man of observation, though too sarcastic to please a fair enquirer; and from the picture given by him of the first Christians, their *maxims*, and their *modes of teaching*, and the subjects they chose for converts, it appears, that they were the exact prototypes of the *Methodists* and *Shakers* of the present day, both sects which contain excellent people, with hardly any fault but credulity.

> "If they (i.e. the teachers of Christianity,) say "*do not examine*," and the like; it is however incumbent on them to teach what those things are which they assert, and whence they are derived."

> "Wisdom in life is a bad thing, but folly is good."

> "Why should Jesus, when an infant, be carried into Egypt, lest he should be murdered? God should not fear being put to death."

> "You say that God was sent to *sinners*: but why not to those who are free from sin? What harm is it not to have sinned?"

"You encourage sinners, because you are not able to persuade any really good men: therefore you open the doors to the most wicked and abandoned."

"Some of them say '*do not examine*, but *believe*, and *thy faith* shall save thee."

"These are our institutions, say they, let not any man of learning come here, nor any wise man, nor any man of prudence: for these things are reckoned evil by us. But whoever is unlearned, ignorant, and silly, let him come without fear! Thus they own that they can gain only the foolish, the vulgar, the stupid, slaves, women, and children."

"At first, when they were but few, they agreed. But when they became a multitude, they were rent again, and again, and each will have their own factions: for factious spirits they had from the beginning."

"All wise men are excluded from the doctrine of their faith; they called to it only fools, and men of a servile spirit."

"The preachers of their Divine Word only attempt to persuade silly, mean, senseless persons, slaves, women, and children. What harm is there in being well-informed; and both in being, and appearing a man of knowledge? What obstacle can this be to the knowledge of God? Must it not be an advantage?"

"We see these *Itinerants* shewing readily their tricks to the vulgar, but not approaching the assemblies of wise men nor daring there to show themselves. But wherever they see *boys*, a crowd of *slaves*, and ignorant men, there they thrust in themselves, and show off their doctrine."

"You may see weavers, tailors, and fullers, illiterate and rustic men, not daring to utter a word before persons of age, experience, and respectability; but when they get hold of boys privately, and silly women, they recount wonderful things; that they must not mind their fathers, or their tutors, but obey *them*; as their fathers, or guardians are quite ignorant, and in the dark; but themselves alone have the *true wisdom*. And if the children obey them, they pronounce them happy, and direct them to leave their fathers, and tutors, and go with the women, and their playfellows, into the chambers of the females, or into a tailor's, or fuller's shop, *that they may learn perfection.*"

Celsus compares a Christian teacher to *a quack*—"who promises to heal the sick, on condition that they keep from intelligent practitioners, lest his ignorance be detected."

"If one sort of them introduces *one doctrine*, another, *another*, and *all join* in saying '*Believe* if you would be saved, or *depart:*' what are they to do, who desire really to be saved? Are they to determine by the throw of a die, where they are to turn themselves, or which of these demanders of implicit faith they are to believe?"

Omitting what Celsus says reproachfully of the *moral characters* of the Apostles, and the first teachers of Christianity, for which we certainly shall not take *his* word; it is easy to perceive from the above quotations, that they had more success among simple, and credulous people, than among the intelligent, and well-informed. Their introductory lesson to their pupils, was, "*Believe*, but do not *examine;*" and their succeeding instructions seem to have been a continued repetition, and practice of the dogma of *implicit faith.**

---

*Jerome, in his Commentary on the Epistle to the Galatians, says, that "The Church of Christ was not gathered from the Academy, or the Lyceum, but from the lowest of the People." (Vili Plebecula.) And Caecilius' in Minutius Felix, says, that the Christian assemblies were made up "de ultima faece collectis, imperitoribus, et mulieribus credulis sexus suae facilitate labentibus," i.e. "that they consisted of the lowest of the mob, simple and unlearned men, and credulous women."

The president of a province is introduced by Prudentius as thus addressing a martyr.

"Tu qui Doctor, ait, seris novellum

Commenti genus, ut LEVES PUELLAE,

Lucos destituunt, Jovem relinquant;

Damnes, si sapias, ANILE DOGMA."

["'You,' he said, 'who are the teacher and propagator of this modern falsehood, seeking to make light-minded girls desert the sacred groves and abandon Jupiter, if you are sensible you will condemn your old wives' teaching.'" H. J. Thomson, *Prudentius* (Cambridge, MA: Harvard University Press, 1929), 2: 205–207.]

The Christian Fathers confess, and glory in it, that the *greater part* of their congregations consisted of women and children, slaves, beggars, and vagabonds.

The Jewish Christians were, as appears evidently from the New Testament, exceedingly poor, and therefore there is frequent mention made of *contributions* for "the poor Saints at Jerusalem." From thence it was that the Jewish Christians got the name of *Ebionites*, i.e. *Poor*. The Jewish Christian Church consisied of the dregs of the Jewish people, simple and ignorant men, Samaritans, &c. No person in Judea of eminence, or learning, appears to have joined the sect of the Nazarenes, except Paul; after the destruction of Jerusalem they gradually dwindled in number, and became extinct.

CHAPTER X.

MATTHEW, ch. v., Jesus says, "Ye have heard that it was said, "Thou shalt love thy neighbour and hate thine enemy." But this is no where said in the Law or the Prophets; but, on the contrary, we read directly the reverse. For it is written, Ex. xxiii. "If thou find the ox of thine enemy, or his ass going astray, thou shalt certainly bring him back to him." "If thou seest the ass of him that hateth thee lying under his burden, and wouldst forbear to help him, thou shalt surely help him." Again, Levit. xix., "Thou shalt not hate thy brother in thine heart, rebuke thy neighbour, nor suffer sin upon him. Thou shalt *not revenge*, nor keep anger, (or bear any grudge,) against the children of thy people, but thou shalt love thy neighbour as thyself, I am the Lord." So also in Prov. xxxiv. "When thine enemy falleth, do not triumph, and when he stumbleth, let not thine heart exult." So also in ch. xxv. "If thine enemy hunger, give him food, if he thirst, give him to drink." These precepts are to the purpose, and are practicable; but this command of Jesus, "*Love your enemies*," if by loving, he means, "*do them good*," it is commanded in the above passages in the Hebrew Law. But if by "*love*" he means to look upon them with the *same affection* that we feel for those who love us, and with whom we are connected by the tenderest ties of nature, and friendship, the command is *impracticable*; and the fulfillment of it contrary to nature, and those very instincts given us by our Creator. And therefore, whoever thinks he fulfills, *really fulfills* this command, does in fact play the hypocrite *unknown to himself*; for though we *can*, and *ought* to do good to our enemy, yet to *love him* is as unnatural as to hate our friends.

In Mark ch. ii. 25, Jesus says to the Pharisees, "Have ye not read what David did when he hungered, and those that were with him. How that he entered into the house of the Lord, in the time of *Abiathar* the High Priest, and did eat of the shew-bread, &c." See the same also in Matthew, ch. xii. 3. Luke vi. 3. Now here is a great blunder: for this thing happened in the time of Achimelech, not in the time of Abiathar; for so it is written, 1 Sam. xxi. "and David came to Nob, to Achimelech the Priest, &c." And in the 22nd chapter it is said that *Abiathar* was his son.

In Luke ch. 1. 26, the Angel Gabriel is said to have come from God to Mary, when she was yet a virgin, espoused to Joseph, who was of the house of David, and announced to her that she should conceive, and bear a son, and should call his name Jesus; that her holy Offspring should be called the Son of God, and that God should give unto Him "the throne of David his Father, and that he should rule the house of Jacob forever, and that to his kingdom there should be no end." Now this story is encumbered with many difficulties, which I shall not consider; but confine myself to asking, Wherefore, if these things were true, did not the Mother of Jesus and his brethren, knowing these extraordinary things, *obey his teachings*? For it is certain, that they did not at first believe him, but, as appears from the 7th chap. of John, derided him. Besides, neither did his mother nor his brethren, when they came to the house where he was preaching to simple and credulous men, come for the purpose of being edified, but "to lay hold of him," to carry him home, for said they he is mad, or "beside himself," (Mark iii. 21) which certainly they would not have dared to do, if this story of Luke were true. For their mother would have taught them of his miraculous conception, and extraordinary character. Moreover, how was it that God *did not* give him the throne of David, as was promised by the Angel to his Mother? For he did not sit upon the throne of David, nor exercise any authority in Israel. Moreover, how comes it that David is called the Father of Jesus, since Jesus was *not* the son of Joseph, who, according to the Evangelists drew his origin from that King. Finally, the saying "that to his kingdom there should be no end," is directly contradicted by Paul in the 1st Ep. to the Cor. ch. xv: for he says therein "that Jesus shall render up his kingdom unto the Father, and be himself subject unto him." Here you see, that the kingdom of Jesus is to have an end; for when he renders up his kingdom to the Father, he certainly must divest himself of his authority. How then can it be said, that "to his kingdom there shall be no end?"

Jesus says, John v. 39, "And the Father himself which hath sent me, hath borne witness of me; ye have neither heard his voice at any time, &c." But how does this agree with Moses, who says, Deut. iv. 33, "Did ever People *hear the voice of God* speaking out of the midst of fire, as *thou hast heard*?"—"And *we heard* his voice out of the midst of the fire; we have seen this day, that God doth talk with man, and he liveth." Deut. v. 24.

Luke, ch. 4, 17, "And they gave to Jesus the Book of Isaiah the Prophet, and he opened the Book, and found this place, where it was written, 'The Spirit of the Lord is upon me, therefore hath he anointed me; to preach the Gospel to the poor hath he sent me, that I should bind up the broken in heart, proclaim liberty to the captives, *and sight to the blind*; that I should preach the acceptable year of the Lord.' And shutting the Book, he gave it to the minister, and afterwards addressed them, saying, 'This day is this Scripture fulfilled in your ears.' Here you see the words which gave offence; and by turning to Is. in loco, chap. lxi you may see the reason why the inhabitants of Nazareth arose up in wrath against him. For 1. these words alleged in Luke, are somewhat perverted from the original in Isaiah: for these words, "and sight to the blind," are *not* in Isaiah, but are inserted in Luke for purposes very obvious. And 2. he neglects the words following, "and the day of vengeance of our God, and of consolation to all who mourn. To give consolation to the mourners of Zion; to give them beauty instead of ashes, and the oil of joy instead of grief; a garment of praise instead of a broken heart, &c." to the end of the chapter. From this it is very clear, that this prophecy has no reference to Jesus: but Isaiah speaks these things of *himself*; and the words "the Lord hath anointed me," signifying, "God hath chosen, established me to declare"—what follows. This exposition of anointing is confirmed from these passages. 1 Kings, xix. ch. "*Anoint* a Prophet in thy stead," where the sense is, "*constitute* a Prophet in thy place." Again, "touch not mine anointed ones, and do my Prophets no harm," i. e. "Touch not my chosen servants;" and so in several other places. The meaning, therefore, of Isaiah is, that God had appointed, and constituted *him* a Prophet to announce these consolations to the Israelites, who were to be in captivity, in order that they should not despair of liberation; and that they should have hope, when they read these comfortable words spoken by the mouth of Isaiah, at the command of God. For he calls the subjects of his message "the broken in heart," "*the captives*," "the *mourners of Zion*, &c." all which terms are applicable *only* to the Israelites. That this is the true interpretation, will be made further evident to any impartial person, by reading the context preceding, and following.

Jo. ch. ii. v. 18. "The Jews said to Jesus, what sign shewest thou to us, that thou doest these things? Jesus answered and said unto them, Destroy this temple, and in three days I will raise it up. The Jews answered, saying, *forty and six years* was this temple in building, and wilt thou build it in three days?" The Jews could never have spoken these words here related: for the temple then standing was built by *Herod*, who reigned but *thirty-seven* years, and built it in *eight* years. This, therefore, must be a blunder of the Evangelist.

Jo. xiii. v. 21. Jesus says to his Disciples, "a *new* commandment I give unto you, that ye *love* one another." This is not true, for the love of man towards his neighbour, was *not a new* precept but at least as ancient as Moses, who gives it Levit. xix. as the command of God, "Thou shalt love thy neighbour as thyself."

Acts vii. v. 4. "When he (Abraham) went out of the land of the Chaldees, he dwelt in Charran; from thence *after his father was dead*, he led him into this land in which ye dwell." This directly contradicts the chapter in Genesis where the story of Abraham's leaving Haran is related; for it is certain from thence, that Abraham left his father Terah in Haran alive when he departed thence. And he did not die till many years afterwards. This chronogical contradiction has given much trouble to Christian Commentators, as may be seen in *Whitby, Hammond,* &c. &c.

V. 14, Stephen says, "Jacob therefore descended into Egypt, and our Fathers, and there died. And they were carried to Sichem, and buried in the sepulchre which *Abraham* bought from the Sons of Hemor the Father of Sichem." Here is another blunder; for this piece of land was *not* purchased by *Abraham*, but by *Jacob*. Gen. xlix. 29: so also see the end of Joshua. But it is evident, that Stephen has *confounded* the story of the purchase of the field of Machpalah, recorded in Gen. xxiii. with the circumstances related concerning the purchase by Jacob.

In v. 43 of the same chapter, there is another disagreement between Stephen's quotation from Amos, and the original, which see.

So also there is in the speech of *James*, Acts xv. a quotation from Amos, in which to make it fit the subject, (which after all it does not fit,) is the substitution of the words, the remnant of men, for the words, "remnant of *Edom*" as it is in the original.

All these mistakes, besides others to be met with in almost—I was going to say in every page, of these Histories of Jesus and his Apostles, sufficiently show how superficial was the acquaintance of these men with the Old Testament, and how grossly, either through design or ignorance, they have perverted it. Indeed from these mistakes *alone*, I should be led strongly to suspect, that the Books of the New Testament were written by Gentiles, as I can hardly conceive that any Jew could have quoted his Bible in such a blundering manner.

CHAPTER XI.

A very great part of Dogmatic Theology among Christians, is founded upon the notion, that the Jewish Law was a *temporary* dispensation, only to exist till the coming of Jesus, when it was to be superceded by a more perfect dispensation.

On the contrary, the Jews are persuaded that *their Law* is of perpetual obligation, and the Doctrine of the *Trinity itself* is hardly more offensive to them, and, as they think, more contradictory to the Scriptures, than the notion of the abrogation of it. Now that the Jews are on the right side of this question, i. e. arguing from the Old Testament, I shall endeavour to prove by several arguments. They are all comprised in these positions, 1. That the Mosaic Institutions are most solemnly, and repeatedly declared to be *perpetual*; and we have no account of their *being abrogated*, or *to be abrogated* in the Old Testament. 2. They are declared to be perpetual by Jesus himself, and were adhered to by the twelve apostles.

1. Nothing can be more expressly asserted in the Old Testament, than the perpetual obligation of those rites, which were to distinguish the Jews from other nations. It appears for instance (from the 17 ch. of Genesis,) in the tenor of the covenant made with Abraham, that *circumcision* was to distinguish his posterity to the end of time. It is called "*an everlasting covenant*" to be kept by his posterity through *all their generations*. See the chapter where the condition of the covenant, is that God would give to Abraham, and his posterity the perpetual inheritance of the promised land with whatever privileges were implied in his being *their God*, on condition that their male children were circumcised, in testimony of putting themselves under that covenant. There is *no limitation* with respect to *time*; nay it is expressly said that the covenant should be *perpetual*.

The ordinance of the Passover is also said to be *perpetual*, Ex. xii. 14, &c, "And this day shall be unto you for a memorial, and you shall keep it as a feast to the Lord *throughout your generations*. You shall keep it a feast by an ordinance forever." This is repeated afterwards, and the observance of this rite is confined to Israelites, Proselytes, and Slaves who should be circumcised. v. 48.

The observance of the *Sabbath* was *never* to be *discontinued*, Ex. xxxi. 16. "Wherefore the children of Israel shall keep the Sabbath *throughout their generations*, for *a perpetual covenant*. It is a sign between me and the children of Israel *forever*."

The appointment of the Family of Aaron to be Priests, was to continue as long as the *Israelites should be a nation*, see Lev. vii. 35.

The Feast of Tabernacles was to be *forever*, Lev. xxiii. 41. "It shall be a statute *forever*, in your generations." The observance of this Festival is particularly mentioned in the prophecies, which foretell a future settlement of the Jews in their own land, as obligatory on all the word; as if an union of worship at *Jerusalem* was to be, according to them, effected among all nations by the united observance of this Festival there, see Zech. 14; what he there says is confirmed by what Isaiah prophesied concerning the same period, Is. 2. "It shall come to pass in the last days, that the mountain of the Lord's house shall be established in the top of the mountains, and shall be exalted above the hills, and *all nations* shall flow unto it. And many people shall go, and say, Come ye, and let us go up to the mountain of the Lord, to the house of the God of Jacob, and he *will teach us of his ways*, and we will walk in his paths. For out of Zion shall go forth the Law, and the word of the Lord from Jerusalem. And he shall judge among the nations, and rebuke many people, and they shall beat their swords into ploughshares, and their spears into pruning hooks. Nation shall not lift up sword against nation, neither shall they learn war any more."

With respect to all the Laws of Moses, it is evident from the manner in which they were promulgated, that they were intended to be of perpetual obligation upon the Hebrew nation, and that by the observance of them they were to be distinguished from the other nations, see Deut. xxvi. 16.

The observance of their peculiar Laws was the express condition on which the Israelites were to continue in possession of the promised land; and though on account of their disobedience they were to be driven out of it, they had the strongest assurances given them that they should never be utterly destroyed, like many other nations who should oppress them; but that on their repentance, God would gather them from the remote parts of the world, and bring them to their own country again. And both Moses, and the later Prophets assure them, that in consequence of their becoming obedient to God in all things, which it is asserted they will, (and which may be the natural consequence of the Discipline they will have gone through,) they shall be continued in the peaceable enjoyment of the land of promise, in *its greatest* extent to the end of Time, see to this purpose Deut. iv. 25, &c. also Deut. 30, where it is thus written.

"And it shall come to pass, when all these things are come upon thee, the blessing and the curse, which I have set before thee, and thou shalt call them to mind among all the nations whither the Lord thy God hath driven thee; and shalt return unto the Lord thy God, and shalt obey his voice according to all that I command thee this day, thou and thy children, with all thy heart, and with all thy soul; that then the Lord thy God will *turn thy captivity*, and have compassion upon thee, and will return, and gather thee from *all the nations* whither the Lord thy God hath *scattered thee*. If any of thine be driven out unto the utmost parts of heaven, from thence will the Lord thy God gather thee, and from thence will he fetch thee. And the Lord thy God will bring thee unto the Land which thy Fathers possessed, and thou shalt possess it, and He will do thee good, and multiply thee above thy Fathers. And the Lord thy God will circumcise thy heart, and the heart of thy seed, to love the Lord thy God with all thy heart, and with all thy soul, that thou mayest live; and the Lord thy God will put all these curses upon thine enemies, and on them that hate thee, which *persecuted thee*. And thou shalt return, and obey the voice of the Lord, and *do all his commandments which I command thee this day, &c.*"

"What an extent of prophecy, and how firm a faith in the whole of it do we see here! (says Dr. Priestley.) The Israelites were not *then* in the land of Canaan. It was occupied by nations far more numerous, and powerful than they; and yet it is distinctly foretold in the 4th ch. that they would soon take possession of it, and multiply in it: and that afterwards they would offend God by their idolatry, and wickedness, and would in consequence of it be driven out of their country; and without being exterminated or lost, be scattered among the nations of the world; that by this dispersion, and their calamities, they would at length be reformed, and restored to the divine favour, and that then (as in the quotation) in *the latter days* they would be gathered from all nations, and restored to their own country, when they *would observe all the laws which were then prescribed to them.* Past history and present appearances correspond with such wonderful exactness to what *has been* fulfilled of this prophecy, that we can have no doubt with respect to the complete accomplishment of what *remains* to be fulfilled of it."

What was first announced by Moses is repeated by Isaiah, and other Prophets, assuring them of their certain return wherever dispersed, to their own land in *the latter days*; and that they should have the undisturbed possession of it to the end of time.

It has been objected, that the term *"forever"* is not always to be understood in its greatest extent, but is to be interpreted according to circumstances. This for the sake of saving time I will acknowledge. But the circumstances in which this phrase is used in the passages already adduced, and in a number of others of similar import which might be adduced, clearly indicate, that it is to be understood in those passages to mean a period *as long as the duration of the Israelitish nation*, which elsewhere is said to continue *to the end of the world.*

For this reason, among others, this final return of the Jews from their dispersed state, cannot at any rate be said to have been *accomplished* at their return from the Babylonish captivity.

For that captivity was not by any means such a *total dispersion* of the people *among all nations*, as Moses, and the later Prophets have foretold. Nor does their possession of the country subsequent to it at all correspond to that state of peace, and prosperity, which was promised to succeed this final return.

Figures of speech must no doubt be allowed for. But if the whole of the Jewish polity was to terminate at the destruction of Jerusalem by Titus, (as is maintained by Christians,) *while the world is still to continue*, the magnificent promises made to Abraham, and his posterity, and to the nation in general afterwards, have *never* had any *proper accomplishment at all*: because with respect to *external prosperity*, which is contained in the promises, many nations have *hitherto* been more distinguished by God, than the Jews. *Hitherto* the posterity of Ishmael has had a much happier lot than that of Isaac. To say, as Christians do, that these prophecies have had a *spiritual* accomplishment in the spread of the Gospel, when there is nothing in the phraseology in which the promises are expressed, that could possibly suggest any such ideas, nay when the promise itself in the most definite language expresses the contrary, is so *arbitrary* a construction as nothing can warrant. By this mode of interpretation, *any event* may be said to be the fulfillment of *any prophecy whatever.*

Besides, it is perfectly evident, that these prophecies, whether they *will* be fulfilled, or not, cannot *yet* have been fulfilled. For all the calamity that was ever to befall the Jewish nation is expressly said *to bear no sensible proportion* to their subsequent prosperity: whereas, their prosperity has *hitherto* borne a small proportion to their calamity; so that had Abraham really foreseen the fate of his posterity, he would, on this idea, have had little reason to rejoice in the prospect.

It may be said, that the prosperity of the descendants of Abraham, was to depend *on a condition*, viz. their obedience and that this condition was not fulfilled. But besides that the Divine Being must have foreseen this circumstance, and therefore must have known that he was only tantalizing Abraham with a promise which would never be accomplished; this disobedience, and the consequences of it are expressly mentioned by Moses, and the other Prophets, only as a *temporary thing*, and what was to be succeeded by an effectual repentance, and perpetual obedience and prosperity.

Among others, let the following prophecy of Isaiah (in which the future security of Israel is compared to the security of the world from a second deluge) be considered, and let any impartial person say, whether the language does not necessarily lead those who believe the Old Testament, to the expectation of a much more durable state of Glory and Happiness, than has yet fallen to the lot of the posterity of Abraham.

Is. 54, 7. "For a small moment have I forsaken thee, but with great mercies will I gather thee. In a little wrath I hid my face from thee for a moment, but with everlasting kindness will I have mercy on thee, saith the Lord thy Redeemer. For this is as the waters of Noah unto me. For as I have sworn that the waters of Noah should no more go over the earth, so have I sworn, that I would not be wroth with thee, nor rebuke thee. For the mountains shall (or "may") depart, and the hills be removed, but my kindness shall not depart from thee, neither shall the covenant of my peace be removed, saith the Lord that hath mercy on thee.—All thy children shall be taught of the Lord, and great shall be the peace of thy children. In righteousness shalt thou be established. Thou shalt be far from oppression, for thou shalt not fear, and from terror, for it shall not come nigh thee. No weapon formed against thee shall prosper, and every tongue that shall rise against thee in judgment, thou shalt condemn. This is the heritage of the servants of the Lord, and their righteousness is of me, saith the Lord."

Here, as also in Moses, and other Prophets, an establishment in righteousness is promised to the Israelites, such as shall secure their future prosperity; and this promise has *not yet* been fulfilled. The promise of future virtue, as connected with their future happiness, is also clearly expressed in Jer. ch. iii. 18.

Had the Jewish nation become *extinct*, or likely to become so, it might with some plausibility have been said by Christians, that the purposes of God concerning them were actually fulfilled, and therefore, that the words of the promise must have had some other signification than that which was most obvious. But the Jews are as much a distinct people as they ever were, and therefore, seem reserved for some future strange destination.

On the whole, it must be allowed, that the settlement of Israel in the land of Canaan, foretold with such emphasis by the Prophets, is a settlement which has not yet taken place, but may take place in that period so frequently, and so emphatically distinguished by the title of "*the latter days;*" and *therefore*, that whatever is said of Jewish customs, or modes of worship in "*the latter days,*" is a *proof* of the meant restoration of their *ancient religious rites.*

That the institutions of the Mosaic Law are to be continued on the restoration of the Jews to their own land after their utter dispersion, is asserted by Moses himself in one of the passages already quoted; but is more clearly expressed by the subsequent Prophets. In some of their prophecies particular mention is made of the observance of Jewish festivals, and of sacrifices; and in Ezechiel we find a description of a magnificent Temple which, being closely connected with his prophecy of the future happy state of the Israelites in their own land, cannot be understood of any other than a Temple, which is then, according to the Hebrew

Prophets, to be reared with greater magnificence than ever. Mention is also made of "*the Glory of the Lord*," or that effulgent Shechinah which was the symbol of the divine presence, filling this Temple, as it did that of Solomon.

Ezech. xliii. 1, &c. "Afterward he brought me to the gate, even the gate that looketh toward the East; and behold the glory of the Lord came from the way of the East, and his voice was like the noise of many waters, and the Earth shined with his Glory.—And the Glory of the Lord came into the house by the way of the gate, whose prospect is toward the East. So the Spirit took me up, and brought me into into the inner court, and behold the Glory of the Lord filled the house.—And he said unto me, Son of man, the place of my Throne, and the place of the soles of my feet, where I will dwell in the midst of the children of Israel *forever*, and my holy name shall the house of Israel no more defile," &c.

Towards the end of the same chapter we read an account of the *dedication* of this new Temple by sacrifices; and particular directions are given in the succeeding chapters for the Priests, and for the *Prince*. If, therefore, there be any truth in these prophecies, the Jews are not only to return to their own country, and to be distinguished among the nations, but are to rebuild the Temple, and to restore the ancient Worship.

Having proved that the Old Testament declares the perpetuity of the Mosaic Law, I proceed 2ndly to prove, that it is declared to be perpetual by Jesus himself.

But before I adduce my proofs, I beg leave to premise, that when any Law is *solemnly enacted*, we expect that the *abrogation* of it should be *equally solemn* and *express*, in order that no room for dispute may remain upon the subject. Accordingly, it is the custom, I believe, in all countries, not to make any *new* Law *contradictory* to another before subsisting, without a *previous express abrogation* of the *old* one. And certainly it appears to me a strange notion to suppose, that the elaborate and noble Law given from Mount Sinai amidst circumstances unexampled, awful, and tremendously magnificent, and believed to have been declared by the voice of God to be a perpetual and everlasting Code, should vanish, perish, and be annihilated by the *mere dictum* of twelve fishermen!!

But the fact is otherwise, for Jesus was so far from teaching the *abrogation* of that law, that he expressly says—"Think not that I am come to destroy the law, or the Prophets, I am not come to destroy, but to fulfil. For verily I say unto you, till Heaven and Earth pass, one jot, or one tittle, shall in no wise pass from the law till all be fulfilled." This is a most explicit declaration that not the smallest punctilio in the law of Moses was *intended* to be set aside by the *Gospel*. Nay more, he expressly commanded his Disciples to the same purpose—"The Scribes and Pharisees (says he) sit in Moses' seat; all, therefore, whatsoever they command you, that *observe*, and *do*."

It is said in answer to this by Christian Divines, that his discourse relates to things of a *moral nature*, and that he only meant that no part of the *Moral Law* was to be abolished. But besides that the expression is *general*, there could be no occasion to make so solemn a declaration against what he could not have been suspected of intending, viz. of *abolishing the moral law*. He seems in his discourse to have had in view the additions that had been made to the law. These he sets aside, but no part of the original law itself.

It has also been urged that by *fulfilling*, may be meant such an *accomplishment* of it as would imply the *superceding* of it when the purposes for which it was instituted should be answered. To silence this explication it will be sufficient to produce a few out of many passages of the New Testament where the term *fulfil* occurs in connexion with the term law. Thus Paul says, Gal. v. 14—"And all the law is *fulfilled* in one word, even in this, thou shalt love thy neighbour as thyself," and again, Rom. xiii. 8— "He that loveth another hath *fulfilled the law*." But certainly notwithstanding this *fulfillment* of the *moral law*, it remains in as full force as ever.

The Apostles understood Jesus to mean as we have asserted. For it is evident from the Acts, that the Christians at Jerusalem were zealous in attachment to the law of Moses; this is evident from their surprise at Peter's conduct with regard to *Cornelius*; and in the dispute about imposing circumcision upon the *Gentiles: observe*, there was no dispute about its being obligatory upon Jews.

Paul was indeed vehemently accused of teaching a contrary doctrine, as we find in the history of the transactions respecting him in his last journey to Jerusalem. Acts xxi. 21—"They (i. e. the Christians) are informed of thee (says James to Paul) that thou teachest all the Jews which are among the Gentiles, to *forsake Moses*, saying that they *ought not* to circumcise their children, neither to walk after the customs." Here James gives Paul to understand that he considered the report as *a calumny*, and accordingly, to convince the Jewish Christians that it was *a false report*, he advises Paul to be at charges with some Jewish Christians, who were under a vow of *Nazaritism*, (which is an instance in point to prove that the first Christians kept the law,) and thus publicly manifest that he himself "walked orderly, and kept the law." Paul complies with this advice, and purified himself in the Temple, and did what was done in like cases by the strictest Jews. He also circumcised Timothy, who was a convert to Christianity, *because* he was the son of a *Jewish Mother*. And he solemnly declared in open court. Acts xxv. 8—"Against *the law* of the Jews, neither against *the Temple*, have I offended *any thing at all*," and again to the Jews at Rome, Acts xxviii. 7, he assures them that "he had done nothing against the people, or the *customs of the Fathers.*"

But some men will say, "did not *Paul* expressly teach the abrogation of the law in his Epistles, especially in that to the Galatians?" I answer, he undoubtedly *did*; and in so doing he contradicted the Old Testament, his master Jesus, the twelve Apostles, and *himself* too. But how can this be? I answer, it is none of my concern to reconcile the conduct of *Paul*, or to defend his equivocations. It is pretty clear, that he did not dare to preach this doctrine at Jerusalem. He confined this *"hidden wisdom,"* to the Gentiles. To the Jews he became as a Jew; and to the uncircumcised as one uncircumcised, he was *"all things to all men!"* and for this conduct he gives you his reason, viz. "that he was determined at *any rate* to *gain some.*" If this be double dealing, dissimulation, and equivocation, I cannot help it; it is none of my concern, I leave it to the cornmentators, and the Reconciliators, the Disciples of *Surenhusius*; let them look to it; perhaps they can hunt up some "traditionary rules of interpretation among the Jews," that will help them to explain the matter.

Lastly, it has been said that there was no occasion for Jesus, or his Apostles to be very explicit with respect to the abolition of the laws of Moses, since the Temple was to be soon destroyed, when the Jewish worship would cease of course.

This argument, flimsy as it is, is nevertheless the *instar omnium* of the Christian Divines to prove the abolishment of this Law: (for the other arguments adduced by them as *prophecies* of it from the 1 ch. of Isaiah, and some of the Psalms, are nothing to the purpose; they being merely declarations of God, that he preferred obedience in the weightier matters of the Law, Justice, Mercy, and Holiness, to *ceremonial* observances; and that repentance was of more avail with him, than offering thousands of rams, and fed beasts, and this argument, like so many others, when weighed in the balance will be "found wanting."

For, as the destruction of the Temple by *Nebuchadnezzar* certainly did *not* abolish the Law, so neither did the destruction by Titus do it. And as it would be *notoriously absurd* to maintain the *first*, so it is equally so, to maintain the *last position*. Besides a very considerable part of that law *can be*, and for these *seventeen hundred years has been* kept *without* the Temple. As for example, circumcision, distinction of meats, and many others. And when, if ever, they shall return to their own land, and rebuild the Temple, they will then, according to the Old Testament, observe *the Whole*, and with greater splendour than ever.

CHAPTER XII.

As Christians lay great stress upon their argument for the truth of their Religion, derived from the supposed miraculous conversion of *Paul*; and since almost the whole of Systematic Christianity is built upon the foundation of the Epistles ascribed to him; we shall pay a little more attention to his character and writings.

Paul was evidently a man of no small capacity, a fiery temper, great subtilty, and considerably well versed in Jewish Traditionary, and Cabbalistic Learning, and not unacquainted with the principles of the Philosophy called "the Oriental." He is said by Luke to have been converted to Christianity by a splendid apparition of Jesus, who struck him to the ground by the glory of his appearance. But by the Jews and *the Nazarene Christians*, he is represented as having been converted to Christianity from a different cause. They say that being a man of tried abilities and of some note, he demanded the High Priest's daughter in marriage, and being refused, his rash and rageful temper, and a desire of revenge, drove him to join the "sect of the Nazarenes," at that time beginning to become troublesome to the Sanhedrim. However this may be, whether he became a Christian from *conviction*, or from *ambition*; it is certain from the Acts that he always was considered by the Jewish Christians, as a *suspected* character; and it is evident that he taught a *different Doctrine* from that promulgated by the twelve Apostles. And this was the true cause of the great difficulty he was evidently under of keeping steady to him his Gentile converts, for it is evident from the Epistles to the Galatians, and the Corinthians, that *the Jewish Christians* represented Paul to them as not "sound in the Faith," but as teaching a different Doctrine from that of the Twelve, and so influential were these representations, that Paul had the greatest difficulty in keeping them to his System.

That there were two *Parties*, or *Schools* in the first Christian church, viz. the adherents of the *Apostles*, and the Disciples of *Paul*, is evident from the New Testament, and has been fully, and unanswerably *proved* by the learned Semler, the greatest Scholar certainly in Christian Antiquities that ever lived. The knowledge of this secret, accounts for the different conduct of Paul when among his *Gentile* converts, from that which he pursued when with the apostles at *Jerusalem*. He had a difficult part to act, and he managed admirably. He was indeed, as he says himself, "all things to all men," a Jew with the Jews, and as one uncircumcised among the uncircumcised. To the Jews, he asserted, that he "taught nothing contrary to the Law and the Prophets," and when brought before the Sanhedrim for teaching otherwise than he said, he dexterously got himself out of tribulation, by throwing a bone of contention among the Council, and setting his Judges together by the ears. "And when *Paul perceived* that the one part (of the Council) were *Sadducees*, and the other *Pharisees*, he cried out in the Council: Brethren *I am a Pharisee*, and the son of *a Pharisee*; concerning *the hope of the resurrection of the dead*, I am *now judged*. And when he had said this, *a dissention* arose between the Pharisees, and the Sadducees, and the multitude was divided. For the *Sadducees* say there is *no resurrection*, neither angel, nor spirit; but the Pharisees confess both. And there was *a great cry*, and the Scribes that were on the part of the Pharisees arose and *strove*, saying, We find no evil in this man, &c." This indeed was a masterly manoeuvre, and produced the desired effect; and Paul by this shows his knowledge of *the human heart*, in trusting to make his Judges forget what he was accused of, by making an appeal to their *sectarian passions*. For in truth, he was *not* accused concerning his opinion about "the hope, and the resurrection of the dead." But for the following cause, as his accusers vociferated (in the xxi. ch.) when they seized him in the Temple, "Men of Israel, Help! *This* is the man, who teacheth all men every where against the people, and *the Law*, and this place."

These strokes of character enable us to understand the man: and I shall now go into the consideration of some of the arguments he has deduced from passages in the Old Testament in support of his opinions, after premising that the truth of the story of the manner of his conversion depends entirely upon *his own assertion*; and whether his credibility be *absolutely* unimpeachable, can be easily determined by an impartial consideration of the history of his conduct already mentioned. I will only add upon this subject, that in telling the story of his conversion, he ought to have had a better memory. For in telling it once in the xxvi. ch. of Acts, he says, in describing his miraculous vision, that "those that were with me, saw indeed the light, and were afraid, but *heard not* the words of him that spake to me," and thus he directly contradicts the story of it recorded in Acts ix. where it is said "that the men who journeyed with him stood speechless, *hearing the voice*, but seeing no one."

In the 9 ch. of the Epistle to the Romans, v. 24, he thus proves that the Old Testament prophesied of the conversion of the Gentiles to the Gospel—"Even us whom he hath called, not of the Jews only, but also of the Gentiles, as he saith also in *Hosea* "I will call them my people, which were not my people; and her beloved, which was not beloved. And it shall come to pass, that in the place where it was said unto them, ye are not my people, there shall they be called the sons of the living God."—Is not this to the purpose? yet in applying this passage to the Gentiles, Paul has *wilfully*, (yes *wilfully*, for Paul was a learned man, and knew better) *perverted* the original from its proper reference, and has passed upon his simple converts, who did not know so much of the Jewish Scriptures, as he did, a prophecy relating entirely to the *Jews*, as referring to the *Gentiles!!* By turning to *Hosea*, Reader, you will find this to be verily the case; here is the passage. "Then said God, call his name (Hosea's son) Loammi, for *ye* (the Israelites) are not my people, and I will not be your God, yet the number of *the children of Israel* shall be as the sand of the sea, which cannot be measured, nor numbered. And it shall come to pass, that in the place where it was said unto *them*, ye are not my people, there shall it be said unto *them*, ye are the sons of the living God." Hos. ch. 1.

Again, v. 33. "As it is written, Behold I lay in Zion a stone of stumbling, and a rock of offence, and every one who believeth in him shall not be ashamed." Here Paul has *pieced two passages together*, which in the original are disconnected. For in the 8th chapter of Is. it is written, "Sanctify the Lord of Hosts himself and let *him* be your fear, and let *him* be your dread. And *he* shall be for a sanctuary; but for a stone of stumbling, and for a rock of offence, to both the houses of Israel, for a gin, and for a snare to the inhabitants of Jerusalem." And in the 28th chapter it is written, "therefore thus saith the Lord God. Behold I lay in Zion for a foundation, a stone, a tried stone, a precious corner stone, a sure foundation, he *that believeth* shall not be ashamed," (or disappointed.) Here you see Reader, that he jams two distant passages together no ways related; and alters some words, and applies them to *Jesus*, with whom, it appears from the context of Isaiah, they have no concern.

Ch. x. v. 6. "The scripture saith, 'say not in thine heart, "who shall ascend into Heaven?"'" (that is that he may bring down Jesus from above,) again, 'who shall descend into the abyss?' (that is, that he may bring up Jesus from the dead.) But what saith it? 'The word is very nigh unto thee, in thy mouth, and in thy heart,' (that is the word of Faith which we speak.) For if thou confess Jesus with thy mouth, and believe in thine heart that God raised him from the dead, thou shalt be saved." Here you will see another instance of misapplication of Scripture by Paul, in order to dazzle the eyes of his simple, and credulous converts, for let any one look at the place in the Scripture whence the quotation is taken, and he will immediately see the inapplicability of the words, and the adulteration of those of the original, in order to make them apply. For the Scripture quoted speaks of, and refers to *penitence*, and not at all about believing on, or bringing down Jesus from Heaven, or up from the dead; for here are the words, Deut. 30.—"If thou be converted to the Lord thy God with all thy heart, and with all thy mind."— Immediately is subjoined—"For this Law which I command you this day is not far from thee; neither is it afar off. It is not in Heaven, that thou shouldst say, who shall ascend for us into Heaven, that he may bring it unto us, and declare it to us that we might do it, &c." The sense of the whole is, that God wills us to repent of sin; and that you may know when you have sinned, you have only to look at *his Law*, which is not in Heaven, nor afar off, but is put in your own hands, and is perfectly familiar with your heart, and lips.

1 Cor. ch. v. 1. Paul accuses one of the Christians of the church of Corinth of the crime of incest, because he had married his step-mother, and orders them to excommunicate him. But Paul, in all his Epistles and teachings to *the Gentiles*, pronounced them *free* from the Law of Moses. Wherefore then, for the violation of one of those Laws interdicting such a marriage, does he so vehemently blame them? Such a marriage is not forbidden in the Gospel, it was forbidden to them no where in the Scriptures but in the Mosaic Code. Therefore Paul must have founded his judgment against the criminal, upon the *dictum* of that Law in such cases. Paul puts the man under *a curse*; and it is the Mosaic Law which say Deut. 27. "Cursed is he who lieth with his Father's wife." It seems therefore that Jesus did *not* deliver his followers from *"the curse of the Law,"* as Paul taught them it *did* in Gal. iii. 13.

Ch. 10. 1 Cor. "and let us not pollute ourselves with fornication as some of them were polluted, and fell in one day to the number of twenty *three* thousand." Here is a blunder, for it is written "twenty *four* thousand" Num. 25.

Gal. iii. 13. Paul says, "Christ hath redeemed us from the curse of the Law being made a curse for us, for it is written, cursed is every one that hangeth on a tree." What he says of the Christ, or the Messiah redeeming from the curses written in the Law, that by no means agrees with truth. For no Jew can be freed from the curses of the Law, but by repenting of his sins, and becoming obedient to it. And in alleging the words "cursed is every one that hangeth on a tree," from Deut. 21, he, as usual, applies them irrelevantly.

Paul says, Gal. iii. 10. "For as many as are of the works of the Law are under the curse, for it is written, (Deut. xxvii. 26.) "Cursed is every one that continueth not in ALL things written in the Book of the Law to do them." And he interprets this to mean that all *mankind*, Jews and Gentiles, are liable to Damnation, (except those who are saved by Faith) because no man ever *did* continue in *all* things written in the Law.—Now in the first place I would observe, that Paul has dared to *forge*, and insert the word "all" in the passage he quotes from Deut. (in the original of which it is *not*) in order to make it support his system; for *the whole* of his argument is built upon this one surreptitiously inserted word. 2. The words according to the original are simply these "Cursed is he that confirmeth not the words of this Law to do them," i. e. He who disobeys, or neglects to fulfil the commands of the Law, shall be under the curse denounced upon the disobedient. But who would conclude from this, that repentance would not remove the curse? Does not God expressly declare in the 30 chapter of Deut. that if they *repent*, the curses written *shall* be removed from them? and have we not innumerable instances recorded in the Old Testament of sinners, and transgressors of this very Law, received to pardon, and favour, upon repentance, and amendment? So that this argument founded upon forgery, and supported by bad Logic, is every way *bad* and insulting to God, and his (by Paul acknowledged) word.

Gal. ch. iii. 16. To Abraham, and his *seed* were the promises made, He saith not "and to *seeds*," (as of *many*) but as of *one*, "and to thy *seed*, which is Christ." Here is an argument which one would think too far fetched, even for Paul; and it is built on a perversion of a passage from Genesis, which Paul, bold as he was in these matters, certainly would not have *ventured*, if he had not the most assured confidence in the blinking credulity of his Galatian converts. His argument in this place is drawn from the use of the word "*seed*" in the *singular* number, in the passage of Genesis from whence he quotes. And because the word seed is in the *singular* number, he tells the "*foolish Galatians*," as he justly calls them, that this "seed" must mean *one individual* (and not many,) "which, says he, is *Christ*." Now let us look at the 15 chapter of Gen. from whence he quotes, and we shall see the force of this *singular* argument derived from the use of the *singular* number.—"And he (God) brought him (Abraham) forth abroad, and said, Look now towards Heaven, and tell *the stars* if thou be able to number them, and he said unto him, so *shall thy seed be*.—And he said, know of a surety that *thy seed* shall be a stranger in a land that is not *theirs*, and they shall afflict *them*, &c. afterwards *they* shall come out with great substance.—In that same day the Lord made a covenant with Abraham saying, unto thy seed have I given this land, &c. Again, ch. 22. God said to Abraham by his Angel, "I will multiply *thy seed* as the *stars* of Heaven, and as the *sand* which is upon the sea shore, and thy seed shall possess the gate of his, (or its) enemies, and in *thy seed* shall all the nations of the earth be blessed, because thou hast obeyed my voice!

Reader, what do you think now of Paul's argument from the use of the *singular* number? which is most to be admired, his impudence in palming such an argument upon the Galatians; (for being a learned man, he certainly knew, that the argument was nought,) or *their* credulity in receiving such reasoning as *Divine*? Really, I fear there is some reason for admitting as true, what Celsus maliciously says of the simplicity of the Primitive Christians, if Paul could with impunity feed his "spiritual babes" with such pap as this!

I intended to have concluded this subject, by bringing under examination some of the arguments, and quotations in the Epistle to the Hebrews. But upon looking over that Epistle, and contemplating my task, I confess I shrink from it. That Epistle is so replete with daring, ridiculous, and impious applications of the words of the Old Testament, that I am glad to omit it: and I think after the specimens which have been already brought forward, that my reader is quite as much satiated as myself. I will therefore bring forward only one quotation, which is alleged in that Epistle to prove the abolition of the law of Moses. And as for the rest, I content myself with referring those who want to know more of it, to the Pieces written by the celebrated Dr. Priestley upon Paul's arguments in general, and those in that Epistle in particular, preserved in his Theological Repository, where he will see absurdity in reasoning, and something worse, in quotation, exposed in a masterly manner. Indeed some learned Christians are so sensible of the insuperable difficulties attending every attempt to reconcile that Epistle to the Doctrine of Inspiration, or even to common sense, that they avoid the trouble, by denying that Paul could have been the author of such a work, and attribute it to the *same*, or a *similar* hand with that, which forged the marvellous Epistle ascribed to Barnabas.

The quotation brought forward in the Epistle to the Hebrews to prove the abrogation of the Mosaic Law, and the substitution of a *new* one is taken from Jer. xxxi. 31, &c. "Behold the days come saith the Lord, that I will make a *new covenant* with the house of Judah. Not according to the covenant which I made with their Fathers, in the day that I took them by the hand to bring them out of the land of Egypt, (which my covenant they brake, although I was an husband unto them, saith the Lord.) But this shall be the covenant that I will make with the house of Israel. After those days saith the Lord, I will put *My Law* in their inward parts, and *write it in their hearts*; and will be their God, and they shall be my people, and they shall teach no more every man his neighbour saying, know the Lord, for they shall all know me from the least of them unto the greatest of them, saith the Lord, for I will forgive their iniquity, and will remember their sins no more." Upon this passage the Author of the Epistle observes "in that he saith 'a *new* covenant,' he hath made the first old," and he sagely concludes 'now that which decayeth, and waxeth *old*, is ready to *vanish away!!*' and takes the quotation to be a *prophecy* of the *abolition* of the old Law, and the introduction of the Gospel Dispensation.

Now I would observe on his reasoning, in the first place, that allowing for a moment his interpretation of the prophecy to be correct, (i.e. that it signifies the abolishment of the *old*, and an introduction of a *new* Law) the prophecy at any rate *cannot* refer to Jesus, or the Gospel: for so far from having been fulfilled in the time of Jesus, or his Apostles, it has not been fulfilled *to this day*; for certainly God has not yet made a *new covenant* with the *Jews* to whom the prophecy refers, nor has he yet *put his Law in their hearts*; nor *caused them to walk in it*; neither has he yet *forgiven their sins*, or *forgotten their iniquities*, since they are *even now* suffering the consequences of them.

I will now retract what I granted, and assert that the Prophet did not mean an *abolition* of the *Mosaic*, and the *introduction* of a *new Law*. For though the Prophet speaks of a new *covenant*, he says *nothing* of a new *Law*; but *on the contrary* asserts that this new Covenant would be effectual to make them *obey the Law*. God promised to put *his Law within their hearts*; (not *out of remembrance*, as the Catechisms say,) and in this alone, this covenant differs from the one entered into at Mount Sinai. For *then*, though the Law was given them, it was *not* "put within their hearts," but they were apt to their own controul, to obey it, or not; being assured however, that happiness should be the reward of obedience, and death, and excision the punishment for revolt, and disobedience. And you will moreover observe, that notwithstanding what is here called a *new covenant*, nothing is here said of the *abrogation* of any *former* covenant, or constitution, or of any new *terms*, that would be required by God on the part of the Israelites. The Prophet, by expanding his idea, sufficiently explains his whole meaning, which is evidently this, viz. That God would make a new, and solemn promise to the Israelites, that they should be no more out of favour with him, that their hearts would be hereafter so right with God, that in consequence of it they would continue in the quiet possession of their country to the end of time. And all this, is intimated by Moses, in the quotation from Deuteronomy quoted in the last chapter.

Thus is this passage perfectly consistent with those in the Old Testament, which affirm, whether right or wrong, is not my concern, the perfection, and perpetuity of the Mosaic Law. "*Remember*," are the last words of the last of the Prophets, Malachi, "Remember the Law of Moses, my servant which I commanded unto him in Horeb, with the Statutes, and Judgments." Also in the Psalms, "The Law of the Lord is *Perfect*, converting the soul. The Testimony of the Lord is faithful, bringing wisdom to the simple. The Precepts of the Lord are *right*, rejoicing the heart, and enlightening the eyes." "The works of *his* hands are Truth, and Judgment. *All* his Precepts are *sure*. They *stand fast forever and ever*: being done in *Truth*, and *Uprightness*."

CHAPTER XIII.

I have said in the preceding chapter, that Paul was well versed in Cabbalistic Learning, and not unacquainted with the principles of the Philosophy styled "the Oriental:" and to prove, and exemplify this assertion is the subject and intention of this chapter. None but the learned know, how much of *Systematic Christianity* is derived from the *Cabbalism* of the Jews; the Religion of *the Magi of Persia*; and the Philosophy of the *Bramins of Indostan*. I shall attempt to lay open these *Theological Arcana*, and make them known to those who ought to know what they have been kept in ignorance of.

Many of my Readers have no doubt frequently puzzled themselves over these words of Paul Eph. v. 30, "For we are members of his (Christ's) *body*, of his *flesh*, and of his *bones*. Because of this, a man shall leave his father, and mother, and shall cleave to his wife, and they two shall be one flesh. This mystery is great, but I speak concerning Christ, and the Church." This passage exemplifies the connexion between *Christ* and *the Church*, by that which subsists between a man, and his wife: and this Paul calls "a great mystery," and it no doubt must be a very mysterious passage to all those who are unacquainted with the cabbalistic notion to which it alludes, and refers. To illustrate the passage, and to prove that Paul mixed his *Cabbalism* with his Religion, I shall set down here the note of Dr. Whitby the Christian Commentator upon the text of Paul.[24]

"The learned Dr. Allix saith,[25] The first match between Adam and Eve was a Type of that between Christ, and his Church; and in this, saith he, the Apostle follows the Jewish notions. The Jews say, the mystery of Adam is the mystery of the Messiah, who is the Bridegroom of the Church. These two persons therefore confirm the observation of *Munster*,[26] that the creation of the woman from the rib of the man, was made by the Jews to signify the marriage of *the Celestial man* who is blessed, or of the *Messiah*, with the *Church*; whence the Apostle applies the very words which Adam said concerning Eve his spouse, to the *Church*, who is the spouse of *Christ*; saying "for we are members of his body, of his flesh, and of his bones." For the explanation of these words take what follows. "The profoundest of the Jewish Divines whom they now call *Cabbalists*, having such a notion as this among them, *that sensible things are but an imitation of things above*, conceived from thence, that there was an *original* pattern of Love, and Union, which is between a man, and his wife, in *this* world. This being expressed by the kindness of *Tiphiret* and *Malcuth*, which are the names they give to the invisible *Bridegroom* and *Bride* in *the upper world*. And this *Tiphiret* or the *Celestial Adam*, is so called in opposition to the terrestial Adam; as *Malcuth* also, (i. e. the kingdom) they call by the name of Chinnereth Israel, the congregation of Israel, who is, they say, united to the *Celestial Adam*, as *Eve* was to the *terrestrial*. So that in sum, they seem to say the same that Paul doth, when he tells us, that "marriage is a great mystery, but he speaks concerning Christ and his Church." For the marriage of *Tiphiret*, and *Malcuth*, is the marriage of Christ "the Lord from Heaven," ("the *first* man was of the Earth, earthly, the *second man* is *the Lord from Heaven*" says Paul 1 Cor. 15,) with his spouse the Church, which is the conjunction of Adam, and Eve, and of all other men and women descended from them. *Origen* also seems to have had some notion of the relation of this passage to Adam and Eve, when he speaks thus, "If any man deride us for using the example of Adam and Eve, in these words, 'and Adam knew his wife;' when we treat of the knowledge of God, let him consider these words—'This is a great mystery.' Tertullian frequently alludes to the same thing, saying—"this is a great sacrament *carnally* in Adam, *spiritually* in Christ; because of the *spiritual marriage* between Christ, and the Church."

Thus far Dr. Whitby; and the intelligent reader, who is acquainted with the Dogmas, and Philosophy of *Indostan*, will not fail to see through this cloud of words, the *origin* of this analogy of Paul's. The fact is, that in *India*, and in *Egypt*, the *Divine creative power* which produced all things, and *energizes* in every thing, was symbolized by the *Phallus*; and to this day, in *Hindostan*, the *operation of Deity upon matter* is symbolized by Images of the male, and female generative organs; and in the darkest recesses of their Temples, which none but *the initiated* were permitted to enter, the *Phallus of stone* is the solitary idol, before which the *illuminated* bowed. This symbol, though shameful and abominable, is yet looked upon in India with the profoundest veneration, and is not with them, the occasion of shame, or reproach. It is, however, a blasphemous abomination, and the marriage between Christ and the Church ought not to have been thus illustrated by *Paul*, who reproached the Heathen mysteries as "works of darkness," which mysteries, in fact, consisted principally in exhibiting *these symbols*, and similar abominations.

But it may be asked, what is the meaning of the other clause of the verse, what could Paul mean by the strong language "We are members of his *body*, of his *flesh*, and of his *bones*?" Why my reader, he meant that Christians were really part of the body of Christ; and if you desire to know how he imagined this union *to be effected*, I request you to turn to the 10th chapter of the 1st Epistle to the Corinthians, where at the 16th verse he thus writes to them, "The cup of blessing which we bless, is it not a participation of *the blood of Christ*? The *loaf* (ac. to the Greek original,) which we break, is it not a participation of *the body* of Christ? for, because *the loaf* is *one*, we, though *many*, are *one body*, for we all *partake* of that *one loaf*." Again, ch. xi. 29, "For he that eateth and drinketh unworthily, eateth and drinketh judgment to himself, not distinguishing (or discovering) the *Lord's body*," and in ch. xii. 27, he says to them, "Ye are the body of Christ, and his members severally." (See the original of these passages in Griesbach's Greek Testament.) Thus you see, reader, that Paul considered Christians "as members of his (Christ's) *body*, of his *flesh*, and of his *bones*," because they partook of *one loaf*, which was the body of Christ. The Papists are in the right! and have been much slandered by the Protestants: for the doctrine of *Transubstantiation*, or at least the *Real Presence*, is as plainly taught in the New Testament, as the doctrine of the Atonement. You have seen what Paul believed upon this subject, and I shall corroborate the sense I put upon his words, by the words of Jesus his master, and by quotations from the earliest Fathers.

Jesus says, Jo. vi., "I am the living bread which came down from Heaven; if any man eat of this bread, he shall live forever, and the bread which I will give, is *my flesh*, which I will give for the life of the world." The Jews, therefore, contended among themselves, saying "How can thy man give us his flesh to eat?" Jesus therefore said unto them, "*Verily, Verily*, I say unto you, Unless ye eat *the flesh* of the son of man, and drink *his blood*, ye have not life in you. He that eateth my flesh, and drinketh my blood, hath everlasting life; and I will raise him up at the last day.— For *my flesh* is *verily food*, and my *blood* is *verily drink*. He that eateth my flesh, and drinketh my blood, *abideth in me*, and *I in him*. As the living Father hath sent me, and I live by the Father! (here is an oath!) so he likewise that *eateth me*, shall live by me."

This strange Doctrine was the faith of the Primitive Christians as is well known to the learned Protestants, though they do not like to say so to their "weaker brethren."

Ignatius says, "There is one flesh of our Lord Jesus Christ, and one cup in the unity of his blood," and of certain Heretics he says, "they confess not the Eucharist to be *the flesh of our Saviour, Jesus Christ*."

Justin Martyr, in his apology, asserts, that the consecrated bread "is *some how or other*, the *flesh of Christ*."

In the dispute with Latimer about Transubstantiation, it is acknowledged by the most candid writers, that the Roman Catholics had much the advantage.[27] It must have been so, where quotations from the Fathers were allowed as arguments. For what answer can be made to the following extracts? "What a miracle is this! He who sits above with the Father, at the same *instant, is handled* by *the hands of men*." (Chrysostom.) Again, from the same, "That which is in the cup is *the same* which flowed from the side of Christ." Again, "Because we abhor the eating of raw flesh, therefore it *appeareth bread* though it *be flesh.*" (Theophylact.) Or to this? "Christ was carried *in his own hands,* when he said *"this is my body."* [Austin.][28] Or to this? "We are taught that when this nourishing food is consecrated, it becomes the *body* and *blood* of our Saviour," [Justin Martyr.] Or lastly, to this? [from Ambrose.]—"It is bread *before* consecration, but *after* that ceremony, it becomes the flesh of Christ."

Another Doctrine which Paul derived from the Oriental Philosophy, and which makes a great figure in his writings, is the notion, that *moral corruption* originates in the influence of *the body* upon *the mind.*

It was one of the principal tenets of the Oriental Philosophy, that all evil resulted from *matter,* and its first founder appears to have argued in the following manner. "There are many evils in the world, and men seem impelled by a natural instinct to the practice of those things which reason condemns. But that Eternal mind, from which all spirits derive their existence, must be inaccessible to all kinds of evil, and also of a most perfect, and beneficent nature; therefore, the origin of these evils, with which the world abounds, must be sought *somewhere else,* than in the Diety. It cannot reside *in him* who is all perfection, and therefore it must be *without him.* Now there is nothing *without,* or beyond the Deity but *matter,* therefore *matter* is the centre, and source of all *evil,* of *all vice.*"

One of the consequences they drew from this Hypothesis was, that since all evil resulted from *matter,* the depravity of mankind arose from the pollution derived to the *human soul,* from its connexion with the *material body* which it inhabits; and therefore the only means by which the mind could purify itself from the *defilement,* and liberate itself from *the bondage* imposed upon it by the body, was to emaciate and humble the body by *frequent fasting,* and to invigorate the mind to overcome and subdue it, by *retirement* and *contemplation.*

The New Testament though it does not recognise this principle of the Oriental Philosophy, "that *Evil* originates from *matter*" yet coincides with it, in strenuously asserting that the corruption of the *human mind,* is derived from its connexion with the *human body.*

To prove this proposition, I shall show that Paul calls all crimes— *"the works of the flesh."* "Now the works of the flesh are manifest, (says he Gal. v. 19,) which are these: adultery, fornication, uncleanness, lasciviousness, idolatry, sorcery, hatred, contentions, rivalries, wrath, disputes, divisions, heresies, envyings, murthers, drunkenness, revellings, and such like." He also describes the conflict between the flesh, and the spirit or mind, in these terms. "For I know that in me, that is, in *my flesh* dwelleth no good, for to will is present with me, but to perform that which is good, I find not, but the evil which I would not, that I do. For I delight in the Law of God according to the *inner man*, but I see another Law in my members warring against the Law of my mind, and bringing me into captivity to the Law of my sin in my members. O wretched man that I am! who will deliver me from the body of this death?" (or this body of Death?) And he goes on to observe, "that I, the same man, with *my mind* serve the Law of God, but with my flesh the Law of sin, (Rom. vii.)" "For the flesh desireth, against (or in opposition to) the spirit, and the spirit against the flesh, and *these are contrary* the one to the other, so that ye cannot do the things that ye would."—"Those that are Christ's, says Paul, Gal. v. 24, have *crucified* the flesh, with its passions, and desires." And they are commanded (Rom. vi. 12. and viii. 13.) "to *mortify*" or according to the original, "*put to death*" or kill their members, and Paul himself uses language upon this subject exceedingly strong. He represents (1 Cor. ix. 27,) his mind and body as engaged in combat, and says, "I buffet my body, and *subject it.*" The word here translated, "*subject*" in the original, means "to carry into servitude," and is a term taken from the language of the Olympic Games, where the Boxers dragged off the Arena, their conquered, disabled, and helpless antagonists like slaves, in which humbled condition the Apostle represents his body to be with respect to his mind.

From this notion of the sinfulness of "*the Flesh*" we are enabled to apprehend Paul's reasonings about the sufferings of Jesus "*in the flesh.*" "Since the children are partakers of flesh and blood, Christ himself also in like manner partook of them." Heb. ii. 14. "For (says Paul) what the Law could not do, in that it was weak *through the flesh*, God hath done, who by having sent his own son in *the likeness of sinful flesh*, and *on account of sin*, hath *condemned sin in the flesh*" (Rom. viii. 3.) "But now, through Christ Jesus, ye who formerly were far off, are brought near *by the blood of Christ*—For he is our Peace who hath made both one, and hath broken down the middle wall of partition between us, having abolished by *his flesh* the cause of enmity." (Ephes. ii. 16.) "You that were formerly aliens and enemies in your mind by wicked works, yet he hath now reconciled by *his fleshly body*, through *his death*," (Col. i. 20.)

Though these notions are sufficiently *strange*, yet they are not so very remarkable as the one I am about to consider. It is a singular, and a demonstrable fact, that *the fundamental scheme of Christianity* was derived from *the Religion of the ancient Persians*. The whole of the New Testament scheme is *built* upon the Hypothesis, that there is a powerful and malignant Being called *the Devil*, and *Satan*, the Chief of unknown myriads of other evil spirits; that he is, by the sufferance of God, the Prince of this world, and is the Author of Sin, Woe, and Death; the Tempter; the Tormentor of men; and the Tyrant of the Earth; that the Son of God, to deliver mankind from the vassalage of this monster, descended from Heaven, and purchased their ransom of the Tyrant, at *the price of his Blood*; for observe, my reader! that the idea of the death of Christ being *an atonement to God* for the sins of men, is a *modern* notion, for the primitive Christians, *all of them*, considered the death of Christ as a *ransom* paid to *the Devil*; as may be proved from Origen, and other Fathers. That the New Testament represents this character as *the sovereign of the world*, may be proved by the following passages. "All this power will I give thee, and the Glory of them, (said the Tempter to Jesus, when he showed him all the kingdoms of the Earth,) for it is delivered unto me, and to whomsoever *I will*, I give it." Luke 4., Jesus calls him "the Prince of this world;" Jo. 12, and elsewhere. In his commission to Paul, he calls embracing his Religion, "turning from darkness unto light, and from the Power of *Satan* to *God*."—Acts xxvi. 18. Accordingly we find that to become a Christian, was considered as being freed from the tyranny of Satan. "God hath given life to you, (says Paul,) who were dead in offences and sins; in which ye formerly walked, according to the course, (or constitution) of this world, according to the *Prince of the Power of the air*," Ephes. ii. 1, and again, "If our Gospel be covered, (or hid,) it is covered among those that are lost, among those unbelievers, whose minds the *God of this world* hath blinded, to the end that the glorious Gospel of Christ should not enlighten them." 2 Cor. iv. 4., John says in his Epistle, that "the whole world lieth in the power of the wicked one," and Jesus in the Gospels compares *him* to "a strong man armed keeping his goods; and *himself* to one stronger than he, who stripeth him of the arms in which he trusted, and spoileth his goods. "For this purpose was the Son of God manifested, that *he might destroy the works of the Devil.*" 1 Jo. iii. 8. And it is said, that he "came to send forth the captive into liberty, and to *heal* those who were *oppressed of the Devil.*" Men are also said to have been "taken captive of the Devil, to fulfil his will." 2 Tim. ii. 26. And we find, that the Christians attributed all their sufferings to the opposition of this Being. "Put on (says Paul,) the whole Armour of God, that ye may be able to stand against the wiles of the Devil. For we struggle not against flesh and blood only; but against Principalities, against Powers, against the rulers of the darkness of this world, against wicked spirits in high places." Ephes. vi. 12. Christians are also said to be delivered by God from the power of Darkness, and to be *translated* into the kingdom of his dear Son, that is, as Christians were considered as being the subjects of *Jesus*, and the rest of the world as being of the kingdom of *Satan*, when a man became a *Christian* he was translated from the kingdom of *one*, to the kingdom of the *other*. Jesus accused the Devil as being the Author of all *evil*, as *a liar*, and the Father of lies, and a murderer of men and of women too, as appears in the Gospel, from the account of the old Lady whose back the Devil had bowed down, for eighteen years, Luke xiii. 10, (on what account it does not appear.) In short, the New Testament represents him as being the source of all evil, and mischief, and the promoter of it; and the whole world as being *his subjects*, and *combined with him* against all good.

But how does all this prove that these notions were derived from the Religion of the ancient Persians? I answer by requesting you, my reader, to peruse attentively the following account of the fundamental principles of the Religion of Zoroaster, the Prophet of the Persians.

The Doctrine of Zoroaster was, that there was one supreme Being, independent, and self-existing from all Eternity; that inferior to him, there were *two Angels*, one, the *Angel of Light*, who is the Author and Director of all *Good*; and the other, the *Angel of Darkness*, who is the Author and Director of all *Evil*; that *these two* are in *a perpetual struggle* with each other; and that where the Angel of Light prevails, there the most is good; and where the Angel of Darkness prevails, there the most is evil. That this struggle shall continue to the end of the world; that then there shall be a general resurrection, and a day of Judgment, wherein just retribution shall be rendered to all according to their works; after which, the Angel of Darkness, and his followers, shall go into a world of their own, where they shall suffer in darkness the punishment of their *evil* deeds. And the Angel of Light, and his followers shall also go into a world of their own, where they shall receive in everlasting Light the reward due to their *good* deeds.

It is impossible but that the reader must see the agreement of the Doctrines of the New Testament, with all this; and since it is undoubted, that these tenets of Zoroaster are far more ancient than the New Testament, and since, as we have seen, that that book is much indebted to *Oriental notions* for many of its Dogmas, there is no way of accounting for this coincidence (that I know of) besides supposing the Devil of the New Testament to be of Persian origin. It is however in my power to make this coincidence still more striking, from the words of Jesus himself, who says, Mat. xiii. 24, "The Kingdom of Heaven is like a man who sowed good seed in his field, but while men slept, *his enemy* (mark the expression!) *his* enemy came, and sowed tares among the wheat. But when the blades sprung up, and brought forth fruit, then appeared the tares also. So the servants of the householder came near, and said unto him, 'Sir! didst thou not sow good seed in thy field? whence then hath it tares?' And he saith unto them *an enemy* hath done this," you know the rest of the Parable. The explanation of it is as follows, "He who soweth the good seed is *the Son of Man*, and the field is the *world*; and the good seed are the Sons of the kingdom, and the tares are the Sons of the *Evil One*, and *the Enemy* who sowed them is *the Devil*." Here you see, as far as it goes, a precise agreement with the Doctrine of Zoroaster; and to complete the resemblance, you need but to recollect, that at the Day of Judgment, according to the words of Jesus, the wicked go into the fire prepared for the *Devil and his Angels*; and the righteous go into *Life Eternal* with *the Son of God*.

But is there not a *Satan* mentioned in the Old Testament; and is he not there represented as an evil and malevolent Angel? I think not. This notion probably arises from the habit of interpreting the Old Testament by the *New*. The Satan mentioned in the Old Testament, is represented as God's minister of punishment, and as much his faithful servant as any of his Angels. The Prologue to the book of Job certainly supposes, that this

Angel of punishment by *Office*, appeared in the court of Heaven, nay, he is ranked among "the Sons of God." This Satan is merely the supposed Chief of those ministers of God's will, whose office is to execute his ordered commands upon the guilty, and who may be sometimes, as in the case of Job, the minister of *Probation* only, rather than of Punishment; and there is no reason why *he* should be ashamed of *his* office more than the *General of an army*, or the *Judges* of the criminal courts; who, though they are not unfrequently ministers of punishment, are not therefore excluded the royal presence; but on the contrary, their office is considered as *honourable*; i. e., punishment without *malevolence* does not pollute the inflictor. Consider the story of the destruction of Sodom, Gen. xix., of Egypt, Ex. xxii. of Sennacherib, 1 Kings xxix. 35, also Joshua v. 13. The term Satan signifies an *adversary*, and is applied to *any angel* sent upon an errand of punishment. For example, Num. xxii. 23, "The Angel *of the Lord* stood in the way, for an *adversary* (literally for a *Satan*) against Balaam, with his sword drawn in his hand." "Curse ye Meroz saith the Angel of the Lord," whose office is to punish. So also Ps. xxxv. 5, "Let the Angel (of punishment) of the Lord *chase* them, (i. e. drive them before him; in a military manner, pursue them) let their way be dark and slippery, and the Angel of the Lord following them."

2 Sam. xxiv. 16, "The Lord sent a pestilence upon Israel—the Angel (of punishment,) stretched forth his hand and smote the people." 1 Chron. xxi. 16, "David saw the angel (of punishment) having a drawn sword in his hand."

This notion is referred to in the Apocryphal History of Susannah, verse 59. "The Angel of the Lord waiteth with his sword that he may cut thee in two."

Thus we see, that the term *Satan* is in the Old Testament applied to *any Angel of the Lord* sent upon an errand of punishment. And the term itself is so far from being *reproachful* (for David is said, 1 Sam. xxix. 4, to have been "*a Satan* to the Philistines,") that I am not *sure*, that if I had by me a Hebrew concordance, but I could point out places, where *God himself* is represented as saying, that he would be an *Adversary* or *a Satan* to *bad men*, and *wicked nations*. And though there is in the Old Testament *a particular angel* styled by way of eminence, "The Satan," it is so far from being evident, that he is an *evil Being*, that I would undertake to give good reasons to *prove*, that this distinguished Angel, is the *real prototype*, from whence the Impostor Mahomet took the idea of his "*Azrael*," the Angel of Death; who, in the Koran, is certainly represented as being as much the faithful servant of God, as any of the Angelic Hosts.[29]

In fine, the Doctrine of the Old Testament upon this matter may be thus expressed—"*There be spirits created for vengeance*, which in their fury lay on sore strokes; in the *time of Destruction* they pour out their force, and *appease the wrath of him that made them.*—They shall rejoice in his (God's) commandment, and they shall be ready upon earth, when *need is*; and when their time is come, they *shall not transgress his Word.*" Ecclesiasticus, xxxix. 28.

CHAPTER XIV.

Paul, in his 1st Epistle to the Corinthians, speaks to them as possessing several spiritual gifts conferred on them by his ministration; such as the gift of *prophecy*, *discerning of spirits*, and of *speaking in unknown tongues*. He gives them directions about the proper use of their gifts, and speaks to them as absolutely possessing those gifts, with the utmost confidence. Dr. Paley, in his Defence of Christianity, lays great stress upon *the manner* in which Paul addresses the Corinthians upon these miraculous powers: and he considers it as an absolute proof of the Truth of Christianity. Because, he says, it is not conceivable, that Paul could have had the boldness, and presumption to speak to these men concerning the use, and abuse, of these gifts, if they really had them not.

I am ready to confess, that this argument of Dr. Paley puzzled me. For though I was satisfied, that Paul had imposed upon their credulity many irrelevant passages from the Scriptures as proofs of Christianity; yet I could not imagine, that he could presume so much upon their stupidity, as to give them directions about the management of their *miraculous powers*; which being matters of fact known to themselves, therefore *if false*, I conceived must place Paul in their minds in the light of a banterer, when he told them of gifts, which their own consciousness, I thought, must make them sensible they had not. I say I was puzzled with this argument, until I happened to meet with some extracts from Brown's "History of the Shakers,"[30] which convinced me at once, from the obvious likeness between these Shakers and the primitive Christians, that Paul might have written to the Corinthians "concerning their spiritual gifts," with perfect impunity.

This Brown had been a Shaker himself, and while with them, he was as great a believer in his *own*, and *their* gifts, as the Corinthians could be; and since it must be obvious, that the gifts of these Shakers are mere self-delusions, there is then in our own times an example of the gifts of the primitive Christians, which enables us to comprehend their nature, and character, *perfectly well.*

Many of them, (the Shakers,) says Mr. Brown, "professed to have visions, and to *see numbers of spirits*, as plain as they saw their brethren and sisters; and to *look into the invisible world*, and to *converse with many of the departed spirits*, who had lived in the different ages of the world; and to learn, and to see their different states in the world of spirits. Some they saw, they said, were happy, and others miserable. Several declared, that they often were in dark nights surrounded with a light, sometimes in their rooms, but more often, when walking the road, so strong, that they could see to pick up a pin; which light would continue, a considerable time, and enlighten them on their way. Many *had gifts to speak languages*, and many miracles were said to be wrought, and strange signs, and great wonders shown by the believers."

And these poor creatures believed, and at this day *do believe* all this. They are not, you will observe, *artful impostors*, for the Shakers are certainly a harmless and a moral people; and yet they confidently asserted, (and continue to assert,) that they had these miraculous powers of "discerning spirits, speaking with tongues, and doing great signs and wonders." Nevertheless, it must be evident, that these powers were conferred upon them, only by their *enthusiasm*, and *heated imaginations.*

I have heard of the Shakers before, and have been informed, that those in New England are so convinced of their miraculous capabilities, that they have been known, in order to save their neighbours the trouble of applying to the tinman, charitably to offer to join the gaping seams of their worn out tin coffee-pots, and other vessels, "*without the carnal aid of solder*," merely by a touch of their wonderworking fingers.

Mr. Brown, in describing their mode of conduct, in their religious assemblies, unwittingly gives a striking exposition of the 1st Epistle to the Corinthians. He describes "the brethren and sisters," praying, singing, dancing, and preaching in known, and unknown tongues; and sticking out their arms, and extatically following their noses round the church.

He says, respecting such as speak in unknown tongues, "they have a strong faith in this gift; and think a person greatly favoured who has the gift of tongues. And at certain times, when the mind is overloaded with a fiery, strong zeal, it must have vent some way or other; their faith, or belief at the time being in this gift, and a will strikes the mind according to their faith, and then such break out in a fiery, energetic manner, and *speak they know not what*, as *I have done* several times. Part of what I spake at one time, was '*Liero devo jerankeemango, ad sileambano, durem subramo, deviranto diacerimango, jasse vah pe cri evanigalio; de vom grom seb crinom, os vare cremo domo.*'"

"When a person runs on in this manner for any length of time, I now thought it probable that he would strike into different languages, and give some words in each their right pronunciation; as I have heard some men of learning who were present, say, a few words were Hebrew, three or four of Greek, and a few Latin."

In another place he gives an account of his maiden speech in an unknown tongue; and it is easy to conjecture how he came by his gift, by attending to what passed before he broke out. Here it is: "We danced for *near an hour*, several *turned round like tops*, and to crown all, I had a gift to speak in some other language; but the greatest misfortune was, that *neither I, nor any other, understood what I said.*"

My reader will not be surprised after this, at hearing him say, that the spectators of "these signs and wonders," instead of being properly affected, considered the performers as "out of their wits."

Let us now compare this account with what Paul says upon similar subjects, in the 14th chapter of the 1 Ep. to the Corinthians. He advises them in exercising their gifts, to a discreet use of them, as follows: "He who speaketh in an unknown tongue, speaketh not to men, but to God, for *no man understandeth him*; howbeit in the spirit he speaketh mysteries." Again, "For if the trumpet give an uncertain sound, who shall prepare himself to battle? So likewise unless ye utter by the tongue *words to be understood*, how shall it be known what is spoken? for ye will speak to the air." And as others did not understand the Corinthians speaking in unknown tongues, so it seems too, that the Corinthians themselves were in the same unfortunate predicament with the Shakers, in not knowing *the meaning* of what they *themselves* said on these occasions. This is clear from this argument of Paul's, "Wherefore, let him that speaketh in an unknown tongue, *pray that he may interpret.*" Why pray that he may *interpret*, if he understood *himself*? Does a man who speaks *with understanding*, a *foreign language*, need *to pray* that he may be enabled *to interpret* what he says, *in his mother tongue*? Surely every man who understands *himself*, can *naturally* do this? After more to the same purpose, Paul wisely concludes his argument by declaring "that he would rather speak in the church *five words* with his understanding, (i. e. knowing what he said,) that he might instruct others also, than ten thousand words in an unknown tongue." And he fortifies his reasoning by this sensible remark, "If therefore the whole church come together into one place, and *all speak in unknown tongues*, and those that are unlearned, or unbelievers come in, will they not say, *that ye are mad*?" (as the spectators said of the Shakers.)

He advises them therefore, to conduct their assemblies with less uproar than formerly, and exhorts them as follows: "How is it then brethren, when you come together, hath each of you a psalm, hath he a doctrine, hath he an unknown tongue, hath he a revelation? Let all things be done to edifying. Now if any man speak in an unknown tongue, let it be by two, or at most by three, and that in succession, and let one interpret; but if there be no interpreter, let such keep silence in the church, and let him speak to himself and to God. And let two or three Prophets speak, and let the others discern. But if any thing be revealed to another who sitteth by, let the first keep silence. For ye may all prophecy, one by one, that all may learn, and all may be exhorted."

I presume it will be needless to point out more particularly, the perfect correspondence between "the spiritual gifts" of the *Corinthians*, and those of the *Shakers*. And I would ask the venerable Paley, if it were now possible, *whether* an apostolical Epistle of *Ann Lee, William Lee*, or *Whitaker*, (the spiritual mother, and fathers of the Shakers,) addressed to them, and *seriously* giving directions about the use of "their gifts of working miracles, and speaking with tongues," would be *sufficient* to *prove* that they *really* had those gifts. And moreover, (to make the cases more analogous,) suppose that the Shakers from this time become the dominant sect throughout the religious world, and kept the upper hand during a series of a thousand or two thousand years; taking especial care to collect and burn up every writing of their enemies, and opposers; how should we (supposing ourselves all the while invisible spectators of the thing,) how should we pity our posterity, who at the end of that period, should be gravely told by the learned, and mitred advocates of Shakerism, that the miracles of the founders, and first followers of their religion were *certainly* true, *for* that they were *honest* and *good* men, with *no motive* to *deceive*, and had addressed letters to their first converts, wherein they make *express mention* of their possessing these gifts; and give in the simplest, and most unassuming manner, directions for using them. Suppose then that our posterity, having been deprived by the prudential care of the old fathers of the then established church, of the means of detecting the fallacy which we possess; suppose that *they* should *believe* all this: and devoutly praise God every day for confirming the doctrines of his servants *Lee* and *Whitaker*, "with signs following." How should we pity their delusion, and what should we think of the unlucky authors of it?

From all this, I think my reader must be sensible how extremely fallacious are all proofs of doctrines, pretended to be from God, derived from miracles *said to have been* wrought in proof of their Divine authority.

Miracles are related to have been performed in support of all religions without exception: even the followers of Mahomet, though he did not claim the power of working miracles, have said that he did. And they will tell you, that in proof of his mission, he in the presence of hundreds, divided the moon with his finger, and put half of it in his pocket!*

---

*I will here lay before the reader, the arguments advanced by the Mahometans in behalf of the miracles of their Prophet, extracted from the learned Reland's account of Mahometanism. They say that—"the miracles of Mahomet and his followers have been recorded in innumerable volumes of the most famous, learned, pious, and subtle Doctors of the Mahometan Faith, who let nothing pass without the strictest and severest examination, and whose tradition therefore is unexceptionable among them: that they were known throughout all the Regions of Arabia, and transmitted by common, and universal Tradition from Father to Son, from generation to generation; That the books of *Interpreters*, and *Commentators* on the Koran, the books of *Historians*, especially such as give an account of Mahomet's Life, and actions, the books of *Annalists*, and *Lawyers*: the books of *Mathematicians* and *Philosophers*: and last of all, the books of both *Jews* and *Christians* concerning Mahomet, are full of his miracles. That if the authority of *so many* great and wise Doctors be *denied*, then for their part, they cannot see but that a universal scepticism as to all other accounts of miracles

George Bethune English

Speaking of the gift of healing diseases, which the Primitive Christians claimed, Dr. Middleton in his free inquiry observes—"But be that as it will, the pretence of *curing diseases* by a miraculous power, was so successfully maintained in the Heathen world by fraud, and craft, that when it came to be challenged by the Christians, it was not capable of exciting any attention to it among those, who themselves pretended to the *same power*; which, though the certain effect of imposture, was yet managed with so much art, that the Christians could neither *deny* nor *detect* it; but insisted always that it was performed by *Demons*, or evil spirits, deluding mankind to their ruin; and from the *supposed reality of the fact* they inferred the *reasonableness* of believing what was more credibly affirmed

---

(continued from page 165)

must obtain among people of all persuasions. For authority being the only proof of facts done out of our time, or out of our sight, if that be denied, there is no way to come to the certainty of any such, without immediate inspiration; and all accounts of matters recorded in History must be doubtful, and precarious."

"And these witnesses would not have *dared* to assert these miracles unless they were true: for such as forged any miracles for his, which he really did *not*, lay under *a hearty curse* from the Prophet. For it was a received Tradition among the Faithful, that Mahomet denounced Hell and Damnation to all those who should tell any lies of him. So that none who believed in Mahomet *durst* attribute miracles to him which he was not concerned in; and those who *believed not* in him, would certainly never have *given him* the honour of working any, unless he had done so." Christian Reader! thou seest how much can be said, and how many respectable witnesses and authorities can be adduced to prove that Mahomet wrought miracles; canst thou adduce *more*, or *better* authorities in behalf of the miracles or the New Testament? Art thou not rather satisfied how fallacious the evidence of Testimony is in all such cases?

This is not all that the Mahometan might urge in behalf of his Prophet. For he might tell the Christian, boasting that Jesus and his Apostles converted the Roman World from *Idolatry*,—that they overthrew one system of Idolatry, only to build up another; since the worship of Jesus, the Virgin Mary, and the Saints, and their images, was established in a few hundred years after Jesus, and continues to this day; an Idolatry as rank, and much more inexcusable than the worship of the ancient Greeks and Romans. Whereas, Mahomet cut up, root and branch, both Christian and Pagan Idolatry and proclaimed one only God as the object of adoration. And if the Christian should urge the *rapid propagation* of Christianity, the Mahometan might reply, that Mahomet was a poor camel-driver, but that Islamism made more progress in one hundred years, than Christianity did in a thousand; that it was embraced by the noble, the great, the wise, and the learned, almost as soon as it appeared: whereas, Christianity was skulking and creeping among the mob of the Roman Empire for some hundred years before it dared to raise its head in public view. If the Christian should reply to this, by ascribing the success of Mahometanism to the sword, the Mahometan might reply, with truth, that it was a vulgar error; for that vastly more nations embraced Islamism *voluntarily*, than there were who *freely* received Christianity; and he might remind him, how much Christianity owed to the accession of Constantine; to Charlemagne; and the Teutonic Knights; and bid him recollect that the monks were assisted by soldiers to convert to Christianity almost every nation in Modern Europe.

by the Christians to be performed by the power of the true God."[31] "We do *not deny*," says Athenagoras, "that, in different places, cities, and countries, there are some extraordinary works performed *in the name of Idols*, from which some have received benefit, others harm." And then he goes on to prove that they were not performed by God, but by Demons! Doctor Middleton then proceeds, (p. 77.) "whatever proof, then, the primitive Church had among themselves, yet it could have but little effect towards making proselytes among those who pretended to the *same gift*; possessed more *largely*, and *exerted more openly*, than in *the private assemblies* of the Christians. For in the Temple of Esculapius, all kinds of diseases were believed to be publicly cured by the pretended help of that Deity: in proof of which, there were erected in each Temple *columns*, or *tables* of *brass*, and *marble*, on which a distinct narrative of each particular cure was inscribed." He also observes that—"Pausanias writes, 'that in the temple at Epidaurus there were many columns anciently of this kind, and six of them remaining in his time, inscribed with the names of men and women cured by the God, with an account of their several cases, and the method of their cure; and that there was an old pillar besides, which stood apart, dedicated to the memory of Hippolytus, who *had been raised from the dead*!' Strabo,[32] also, another grave writer, informs us, that these temples were constantly filled with the sick, imploring the help of the God; and that they had tables hanging around them, in which all the miraculous cures were described." Dr. Middleton then proceeds thus— "There is a remarkable fragment of one of these tables still extant, and exhibited by *Gruter* in his collection, as it was found in the ruins of Esculapius' Temple, in the island of the Tyber at Rome, which gives an account of *two blind men restored to sight* by Esculapius in the *open view*, and with *loud acclamations of the people, acknowledging the manifest power of the God!!*" Upon which he remarks, that "the learned Montfaucon makes this reflection, '*that in this are seen* either the wiles of the *Devil*, or the *tricks* of *Pagan Priests*, suborning men to counterfeit diseases, and miraculous cures." He then proceeds, (p. 79.) "Now, though nothing can support the belief, or credit of miracles more authentically than *public monuments* erected in *proof* and *memory* of them *at the time* they *were performed*, yet, in defiance of that authority, it is certain all these Heathen miracles were pure forgeries, contrived to delude the multitude; and in truth, this particular claim of *curing diseases miraculously*, affords great room for such a delusion, and a wide field for the exercise of craft."

I need not observe, that by far the greater part of the miracles recorded in the New Testament, are casting out Devils, and healing diseases, Powers claimed by the Heathens as well as these Christians: and these miracles, (undoubtedly *false*) are *as well*, if not *far better* authenticated than those of the New Testament: for books may be *forged*, but *public* monuments of *brass* and *marble* are not so capable of being so: and these are always considered as better evidence for facts than *books*. What then will the Christian say to this? for since these miracles, recorded on brass and marble, inscribed with the narratives of them *almost immediately after the occurrence of them*, are unquestionably *Lies*; what can he pretend to say of those recorded in books, certainly written many years after the events they record, and, as will be proved hereafter, *more than suspected* to be *apocryphal?* And what would become of truth? and who would be able to distinguish truth from falsehood, in matters of Religion, if attested miracles, such as these, are sufficient to establish the divine authority of *Doctrines* said to be confirmed by them? Miracles are as numerous, and *better authenticated* on the part of Jupiter, Apollo, and Esculapius, than on the part of Christianity. They are strong on the part of Popery against Protestantism: for the Roman Catholic Churches in Europe are full of monumental records of miracles wrought by the Virgin Mary and the Saints, in favour of their worshippers. Nay, there never were miracles better proved, as far as *human testimony* could prove them, than the famous miracle mentioned by Gibbon in his History of the Roman Empire, where he relates the story of the Arian Vandals cutting out the tongues of a great number of orthodox Athanasians, who, strange to tell, preached *as much to the purpose*, in favour of the Trinity, without their tongues, as they did with them!! Never was there a miracle better authenticated by *testimony*, than this. It is mentioned by all the Christian writers of that age. It is mentioned by two contemporary Roman historians, one of whom lived in Constantinople, and who says he looked into the mouths of some of these confessors, who had in fact their tongues entirely cut out by the roots; and it is recorded in the archives of the Eastern Empire.

Is not this *testimony* enough; and yet, is it sufficient to prove the doctrine of the *Trinity*? Is it adequate to prove, that the "ancient of days" became a little child; was born of a woman, suckled, &c. &c.; and that "He who liveth for ever and ever," was whipped, was hanged, and *died* upon the cross, and was buried? Can this miracle, well attested as it is, prove for *truths*, such strange, such shocking things as these?

The miracles of the Abbé Paris too, are proved to be true, as far as *testimony* can prove any thing of the kind.—For they happened within a hundred years, were seen by many, and were *sworn to* before the magistrates, by some of the most respectable inhabitants of the City of Paris. How can men, who pretend to believe the miracles of the New Testament upon such meagre evidence as they have in their favour, *consistently* reject the miracles of the Abbé Paris? attested by evidence, recent, respectable, and so strong, that *to this day*, the juggle, and the means by which so many respectable people were imposed upon, have never yet been thoroughly developed and explained.[33]

CHAPTER XV.

In the 18th chapter of Deuteronomy, God says, "The Prophet which shall presume to speak a word in my name, which I have not commanded him to speak, or that shall speak in the name of other Gods, even that Prophet shall die. And if thou say in thine heart, how shall we know (or *distinguish*) the word which the Lord hath not spoken?"—Here is the criterion. "When a Prophet speaketh in the name of the Lord, if the thing *follow not*, nor *come to pass*, that is the thing which the Lord hath *not spoken*. That Prophet hath spoken presumptuously; thou shalt not be afraid of him."

Again, Deut. 13, "If there arise among you, a Prophet, or a dreamer of dreams, and give you *a sign or a wonder* (i. e. a miracle,) and the sign or wonder *come to pass*, whereof he spake unto thee, saying, let us go after other Gods, which thou hast not known, and let us serve them, thou shalt not hearken unto the words of that Prophet, or that dreamer of dream; for the Lord your God *proveth* (or tryeth) *you*, to know whether ye love the Lord your God with all your heart, and with all your soul."

And now Christian reader, I ask you what you think of *miracles*, or "signs and wonders," as proof of a divine mission, to teach doctrines novel and innovating, after such clear and unequivocal language as this, from such high authority? I am sure, that if you are a sincere lover of truth, you must certainly abandon that ground as untenable. For, from these directions, the Jews were commanded these things. 1. That the Prophet who presumes to speak a word, as from God, which God hath not commanded him to speak, must be put to death. 2. That the test, or criterion by which they are to discern a false Prophet from a true one, is this: *not* his *miracles*, but the *fulfilment of his words*. If what he says *comes to pass*, he is a *true Prophet*; if the event foretold does *not take place*, he has spoken presumptuously, and must die the death. 3. "If any man arise in Israel," and advise, or teach them to worship any other besides Jehovah; and in proof of the divinity of his mission promise a sign, or a wonder, and *in fact does bring to pass the sign or wonder promised*, he is nevertheless *not to be hearkened to*; but be put to death. And these criterions, given by God, or Moses, as the means whereby they might know a true Prophet from a false one, most exquisitely prove his wisdom and foresight. For if he had not expressly excluded miracles, or "signs and wonders," from being a proof of the divinity of doctrines; the barriers which divided his religion from those of Idolaters, must have been broken down; since, as we have seen, well attested miracles (meaning always by *miracles*, "signs and wonders," brought to pass by *human agency*,) are related to have been performed in proof of the divinity of every religion under Heaven. But veritable prophecy is, and can be a proof proper only to a *true Revelation*, because none can know what is to come but God, and those sent by him. Accordingly, we find that the Jewish Prophets were not acknowledged as such, but on account of *their foretelling the truth*, or *being supposed to do so*.

Thus it is said, 1 Sam. iii. 20, "And all Israel, from Dan even to Beersheba, knew, that Samuel was established to be a Prophet of the Lord." Why? Because he performed miracles? No! he performed none. But he was known as a Prophet *because* "the Lord was with him, and let none of his words fall to the ground," i. e. fail of their accomplishment. The same may be said of all the Hebrew Prophets, from Nathan to Malachi. For though Elijah, and Elisha performed miracles, yet it *was not in proof of their mission*, for *that* was established *before*; but these miracles were *occasional acts* of beneficence, or protection, but were *never considered,* or *offered* by them as proofs of their being sent from God.

These things being by this time, it is hoped, made plain and evident, let us now test the character of *Jesus* as a true Prophet, by the *criteria*, by Christians, and by the Jews believed to be given by God. If his prophecies *were fulfilled*, and if he taught the worship of no other being besides Jehovah, he was, according to the Old Testament, a true Prophet. But if any of his prophecies were *not* fulfilled, or, if he taught the worship of any other Being besides Jehovah, he was *not* a true Prophet.

And here it must be recollected, that those prophecies of Jesus *only*, can be brought forward in this question, which were *committed to writing, before* the event foretold came to pass; and therefore all Jesus's prophecies concerning the manner, and circumstances of his death, &c. must be *set aside*, as all those events are allowed to have taken place *before* any of the Gospels were written; and of course *it is not certain*, that Jesus *did* actually foretel them. This is acknowledged by Christians; and accordingly they confine themselves to bringing forward as conclusive evidence in their favour, his Prophecy of the Destruction of Jerusalem, and the events following. Here it is, Luke xxi. 21.: "When ye shall see Jerusalem compassed with armies, then know that the desolation thereof is nigh. Then let them which are in Judea flee to the mountains, and them which are in the midst of it, depart out, and let not them which are in the country, enter thereinto. For these be the days of vengeance, that all things *which are written* may be fulfilled. But woe unto them that are with child, and to them which give suck in those days. For there shall be great distress in the land, and wrath upon this people. And they shall fall by the edge of the sword, and shall be led away captive into all nations, and Jerusalem shall be trodden down of the Gentiles, until the times of the Gentiles be fulfilled. And there shall be signs in the sun, and in the moon, and in the stars, and upon the earth, distress of nations with perplexity, the sea and waves roaring, men's hearts failing them for fear, and for looking after those things which are coming on the earth; for the powers of the heavens shall be shaken. And *then* shall they see the Son of Man coming in a cloud, with power, and great glory. And when these things begin to come to pass, then *look up*, and *lift up your heads*; for *your redemption draweth nigh*. And he spake to them a parable, "Behold the fig tree and all the trees. When they now shoot forth, ye see, and know of your own-selves, that summer is now nigh at hand. So likewise ye, when ye see these things come to pass, know ye that the Kingdom of God is nigh at hand. Verily I say unto you, *this generation* shall *not pass away* till *all be fulfilled.* Heaven and earth shall pass away, but my words shall not pass away."

Such is the Prophecy, and on it I would remark, first, that what Jesus here foretells concerning Jerusalem did in fact come to pass. But that was not a fulfilment of *his* prophecy, but of *Daniel's,* who did, as is set down in the 7th chapter of this work, expressly foretell the utter destruction of the city and the temple. And it was from *Daniel* that Jesus obtained his knowledge of the approach of that event. For he *expressly cites Daniel,* Mat. xxiv. 15; Mark xiii. 14; and you will please to observe, reader, that he *refers* to him in this quotation from Luke in the words, "these be the days of vengeance *that all things which are written* may be fulfilled." So that in foretelling the destruction of Jerusalem he did no more than any Jew of that age, who attentively read their Scriptures, could have done, and been no Prophet either.

2. It would have been better for his reputation as a Prophet, if he had stopped short where Daniel stopped. For what he goes on to foretell has *not been* fulfilled. For he proceeds to say, that "there shall be signs in the Sun, and the Moon, and the Stars, &c." All this is taken from the 2nd chapter of Joel, who says that such things shall take place; not however at the *destruction* of *Jerusalem,* but in "the latter days," at the time of the *restoration* of Israel. So that here Jesus has been rather unlucky. For, in truth, there were no signs in the *Sun,* and the *Moon,* and the *Stars,* at that time; neither was there upon earth any "great distress of nations," except in Judea. Nor were "the Powers of Heaven" shaken. Certainly, they did not see Jesus "coming in the clouds of Heaven, with power, and great glory;" and most assuredly, *that generation did* pass away, and many others since, and "all these things" have *not* been fulfilled.

I know very well, and have often smiled over the contrivances by which learned Christians have endeavoured to save the credit of this Prophecy. They say that—it is a *figurative Prophecy* relating *entirely* to the Destruction of Jerusalem, which did in fact take place in that generation; that—the expressions about the "distress of nations," and "the sea and waves roaring," the "signs in Heaven, &c." are *merely poetical*; and that the shaking of "the powers of Heaven" was merely the *shaking* and *pulling down* the stones of the Temple *figuratively* called *Heaven*!! and that the glorious coming of Jesus "in the clouds of Heaven, with power, and great glory," meant merely, that he sent Titus, and the Romans, to destroy Jerusalem, or perhaps might have been an invisible spectator himself.

The reader will easily see, that all this is *nonsense*. And the Commentator Grotius, after meddling a great while in this troublesome business, at length ventures to *insinuate*, that God might have suffered Jesus to be in *a mistake* about the time of his second coming, and to tell the Apostles what he did, for the sake of keeping up their spirits!

But to annihilate the figurative Hypothesis of these well meaning Commentators at once, it will be only necessary to bring forward the testimony following. 1.—The other Evangelists make an *express distinction* between the Destruction of Jerusalem, and the coming of Jesus: and not only so, but represent him as saying, that *after* that event, i. e. of the destruction of Jerusalem, "*in those days*," i.e. in the same area in which that event took place, "the Son of man shall come," &c. Witness for me, Mark, ch. xiii. 24.—"But *in those days*, after *that tribulation*, [i. e. the destruction of Jerusalem] shall the sun be darkened, and the moon shall not give her light, and the stars of Heaven shall fall, and the Powers that are in Heaven shall be shaken. And then shall they see the Son of man coming in the clouds with power and glory; and then shall he send his angels, and shall gather his elect from the four winds, from the uttermost part of the Earth, to the uttermost part of Heaven.—Verily, I say unto you, that this generation shall not pass, till all these things be accomplished." This is decisive, and cannot be evaded.

2. The Apostles, and Primitive Christians believed, that Jesus would come in *that generation*, as is evident from many passages of the New Testament. Paul's Epistles to the Thessalonians prove this, and contain an argument to them intended to allay their terrors, or their impatience. John says in his first Epistle, chapter ii. 18, "Little children, it is *the last hour*; and as ye have heard that Antichrist should come, even now (or already) there are many Antichrists, whereby we *know* that it is *the last hour*." Many passages of similar import might be brought forward. The meaning of it is this—It appears from Paul's 2nd Epistle to the Thessalonians, that

just before the second coming of Jesus there was a personage to appear who was to be called *Antichrist*, i. e. an Enemy to the Messiah. (This notion they got from the interpretation given by the angel of the vision of the "little horn," in Daniel.) John, therefore, seeing many *Antichrists*, i. e. opposers of the pretensions of Jesus, considered the sign, and thus knew that it was "*the last hour*," and that his master was soon to appear.

It appears from the 2nd Epistle of Peter, chapter iii. that there were many in his days who scoffed at his master, saying, contemptuously, "where is the promise of his coming?" And Peter replies by telling them, that their contempt is misplaced, for that "one day is with the Lord as a thousand years, and a thousand years as one day." John, in the 1st chapter of Revelations says, concerning the coming of Jesus, "Behold he cometh with clouds, and every eye shall see him, and they also *which pierced him*, and all kindreds of the earth shall wail because of him." And in the last chapter of Revelations he represents Jesus as saying, "Surely *I come quickly*"!

In short, the Apostles, when they wanted to encourage their desponding Proselytes, they usually did it with such words as these: "be anxious for nothing, *the Lord is at hand*"—"Behold! the Judge *standeth before the door.*"—"Be patient, therefore, Brethren, (says James) for the coming of the Lord *draweth nigh.*" And this persuasion did not end, as might be expected, with that century; for we find that the Heathens frequently laughed at the expectations of the Primitive Christians, who, till the *fourth* century, never gave up the expectation of the impending advent of their master. Nay, so rooted was this idea in their minds, that, understanding the words of Jesus concerning John, "if I will that he tarry till I come, what is that to thee," to mean that that disciple should not die, but survive till the glorious appearance of his Lord, so far were they from being convinced of the vanity of their expectations by that Apostle's *actual decease*, that they insisted, that, though he *was buried*, he was not *dead*, but only *slept*, and that the earth over his body *rose* and *fell* with the action of his *breathing!!*

It is now hardly necessary to add, that Jesus did not at all answer the character of a true Prophet, when *tested* by the criterion laid down in Deuteronomy, for ascertaining the truth of the claims of a prophet to a divine mission.

Let us now see whether he taught the worship of other Beings beside

Jehovah, for if he *did*, the *other test* laid down in Deuteronomy will *also* decide against him. Now did he not command the worship of himself in these words: "all men should honour the Son, *even as they honour the Father*"? This certainly commands to render to Jesus the same homage which is rendered to *God*. I might prove that his Disciples did worship him, by referring to many passages in the New Testament, especially in the *Revelations*; in the latter part of which Jesus is represented as saying, "I am the Alpha, and the Omega, the beginning and the end, the first and the last," terms applied to Jehovah, in Isaiah, where God says, (as if in express opposition to such doctrine) that "there is no God *with him*: He knows not any; there was none before him, neither shall there be any after him." I could also adduce many passages relating to Jehovah of Hosts, quoted from the Old Testament, and applied in the New to *Jesus*. Witness the following: Jo. xii. 41, alludes to Isaiah vi. 5; Rev. i. 8, 11, 17, and ii. 8, to Isaiah xli. 4, xliii. 11, and xliv. 6; Jo. xxi. 16, 17, and Rev. ii. 23, to 1st Kings viii. 39, Po. vii. 9, Jer. xi. 20, and xvii. 20, Rev. xx. 12, to Is. xl. 10;—and, to crown all, Jesus in Rev. i. 13, 14, 15, 16, 17, is described in almost the same words as is the Supreme God, "the Ancient of Days," in Daniel vii. chapter, and were there not other proofs in abundance to this purpose, this resemblance alone would decide me.

I now leave it to the cool judgment of the reader, whether Jesus *prophecied truly*; or *did*, or did *not* teach the duty of paying religious homage to *other Beings* besides God? and if so, it is consequent, according to the tests by Christians acknowledged to be given by *God himself* in Deuteronomy, that Jesus was *not* sent by, or from Him; for if he was— GOD'S OWN WORDS WOULD BE CONTRADICTED BY GOD'S OWN DEEDS.

CHAPTER XVI.

In the preceding Chapters, I have taken the New Testament as I found it, and have argued *upon the supposition* that Jesus and the Apostles *really* said, and reasoned, as has been stated. I shall now endeavour to show, by an examination of the authenticity of the four Gospels, that it is *not certain*, that they were really guilty of such mistakes as are related of them in those Books.

*The Life and Doctrines of Jesus and his Followers, are contained in the pieces composing the Volume called the New Testament. The *genuineness* of the Books, i. e. whether they were written by those to whom they are ascribed, must be judged of, from the external testimony concerning them, and from internal marks in the books themselves. For the miraculous acts therein, and therein *only*, contained and related, cannot prove the truth and authenticity of the BOOKS, because the authority and credibility of the Books themselves must be firmly established, before the miracles related in them can reasonably be admitted as real facts.

Now the *external* evidence in favour of these Books is the testimony of those men called "*the Fathers.*" And as the value of testimony depends upon the character of the witnesses, it would be proper first to state as much as can be learned of these men. As time will not permit me to adduce all that might be said upon this subject, I shall here only take upon me to assert, that they were most credulous, superstitious, and weak men, and, what is worse, made no scruple of telling lies to support and favour what they called "the cause of Truth." For they were writers of Apocryphal Books, attributing them to the Apostles; and moreover great miracle-mongers who vamped up stories of prodigies to delude their followers: and which they themselves *knew* to be *false*. I say I take upon me to assert this, and to confirm, and establish this accusation, I refer the Reader to Dr. Middleton's "Free Enquiry," a learned Christian, who therefore had no interest to misrepresent this matter. And he will there find these accusations amply verified, and traits of character *proved* upon them, by no means favourable to the credibility of their testimony.

The first of these Fathers whose testimony is usually adduced to prove the authenticity of the Gospels, is *Papias*, a Disciple of John. The

*The Reader is requested by the Author to understand, and bear in mind, that it is not at all intended by any of the observations contained in this chapter on the Histories of the four Evangelists, to reflect upon, or to disparage the characters of Matthew, Mark, Luke, and John, under whose names they go; because *he believes*, and thinks it is *proved* in this Chapter, that the real authors of these Histories were *very different Persons* from the Apostles of Jesus: and that in fact the accounts were not written till the middle of the second century, about a hundred years after the *supposed* authors of them were dead. Of course, none of the observations contained in the chapter relative to these Histories, were considered, or intended to apply to any of the twelve Apostles, who were not men who could make such mistakes as will be pointed out. These mistakes belong entirely to the Authors who *have assumed their names*.

character given of him by *Eusebius* is, that "he was a superstitious and credulous man." And this is easily proved by recording some of the stories, concerning Jesus and his followers, written by this Papias in a Book extant in the time of *Eusebius*. One of these stories is mentioned by *Irenaeus* who says, that Papias had it from *John*; who, according to Papias, said, that *Jesus* said, that—"The days shall come, in which there shall be vines, which shall severally have *ten thousand branches*; and every one of these branches shall have *ten thousand lesser branches*; and every one of these branches shall have *ten thousand twigs*; and *every one* of these twigs shall have *ten thousand clusters of grapes*; and *every one* of these grapes *being pressed* shall yield *two hundred and seventy-five gallons of wine*. And when a man shall take hold of any of these sacred bunches, another bunch shall *cry out* "I am a better bunch, take me, and bless the Lord by me!" There's a *Munchausen* for you Reader! Well! this Papias is the first witness who lived after Matthew, who has spoken of his Gospel. He lived about the year 116 after Jesus. And what does he say of it? Why this. "Matthew composed a writing of the Oracles (meaning without doubt the Doctrines of the Gospel,) in the *Hebrew* Language, and every one interpreted them as he was able." So far as this Testimony goes, it is positive evidence, that the only Gospel of Matthew extant in 116, was extant in *Hebrew*; and there was then *no translation of it*, for "every one interpreted as he was able." The *present Gospel* called of Matthew was then not written by him, for it is *in Greek*. And that it has not all *the air* of being a translation is asserted by most of the learned. As it stands then, it was not written by Matthew: and that it cannot be a translation of Matthew's *Hebrew*, is not only plain from the circumstance of its style, and other marks understood by Biblical Critics, but can also be proved by *another story* related by this same Papias concerning the manner of the death of Judas. "His body, and head (says Papias) became *so swollen*, that at length he could not get through a street in Jerusalem, where *two chariots might pass abreast*, and having fallen to the ground——he burst asunder."

Now though this ridiculous story is undoubtedly false, yet it is not credible that Papias, who had so great a reverence for the Apostles, as to collect and gather all *"their sayings"* would so flatly by his story of the death of Judas contradict the story of Matthew, if the *Hebrew* Gospel of

Matthew contained that part of the *Greek* Gospel of Matthew which relates the manner of Judas's death.

Justin Martyr lived *after* Papias, in the middle of the second century and though he relates many circumstances agreeing in the main with those recorded in the Gospels, and appears to quote sayings of Jesus from some book or books; yet it is substantially acknowledged by Dr. Marsh, the learned annotator on Michaelis's Introduction, that these quotations are so unlike the *words*, and *circumstances* in the received Evangelists to which they appear to correspond, that one of two things must be true; either, that Justin, who lived 140 years after Jesus, had *never seen* any of the *present Gospels*; or else, that they *were in his time* in a *very different state* from what *they now are*.

The next Christian Father who mentions the Gospel of Matthew is *Irenaeus*, who says also that "Matthew wrote his Gospel in the *Hebrew Language*." The character of Irenaeus is discoverable from his Work against the Heresies of his time, to that I refer the Reader, who will find him to have been a zealous, though a very credulous, and ignorant man; for he believed the story of Papias just quoted, and many others equally absurd. He however furnishes this important intelligence, that in the second century, the Christian World was overrun with Heresy, "and a swarm of Apocryphal, and spurious Books were received by many as genuine."

The next witness in favour of the Gospel is *Tertullian*, who lived in the latter end of the second century. And the soundness of his Judgment, and his capability to distinguish the genuine Gospels from among a hundred Apocryphal ones and above all *his regard for truth*, may be judged of from these proofs given by himself. He asserts upon *his own knowledge*, "*I know it*," says he—"that the corpse of a dead Christian, at the first breath of the prayer made by the Priest, on occasion *of its own funeral*, removed *its hands from its sides*, into the usual posture of a supplicant: and when the service was ended, restored them again *to their former situation*." (Tertul. de anima c. 51.) And he relates as a fact, which he, and all the orthodox of his time credited, that—, "the body of another Christian already interred *moved itself to one side of the grave* to make room for another corpse which was going to be laid by it." And it is on the testimony of such men as *these*, that the authenticity of the Gospels *entirely depends*, as to external evidence! for these are all the witnesses that can be produced as speaking of them, who lived *within two hundred years* after Jesus: *Three* men, (for Justin cannot be reckoned as a witness in *favour* of the Gospels,) three men, who are all of them evidently *credulous*, and two of them certainly *Liars*.

To convince a thinking man that Histories recording such very extraordinary, ill supported, improbable facts as are contained in the Gospels are *divine*, or even *really* written by the men to whom they are ascribed; and not either some of the many spurious productions with which (as we learn from Irenaeus) that early age abounded, calculated to astonish the credulous, and superstitious, or else writings of authors who were themselves infected with the grossest superstitious credulity; of *what use* can it be to adduce the testimony of the very few writers, of the same, or next succeeding age, when the very reading of their works shews him that *they themselves* were tainted with that same superstitious credulity, of which are accused the real authors of the New Testament?

It is an obvious rule in the admission of evidence in any cause whatsoever, that *the more important the matter to be determined by it is, the more unsullied, and unexceptionable ought the characters of the witnesses to be.* And when no Court of Justice, in determining a question of fraud to the amount of *six pence*, will admit the testimony of *witnesses* who are themselves *notoriously convicted* of the *same offence* of which the defendant is *accused*; how can it be expected, that any reasonable, unprejudiced person, should admit *similar evidence* to be of weight, in a case of the *greatest importance possible*, not to himself only, but to the whole human race?

But there is a still greater defect in the testimony of those early writers, than their superstitious credulity, I mean their disregard of *honour*, and *veracity*, in whatever concerned the cause of their particular System.

Though Luke asserts, that *many* (even before he wrote his histories for the use of Theophilus,) had written upon the same subject: (Who of course must have been of the Jewish nation,) and many more must have been written afterwards, whose writings must have been particularly valuable; yet so singularly industrious have the Fathers, and succeeding sons of the Orthodox Church been, in destroying every writing upon the subject of Christianity, which they could not by some means, or other, apply to the support of their own blasphemous superstition, that no work of importance of any Christian writer, within *the three first centuries*, hath been permitted to come down to us, except *those books* which they have *thought fit* to *adopt*, and transmit to us as *the Canon of Apostolic Scripture*; and the works of a few other writers, who were all of them, not only converts from Paganism, but men who had been educated and well instructed in the Philosophic Schools of the latter Platonists, and Pythagoreans.

The established maxim of these Schools was, that it was not lawful *only* but *commendable* to deceive, and assert falsehoods for the sake of promoting what they considered as the cause of Truth and Piety, and the *effects* of this maxim, which was fully acted upon by both orthodox Christians, and Hereticks, produced a multiplicity of false, and spurious writings, wherewith the second century abounded.

Nay, they did not spare from the operation of this maxim, the *Scriptures themselves*. For they stuffed their copies of the Septuagint with a number of *interpolated pretended prophecies* concerning Jesus, and his death upon the cross;—forgeries as weak, and contemptible, and clumsy in themselves, as they were impious, and wicked. Whoever desires to see a number of them, may find them in the Dispute, or Dialogue of Justin with Trypho the Jew! where he will see the simple Justin bringing them out passage after passage against the stubborn Israelite, who contents himself with coolly answering, that these marvellous prophecies were not to be found in his Hebrew Bible!

There is also another well known, incontrovertible proof of the deceit and falsehood of the leading Christians of early times, of which every person in the least conversant with the Ecclesiastical History of those times must be convinced—their pretended power of working miracles! On this subject I shall say nothing, but refer the Reader to the work of Dr. Middleton already mentioned, for an ample account of their lying wonders, which they imposed as miraculous upon the simple people.

With regard to the *internal evidence* for the authenticity of the writings composing the New Testament, it is *still less satisfactory* than the external evidence.—And this may be well believed, when the Reader is informed that the Great *Semler*, after spending his life in the study of Ecclesiastical History, and antiquities, which he is allowed to have understood better than any before him, affirmed to his astonished Coreligionists, that, except the Gospel of John, and the Apocalypse, the whole New Testament was a collection of *forgeries* written by the Partizans of the Jewish, and Gentile parties in the Christian Church, and entitled *Apostolic*, in order the better to answer their purpose. This opinion has been in part adopted in England, by a learned and shrewd Clergyman named *Evanson*,[34] who has almost demonstrated, that the Greek Gospel of Matthew was written in the second century after the birth of Jesus, by *a Gentile*. For he proves that it could not have been written by a Jew, on account of *Geographical* mistakes, and manifest ignorance of *Jewish customs*.—He also gives good reasons for rejecting the authenticity of some of the Epistles. In short he has poured such a flood of light upon the eyes of his terrified Brethren, as will ere long no doubt enable them to see a little clearer than heretofore.

He gives several instances of Geographical blunders in Matthew. I shall mention only one. Matthew says in the 2d chapter that when Joseph the husband of Mary returned from Egypt, "hearing that Archelaus reigned in Judea, he was afraid to go thither, and therefore turned aside, into the Parts of Galilee." Now this, as will appear from a map of Palestine, is just like saying, "a man at *Philadelphia*, intending to go to the State of *New-York*, on his route heard something which made him afraid to go thither, and therefore he *turned aside—into Boston!*"

That the author of that Gospel was ignorant of Jewish customs will be evident from the following circumstances. He says Jesus told Peter, that before *the cock crew* he would deny him thrice; and that afterwards, when Peter was cursing and swearing, saying "I know not the man! immediately the cock crew." Now it is unfortunate for the credit of this story, that it is well known, that in conformity with Jewish customs, at that time subsisting, no cocks were allowed to be in Jerusalem, where Jesus was apprehended. This is known, and acknowledged by learned Christians; who have extricated themselves from this difficulty by proving, that the crowing of the cock here mentioned does not mean, as it appears to mean, *absolutely* the crowing of a cock, but that it means—what dost thou think reader! why it means—the sound of a *trumpet!!**

According to Luke, as soon as Jesus was dead, Joseph of Arimathea went to Pilate, and begged his body; and *hasted* to bury it, because the *Sabbath* (which began at sunset,) drew on; that his female disciples attended the burial; observed how the body was placed in the Sepulchre, and returned, and prepared spices, and ointments to embalm it with, *before* the Sabbath commenced? and then rested the Sabbath day, according to the commandment.

The pretended Matthew, however, tells us, that "*when the even was come,*" i. e. when the Sabbath day was *actually begun,* Joseph went to beg the body; took it down, wrapped it in linen, and buried it; and that Mary Magdalene, and the other Mary were sitting over against the Sepulchre. From the time that this writer has thought fit to allot for the burial of Jesus, it is evident, that he was not only *no Jew,* but so ignorant of the customs of the Jews, that he did not know, that *their day* always began with *the evening;* or he would never have employed Joseph in doing what no Jew would, nor dared to have done after the *commencement* of the Sabbath. He takes no notice at all of the preparation made by the women, mentioned by Luke; for that would not have agreed with the sequel of his story. But to make up for that omission, he informs us of a circumstance not mentioned at all by the other Evangelists. For he tells us that "on the

---

*That the pretended Gospel of Matthew was not written by Matthew, or by *an inhabitant of Palestine,* may be also inferred, I think, from the blundering attempts of the author of it to give the meaning of some expressions uttered by Jesus, and used by the Jews, *in the language of the country,* which was the Syro Chaldaic; and which the *real* Matthew could hardly be ignorant of. For instance, he says, that *Golgotha* signifies—"*the place of a skull,*" Mat. xxvii. 33. Now this is not true for Golgotha, or as it *should have been* written, *Golgoltha,* does not signify "*the place of* a skull," but simply "*a skull.*" The Gospels according to Mark, and John, are guilty of the same mistake, and thus *betray* the same marks of *Gentilism.* Again, the pretended Matthew says, that Jesus cried on the cross, "Eli Eli lama, sabackthani," which he says meant, " My God, My God, why hast thou forsaken me?" (Mat. xxvii. 46.) If the reader will look at what Michaelis, in his introduction to the New Testament, says upon this subject, he will find the *real* Syro Chaldaic expression which must have been used by Jesus, to be *so different* from the one given by the supposed Matthew, that he will, (and the observation is not meant as a disparagement to the *real* Matthew, who certainly had no hand in the composition of the Gospel covered with his name) I suspect be inclined to believe, that this *pretended* Matthew's knowledge of the vulgar language of the Jews used in Christ's time, must have been about upon a par with the honest *sailor's* knowledge of *French;* who assured his countryman, on his return home, that the French called a *horse* a *shovel,* and a hat *a chopper!*

next day which followeth the day of preparation, the Chief Priests, and Pharisees came together unto Pilate, &c." "The next day which followeth the day of preparation!!"—such is the periphrasis that he uses for the Sabbath day. It is well known that among the Jews it was, and is customary to prepare, and set out, in the afternoon of the Friday, all the food, and necessaries for every family during the Sabbath day. Because they were forbidden to light a fire, or do any servile work on that day; and therefore Friday was very properly called "the day of preparation." But it appears to me next to impossible that any Jew would call *the Sabbath "the day that followeth the day of the preparation."* Yet this singular Historian so denominates it, and moreover goes on to inform us, that the Chief Priests, and Pharisees went to Pilate, to ask for a guard to place round the Sepulchre till the third day, to prevent his Disciples from stealing away his body, and then saying, that he was risen from the dead; and that after obtaining the Governor's permission, *"they went,* and *secured* the Sepulchre by *sealing the stone* that was rolled against it, and setting a watch." Though there appear nothing very strange in this account to a *Christian,* yet I assure my reader that to the Jews, it ever did, and must appear, utterly incredible. For it is *wonderful!* that the *Jewish Rulers* and the *rigorous Pharisees* should, in *so public a manner,* thus violate the precept for observing the Sabbath day; for the penalty of this action of theirs was no less than *death!* More wonderful still is it that they should have so much better attended to, and comprehended the meaning of the prediction of Jesus to his disciples, than his own disciples did; and most wonderful of all, that a *Roman Proconsul* should consent to let his troops keep watch round a tomb, for fear it should be thought that a dead man was come to life again.

But though our author's history of these extraordinary facts is neither consistent with reason and probability, nor with the other histories of the same event; it proceeds in pretty strict conformity to the manner in which it sets out. For to convince us still more fully that the author was totally ignorant of the mode of computing time in use among the *Jews,* and *habituated* to that in use among the *Greeks,* and *Romans*; he reckons the *Sabbath* to *last* till *day light* on Sunday morn, and says, chapter xxviii. "that in the *end* of the *Sabbath,* as it began *to dawn,* towards *the first day* of the week,"—the two Marys before mentioned came, (not as in Luke, to embalm the body, for with a guard round the sepulchre, that would have been impracticable, but) *to see the sepulchre*. Whilst they were there, the author tells us, there was another great earthquake, and an Angel descended, rolled away the stone, and sat upon it, at whose sight the soldiers trembled, and were frighted to death. But to prevent the like effect of his appearance upon the women, he said unto them, fear not *ye*, for I know that ye seek Jesus who was crucified. That the women as well as the soldiers were present at the descent of this Angel, appears not only from there being nobody else, by whom these uncommon circumstances could have been related, but also by the pronoun personal *ye* inserted in the original Greek, which in that language is never done, unless it be emphatically to mark such a distinction, or antithesis, as there was on this occasion between them, and the *Roman Guard*. Here, however, the author is inadvertently inconsistent with *himself*, as well as with the other Evangelists; and *forgetting*, that the sole intent of rolling away the stone, was to *open a passage*, absolutely necessary to *the body of Jesus to come forth out of* the sepulchre; and that if he had *risen*, and come forth *after* the Angel had rolled it away, both *the women*, and *the soldiers* must *have seen him rise*, he makes the Angel bid them look into the sepulchre, to see—that he *was not there!* and tell them that he was *already risen*; and that he was *gone before them into Galilee*, where they *should see him*!! In their way, the author adds, Jesus himself met the women, and said "be not afraid, go tell my Brethren to go into Galilee, and there Shall they see me": He says that the eleven Apostles went into Galilee to an appointed mountain, and saw him there: notwithstanding that some of them were so incredulous, as not to believe even the testimony of their own senses.

In the interim, whilst the women were going to the Apostles, the author tells us, "some of the watch," some strictly disciplined Roman soldiers, left their station, to bring an account of what had passed, not to the *Governor* their *General*, nor to any other of *their own Officers*—but to the *Chief Priests of the Jews!* that *they* assembled a council of the elders upon the occasion, and after deliberating what was to be done, induced the soldiers, by large bribes, to run the risk of being put to death themselves, upon the highly improbable chance of the Jewish rulers having influence sufficient with the Roman Proconsul, to prevail on him to submit to the indelible infamy of neglecting the discipline of the army under his command, to such a degree, as to suffer an entire guard of soldiers *avowedly to sleep* upon their station, without any notice being taken of it! and to say "his disciples came, and stole him away *whilst we slept.*" This incredible story is another instance how necessary it is, that those who do not adhere closely to the truth, should have extraordinary good memories, to enable them to keep clear of absurdities, or palpable contradictions, in their narrations, for consider the circumstances. How were the tongues of these soldiers to be restrained among the inquisitive inhabitants of a large city, (at that time too, greatly crowded on account of the Paschal feast,) not only in their way *to* the Chief Priests; but also during the whole time while the Priests *assembled* the Sanhedrim, and were *deliberating* what was to be done? And if that part of the watch, who the author says came to inform the Chief Priests, were poltroons enough for the sake of a bribe to undergo so shameful a disgrace to themselves, as well as to hazard the resentment of their General, how could they undertake that *all their comrades* who remained at the Sepulchre would do the same? and to *what purpose* could the Jewish council bribe *some*, without a possibility of knowing how *the rest* of the corps would act? And even supposing all these difficulties surmounted, and that the whole guard had *agreed*, and *persisted* in saying, "his disciples stole him away while we slept," of *what service* could that be to the Jewish rulers? for if the guards *were asleep*, they could be no evidence to prove that the body *was taken away*; and it might be just as probable that he might rise to life again while the watch was asleep, as it was if no watch had been set.

In a word, it appears from the numbers of *Latin words* in Greek characters, which this Book contains; from the numerous *Geographical blunders*; and the author's evident ignorance of the customs of the Jews: from *the form of Baptism* enjoined at the conclusion, which was *not in use* in the *first* century as appears from the form mentioned as then used in the Acts: from the Roman Centurion's being made to call Jesus "a Son of a God" which words in the mouth of a Pagan could only mean that he must be a Demi-god, like Bacchus, Hercules, or Esculapius: it is clear that this Gospel is the patched work composition of some convert from the Pagan schools. At any rate his Gospel flatly contradicts the others in several important particulars in the History of the Resurrection. For he represents the Apostles as being commanded by the Angel, and by Jesus *to go to*

Galilee, in order to see him; and that they *went there*, and saw him on a mountain. Yet it is said by *the other Evangelists*, see Luke chapter 24, and Acts 1, that he appeared on the *same day* of the resurrection to *Peter*, at *Jerusalem*; to two other Disciples as they went to Emmaus; and on the *succeeding night* to the *whole* congregation of the Disciples, not in *Galilee*, but in *Jerusalem*, and that by his *express command* the Apostles did *not* go into Galilee, but *remained* at *Jerusalem* till the feast of Pentecost.

But as this Author differs from the other Evangelists, so they also differ among themselves. And the latter part of the last chapter of Mark is so irreconcilable to the other Historians of the Resurrection, that in many Manuscripts it is found *omitted*. And that Gospel ends in *them*, at the eighth verse of the last chapter. And Mr. West,[35] in his attempted reconciliation of their accounts of the Resurrection, is obliged to make a number of postulates, to take a number of things for granted, which might be denied; and after elaborately arranging the stage for the performance, he sets the women, and the Disciples a driving backwards, and forwards, from the City to the Sepulchre, and from the Sepulchre to the City, and so agitated, that they forget to know each other when they cross in their journeys. Notwithstanding his great ingenuity in reconciling contradictions, in which he beats Surenhusius himself, he makes but a sorry piece of work of it after all. He had much better have let it alone; for his work upon the Resurrection which he calls "the main fact of Christianity" displays these contradictions in so *glaring* a light, that *the very laboured ingenuity* of his methods of reconciliation, inevitably suggests "confirmation strong" to the keen-eyed reader, of that irreconcilability which the author endeavors to refute. What rational man therefore can *reasonably* be required to believe the story of resurrection pretended *to have been seen* and known, *only* by *the party interested in making it believed*! when in their Testimony even, they do *not agree*, but contradict each other?

There is really an immense number of discrepencies, and contradictions in the New Testament which the acumen of learned Christians has of late discovered, and pointed out to the world. And Mr. Evanson, in his work on "the Dissonance of the four Evangelists," has collected a mass, enough I should think, to terrify the most *determined* Reconciliator that ever lived. It is a little remarkable, that Mr. Evanson has asserted and proved the spuriousness of the Gospel ascribed to *John*, which Semler spared, in the general wreck which he made of the authenticity of the other Books of the New Testament.[36] Mr. Evanson says, in his examination of it, what has been said before, that the speeches ascribed to Jesus in it are most *incoherent, contradictory*, and falsified by *well-known facts*. And indeed the Author of the Book itself seems to be sensible of this; for he very naturally represents the Jews repeatedly accusing Jesus of being *mad*. "He hath a devil, and is mad, (say they to the multitude) why hear ye him?" and so in other places.—Mr. Evanson considers this work as the composition of a converted Platonist, or of a *Platonizing Jew*, the latter we think to be the most correct opinion, since it is evident that the author of *that* Gospel had the works of Philo at his fingers' ends, which is more than can be supposed of *John*. As Semler excepted the Gospel of John *only*, so Mr. Evanson excepts the Gospel of Luke *only* from the charge of spuriousness: though he says that it is grossly corrupted and interpolated. From these corruptions, and interpolations, he endeavours to purify it; in which attempt we think he has had very indifferent success. In short, his work has proved, (what he did not himself contemplate) that the Providence of the God of Truth has taken care, that so many absurdities, and contradictions should be contained in these Books of the New Testament which were written to establish a mistake, as must, I conceive, satisfy any man who has them once pointed out to him, that the Doctrine of those Books is not, and cannot be from God.

But it may be still asked, "How did this notion of the resurrection of Jesus become current?" "How can you account for the Apostles' believing such a thing?" We answer sincerely—we cannot absolutely ascertain. The Jews of that age have left no Documents upon this business. The origin of the Christian Religion is so extremely obscure, that Josephus takes *no notice of it at all*, (for the passages relating to Christian affairs *now* found in Josephus are notorious interpolations.) And it is evident from the Chronological, and other mistakes about Jesus in *the Talmud*, that the curiosity of the learned Jews had never been interested by Christianity, till so long *after* Jesus, that the memory of him, and his, was almost entirely lost among that nation. And it appears from the last chapter of the Acts, that when Paul was received by the Jews at Rome he had not been considered by the Jews of *Jerusalem* as of *sufficient importance*, as to cause them to warn their Brethren of the dispersion concerning him; for these

Jews tell Paul, on his enquiring, that they had not received any letters concerning him from Jerusalem. So that we can offer nothing but *conjecture*,
to solve the difficulty.

It has been said by some, (and it is by no means an Hypothesis desti-
tute of plausibility,) that Jesus was indeed crucified, but did not actually
die on the cross. It is evident that Pilate was extremely desirous to save
his Life; and is it impossible that the Roman Soldiers who crucified him,
had *secret orders*? Consider the circumstances. He was crucified at our
nine in the morning, and was taken from the cross at about three in the
afternoon. Now crucifixion is not a death which kills men in six hours,
and men have been known to have lived fastened to the cross for more
than *two days*. Consider besides, that when the Soldiers gave the *coup de
grace* to the two robbers, that they *did not* break the legs of *Jesus*. This,
the author of the Gospel according to John says they did, in order to ful-
fill a *prophecy*, but I leave it to my reader whether it is not more likely
that they did so in order to *fulfil secret orders*? But to make up for that
omission, the author adds, that they pierced Jesus with a spear. Now
besides that this is not mentioned by the other Evangelists, the very
manner in which this circumstance is mentioned, and *eagerly* affirmed by
him looks as if the Author was aware of the likelihood of a suspicion of
the fact we are trying to prove probable, and that he wrote this in order to
obviate it. And after all, the Gospel according to John was certainly not
written by him, and therefore what the Author of it observes may be true,
or not. You will observe also reader, that the body of Jesus was given by
Pilate to his friends *immediately*, a favour *never* vouchsafed by the
Romans in such a case, except *"speciali gratia."* You will observe also,
that the body was taken down by *his friends*, no doubt with great care,
probably was washed from the blood, and *rubbed perfectly dry*, and was
deposited in the cave or sepulchre with a large quantity of *spices*, and *aromatics*.—Now suppose that Jesus had only *swooned* on the cross, and that
his naked body after being cleansed as aforesaid, was laid in the new
Sepulchre where the air was cool and fresh, wrapped in a considerable
quantity of *dry linen*, together with *many spices, and aromatics*, what
could be more opportune, or *proper* to stimulate his drowsed senses, and
recall the unfortunate sufferer to life? Suppose then, that on awaking from
his trance, he disengaged himself, and took himself away as secretly as

possible. Might not all this have happened? Is it impossible? And does it not look plausible? It is not improbable that he might after this have shewed himself privately to his particular Disciples; for you will recollect Reader, that the appearances of Jesus to his Disciples *after* his crucifixion were to *them only*, and for the most part in *the night*. And thus it is by no means impossible, that the *twelve Apostles*, who were, I doubt not, well meaning men, though extremely simple, and credulous; I say it is thus by no means impossible, that they might have believed sincerely, that their master had risen from the Dead. This Hypothesis must not be considered only as the brain work of an unbelieving Sceptic; for it has been (in its main principle) advanced, and elaborately defended by Dr. Paulus the professor of divinity in the principal University in Bavaria.[37]

It is true, that it may be said, that this is all *Hypothesis*, and *mere conjecture*. We allow it; it is true; and we assert, that the account given by the Evangelists is *no better*, nay, *worse* than conjecture, as it is a mere forgery of the second century! For no man, we think who knows all that has been made known by Biblical Critics in later years, will now *seriously* contend for the *literal Truth* of that account.*

If all this will not satisfy the man that "believeth all things," our last resource is to *deny the fact* of this resurrection. And this we can do with perfect *sang froid*, as we know very well that it cannot be *proved*; for the *only* testimony in favour of it are the four Evangelists; four witnesses, the like of whose written testimony, (being as contradictory as that is,) *to say no more*, certainly would not, we believe, be received in a modern Court of Justice to settle *the fact* about a debt of *five dollars*. And if it be still urged, that such a story is *unparalleled*, and therefore respectable, we say

---

*As reasons for this assertion, take the following facts, which are now ascertained, and can be proved:—1. Several sects of Christians in the first century, in the apostolic era, *denied* that Jesus was crucified: as the Basildeans, &c. The author of the Epistle ascribed to Barnabas, I think, *denied* it, and the author of the gospel of Thomas certainly did. 2. The Jewish Christians, the *disciples of the twelve Apostles*, never received, but *rejected* every individual book of the present New Testament. They held in especial abomination the writings of *Paul*, whom they called "an apostate," and there is extant in "*Cotelerius' Patres Apostolici*," a letter ascribed to *Peter*, written to James at Jerusalem, wherein he complains bitterly of *Paul*, styling him "*a lawless man*," and a crafty misrepresenter of him (Peter,) and his doctrine, in that Paul represented every where, Peter as being *secretly* of the same opinions with himself; against this he enters his protest, and declares, that he reprobates the doctrine of Paul. (See Appendix A.)

(continued from page 189)

3. It is certain, that from the beginning, the Christians were never agreed *as to points of faith*; and that the Apostles themselves, so far from being considered as *inspired* and *infallible*, were frequently contradicted, thwarted, and set at nought by their own converts: and there were as many sects, heresies, and quarrels, in the *first* century, as in the second or third. 4. Christ and his Apostles were no sooner off the stage, than forgeries of all kinds broke in with irresistible force; Gospels, Epistles, Acts, Revelations without number, published in the names, and under the feigned authority of Jesus and his Apostles, abounded in the Christian church; and as some of these were *as early in time* as any of the writings in the present canon of the New Testament, so they were received *promiscuously with them*, and held in equal credit, and veneration, and read in the public assemblies as of equal authority with those now received. 5. The very learned and pious Dodwell, in his Dissertations on Irenaeus, [Henry Dodwell (1641–1711), *Dissertationes in Irenaeum* (Oxford, 1689) (—*Ed.*)] avows, that he cannot find in Ecclesiastical Antiquities, (which he understood better than any man of his age,) any evidence at all, that the four Gospels were known, or heard of before the time of *Trajan*, and *Adrian*, i. e. before the middle of the second century, i. e. nearly a hundred years after the Apostles *were dead*. (See Appendix B.) Long *before this time* we know, that there were extant numbers of spurious gospels forged, and ascribed to the Apostles; and we have not the least evidence to be depended on, that those now received were not also apocryphal. For they were written nobody certainly knows by *whom*, or *where*, or *when*. They first *appeared* in an age of credulity, when forgeries of this kind abounded, and were received with avidity by those whose opinions they favoured, while they were rejected as spurious by many sects of Christians, who asserted that *they* were possessed of the genuine gospels, which, however, those who received "the four," denied. 6. All the different sects of Christians, without a known exception, altered, interpolated, and without scruple garbled their different copies of their various and discordant gospels, in order to adapt them to their jarring, and whimsical philosophical notions. Celsus accuses them of this, and they accuse each other. And that they were continually tampering with their copies of the books of the New Testament, is evident from the immense number of various readings; and from some whole phrases, and even verses, which for knavish purposes were foisted into the text, but have been detected, and exposed by Griesbach [Jo. Jac. Griesbach (1745–1812)—*Ed.*], and others. They also forged certain rhapsodies under the name of "*Sybiline Oracles*," and then adduced them as prophetic proofs of the truth of their religion. They also interpolated certain clumsy forgeries as prophecies of Jesus into their copies of their Greek version of the Old Testament. 7. The *present* canon of the New Testament has never been sanctioned by the general consent of Christians. The Syrian Church rejects some of its books. Some of its books were not admitted until after long opposition, and not until several hundred years after Christ. The lists of what were considered as canonical books, differ in different ages, and some books now acknowledged by all Christians to be forgeries, were in the second and third centuries considered as equally apostolic as those now received, and as such were publicly read in the Churches. 8. The reason why we have not now extant gospels different, and contradictory to those now received, is because that the sect or party, which finally got the better of its adversaries, and styled itself Catholic, or orthodox, took care to burn and destroy the heretics, and their gospels with them. They likewise took care to hunt up, and burn the books of the Pagan adversaries of Christianity, "because they were shockingly offensive to pious ears." 9. Semler considered the New Testament as a collection of pious frauds, written for pious purposes, in the latter part of the second century, (the very time assigned for their *first appearance* by Dodwell.) Evanson adopts, and gives good reasons for a similar opinion with regard to most of the books which go to compose it. Lastly. The reason why the New Testament canon has been so long respected, seems to have been purely owing to the credulity of the ignorant, and the laziness, indifference, or *fears* of the learned.

(continued from page 190)

Douglas, in his famous "Criterion," [John Douglas (1721–1805), *The Criterion, or, Miracles examined with a view to expose the pretensions of pagans and papists* (London, 1754)—*Ed.*] gives us as infallible tests, by which we may distinguish when written accounts of miracles are fabulous, the following marks.

1. "We have reason to suspect (he says,) the accounts to be *false* when they are not published to the world till *after the time* when they are said to have been performed."

2. "We have reason to suspect them to be *false*, when they are not published *in the place* where it is pretended the facts were wrought, but are propagated only at a great distance from the supposed scene of action."

3. "Supposing the accounts *to have* the two fore-mentioned qualifications, we still have reason to suspect them to be false, if in the time *when*, and at the place *where* they took their rise, they might be suffered to pass without examination."

These are the marks he gives us as infallible tests by which we may distinguish the accounts of miracles in the New Testament to be *true*; and accounts of miracles in other books (though supported by more *testimony* than the former,) to be false; with how much justice may be evident from the following observations.

1. If "we have reason to suspect the accounts to be false, when they are not published to the world till long after the time when they are said to have been performed," then we have reasons to suspect the accounts given in the four Gospels; for we have no proof in the world, that any of them were written till nearly one hundred years after the supposed writers of them were all dead.

2. If "we have reason to suspect them to be false, when they are not published in the *place where* it is pretended the facts were wrought, but are propagated only at a great distance from the supposed scene of action," then it is still further evident that the accounts in question are not true. For they were apparently none of them published in *Judea*, the scene of the events recorded in them. But it is pretty clear that they were written in countries *at a distance from Palestine*. And the facts recorded in them were no where *so little believed* as in Judea, among the people in whose sight they are said to have been wrought, where they ought, *if true*, to have met with most credit. It is, however, evident from the histories themselves, that these stories were laughed at by the learned, and intelligent of the Jewish nation, and disbelieved by the great body of the people. In truth the first Christians were merely one hundred and twenty Galileans, who asserted to their coreligionists, that Jesus of Nazareth was the expected Messiah. It was a mere *national quarrel* between the great body of the Jews, and a few schismatics. This is evident from the Acts, where we find that for several years they confined their preaching to *Jews only*. Till the conversion of Cornelius, they do not appear to have thought the Gentiles any way interested in their dispute with their countrymen. So that it is not improbable, (as the Jewish Christians dwindled very rapidly,) that had it not been for the Gentile proselytes to Judaism, Christianity would have perished in its cradle. These people were very numerous, and formed the connecting link between the Jews and the Gentiles. And it was through the medium of these people, that Christianity became known to the heathens. For we find that after the Apostles could make nothing of the stubborn Jews "they shook their garments, and told them that from henceforth *we go to the Gentiles*." Accordingly, when the Apostles preached in the synagogues, and the Jews "*contradicted*, and *blasphemed*," and made fun of their mode of proving from the Prophets, "that Jesus was the Christ;" yet the "*proselytes* and *devout women*" listened, and believed.

3. If "supposing the accounts to have the two foregoing qualifications, we still may suspect them to be false, if in the time when, and in the place where they took their rise, they might be suffered *to pass without examination*," we have still less reason to believe the Gospels. For one reason

that it is not unparalleled; as we have an account of a false Messiah, who *applied the Prophecies to himself*, had a *forerunner*, and more than two hundred thousand followers who *publicly acknowledged* him for the Messiah, raised contributions, and supported him magnificently. He too *quoted the Prophets* as *speaking concerning him*, and was said to have *worked divers miracles*, and was ultimately put to death by the order of the Grand Seignor at Constantinople; yet nevertheless *was said to have been seen again* by *certain of his followers*, who *wrote Books* in favour of *that fact*, and of *his Messiahship*. Many learned Rabbins enrolled themselves as his Disciples, and *wrote controversial works* in his cause, as *Paul* did. And to conclude, his party was not entirely extinct within a very few years. Yet notwithstanding all this, he was an Impostor; and no man now believes the stories of *his miracles*, or *his resurrection*; notwithstanding that *both* are affirmed by more *recent*, more *learned*, and more *respectable* testimony, than is, or can be offered in favour of the Messiahship of Jesus. The name of this famous Impostor was *Zebathai Tzevi*, and his history is given by Basnage in his History of the Jews.[38]

I wish the Christian Reader to peruse carefully, and coolly, that account: and if he *then* persists in believing the History given by the

---

(continued from page 191) why they might be suffered to pass without examination is, where the miracles proposed coincided with the notions, and superstitious prejudices of those whom they were reported; and who, *on that account*, might be prone to receive them unexamined. Now we have documents in plenty, which abundantly prove, along with the virtues, the extreme credulity, and simplicity of the Primitive Christians; whose maxim was "believe, but do not examine, and thy faith shall save thee." Another very good reason why they might be suffered to pass without examination is, that the miracles of the Gospels were entirely *unknown* to, or at least unacknowledged by any *Heathen* or *Jew* of *the age in which they are recorded to have happened*. Nobody seems to have known a syllable about them but the Apostles and their converts. Even the books of the New Testament were not generally known to the heathens until some hundred years after the birth of Jesus, and it seems from the few fragments of their works come down to us, that the only notice they did take of them was to accuse them, of telling lies, and old wives' fables. And as for the Jews, the origin and early propagation of Christianity was so very obscure, that those who lived nearest the times of the Apostles do not seem to have known any thing about them, or their doctrines.

Though a little out of place, yet I will here adduce a fact which illustrates and exemplifies the power of enthusiasm to make people believe they saw what they did not see. Lucian gives an account of one Peregrinus, a philosophist very famous in his time, who had a great number of disciples. He ended his life by throwing himself, in the presence of assembled thousands, into a burning pile. Yet such was the enthusiastic veneration of his followers, that some of his disciples did solemnly aver, that they had seen him after his death, clothed in white and crowned; and they were believed, insomuch that altars and statues were erected to Peregrinus as to a demigod. See Lucian's account.

Evangelists,—with such faith as *his*, he certainly *ought* to be able to move mountains; and I have no doubt at all, that with such a good natured understanding as his, if he had found in his *New Testament* the story of Jonah *misquoted*, and by a *small transposition à la mode de Surenhusius* representing, that *"Jonah* swallowed *the whale!"* his sturdy "confidence in *things not seen*," would, I doubt not, have enabled him without difficulty to swallow the Prophet *with the whale in his belly.*

CHAPTER XVII.

I have already expressed my respect for the character of Jesus Christ. And I again declare, that I request that it may be distinctly understood, that by nothing that I have said, do I intend to impeach, or to depreciate his *moral character.* Whatever may have been his defects, or whatever were his foibles, they must have been the faults of his mind, not of his heart. For though he *may* have been a mistaken enthusiast, yet I do firmly believe, that, with such a character as he is represented to have possessed, he could not have been either a hypocrite, or a wilful impostor. And if it be replied, that I have, by some observations on his conduct, indirectly impeached the perfection of his moral character, I answer, that if so, it is certainly my misfortune, but it may not be his fault. To explain this observation, I request the reader to recall to mind, that Jesus *wrote nothing himself,* that the only accounts we have of him are contained in books, probably apocryphal, and *certainly* not *generally known* till after the middle of the second century from his birth. The gospels now extant do not appear to have been known to Justin Martyr; and the *earliest* Fathers in their writings generally quote *traditions* concerning Jesus instead of *histories.* Since these things are so, who knows, but that the authors of the histories of him now extant, have attributed to him words and actions of which he was guiltless. We know how prone mankind are to invent falsehoods concerning eminent men; for instance, Mahomet expressly disclaimed the power of working miracles, and yet the writings of his early followers ascribe hundreds to him. Why may it not be possible then, since Jesus wrote nothing himself, that these books ascribe to him words, and actions he neither spake, nor performed? God grant that this may one day be proved! For I should rejoice to find the meek, gentle, and amiable man of Nazareth proved guiltless of the follies, and impieties attributed to him in the New Testament. And though I am obliged in this work, to take the New Testament *as I find it*, and to reason concerning the works, and words of Jesus as I find them there expressed, yet I would earnestly request the reader to consider me willing, and *desirous* to exempt the author, or rather *the cause* of the Christian Religion, from the reproach of the sentiments I am bound by my regard for ONE GOD, and His attributes, to express for the system itself. Yes! I can in my own mind separate *Jesus* from his Religion and his Followers. I read with admiration many of his beautiful parables. I shall ever contemplate his mildness and benevolence with respect: and I peruse with pity, the recital of his sufferings, and cruel death. All this I have done, and I believe I shall ever do; but I cannot! I cannot in effect deny the ONE living, and true GOD, and renounce my reason, and common sense, by believing all the contradictory, and strange doctrines contained in the New Testament.

Having unburthened my mind upon this subject, and frankly expressed my sentiments and feelings with regard to the character of Jesus, I hope I may now be allowed (without incurring the charge of maliciously exposing him, or the twelve Apostles, to reproach) to state my opinions with regard to the merit of the *moral maxims* ascribed to him and them in the New Testament. And I again caution the reader, that he is not *obliged* to lay to *his, or their charge* the mischievous consequences that originated from acting upon these maxims and principles: since it is by no means impossible, that they may have been *falsely* ascribed to him and to them.

Now then, let us attend to the subject of the chapter, viz. the moral maxims *ascribed* to Jesus. These moral maxims consist of 1st. Those which were adopted by him from the Old Testament. 2d. Those of which he himself is described as being the author. With the consideration of those of the first class, I shall not trouble the reader, but shall devote this chapter to the examination of those which are supposed to have originated from him. These are 1st. 'Do to others what you would that others should do to you.' 2nd. 'Resist not the injurious person, but if a man smite thee on one cheek, turn to him the other also.' 3rd. 'If a man ask thy cloak, give him thy coat also.' 4th. 'If thou wouldest be perfect, sell all thou hast, and give to the poor; and come follow me.' 5th. 'Unless a man hate his father, and mother, and wife, and children, and possessions, yea, and his own life also, he cannot be my disciple.' 6th.—'Take no thought for the morrow.'

With regard to the first of these maxims, it does not belong to Jesus *as the author*. It is found in the book of Tobit, ch. iv. 15, and it was a maxim well known to the Rabbins. It is found in the Talmud *verbatim*. "What thou wouldest not have done to thee, do not thou to another. (Tal. Bab. Schabbat fol. 31.) So also Hillel addressed a Proselyte, thus, "what is hateful to thee, do not thou to thy neighbour." Several other expressions of Jesus were, it appears from the Talmud, *proverbial expressions* in use among the Jews. For instance, the original of that saying recorded Mat. vii. 2. "With whatsoever measure ye mete," &c. is found in the Talmud of Babylon (Sanhedrim fol. 100, Sotah ch. 4, 7, 8, 9.) "With whatsoever measure any one metes it shall be measured to him." So also the original of that expression of "Cast out the beam out of thine own eye, and then thou shalt see clearly to cast the mote out of thy brother's eye," is to be found in the Talmud.

What is called by Christians "the Lord's Prayer," is merely a few clauses taken from Jewish Prayers and put together. Very many instances of a similar nature to these might be produced! but as I must be brief, the reader is referred for further satisfaction to the works of Lightfoot,[39] where he will learn by extracts from Jewish writings the source and *meaning* of many more of the sayings of Jesus.

I now proceed to the most disagreeable part of the subject, viz.: the consideration of the *other* maxims mentioned, which it must be allowed do belong to Jesus, or at least to the New Testament, since they are the *peculiar* moral principles of Christianity, and the honour of them can be challenged by, I believe, no other religion.

These precepts are so extremely *hyperbolical*, that they *are not*, and *cannot be perfectly* observed by any Christian, who does not detach himself completely from the business of Society; and these maxims, (which, as I said before, are the only part of the morality of the New Testament, which is *not borrowed*,) never have been obeyed by any but the *Primitive Christians*; and by the *Monks*, and *Anchorets*; for even the *Quakers* and *Shakers*, eminent as they are in Christian morality, have never been able to come *quite up* to the self denial required by the New Testament.

Indeed, the moral maxims *peculiar* to Christianity are impracticable, except by one who confines his wealth to the possession of a suit of clothes, and wooden platter, and who lives in a cave or a monastery. They bear the stamp of enthusiasm upon their very front, and we *have* always seen, and ever shall see, that they are not fit for man; that they lift him out of the sphere in which God designed him to move: that they are useless to society, and frequently produce the most dangerous consequences to it. In a word, in these maxims we find commands, the fulfilment of which is impossible by any man who is a *husband, a father, or a citizen.*

It is an outrage to human nature, and to common sense, to order a virtuous man, in order to reach perfection, to strip himself of his property; to offer the other cheek to receive a new outrage; not to resist the most unjust violence, injury, and insult; not to defend himself or his property when "sued at the law;" to quit his house and goods, and to hate his parents, and brethren, and wife, and children, for the sake of Jesus; to refuse and reject innocent pleasures; to deny himself lawful enjoyments, appointed by the Creator to make the existence of man a blessing to himself and others.

Who does not see in these commands the language of enthusiasm, of hyperbole? These maxims! are they not directly fitted to discourage, and debase a man? to degrade him in his own eyes, and those of others? to plunge him into despair? And would not the *literal* fulfilment of them prove destructive to society? What shall we say of that morality which orders the heart to detach itself from objects, which God, and reason, and nature order it to love? To refuse to enjoy innocent and lawful happiness,—what is it but to despise the benefits of God? What real good can result for society from these melancholy virtues, which Christianity regards as perfections? Will a man become more useful to society when his mind is perpetually inquieted by imaginary terrors, by mournful thoughts, which prevent him from fulfilling the duties he owes to his family, his country, and those with whom he is connected?

It may be safely said, that Enthusiasm is the base of the morality of Christianity, I say, the morality of *Christianity*, meaning thereby, not the morality of those called *Christians*, but the morality *expressed* and *required* in the New Testament. The virtues it recommends, are the virtues caricatured, and rendered extravagant; virtues which divide a man from his neighbour, and plunge him in melancholy, and render him useless, and unhappy. In this world we want *human* virtues, not those which make a man a misanthrope. Society desires, and wants virtues that help to maintain it, which gives it energy and activity. It wants virtues which render families industrious, and united; and which incite, and enable every one to obtain lawful pleasures, and to augment the general felicity. But the peculiar virtues of the New Testament, either debase the mind by overwhelming fears, or intoxicate it with visionary hopes, both which are equally fitted to turn away men from their proper duties.

In truth, what advantages can society derive from those virtues styled by Christians *Evangelical*? which they prefer to the social virtues, the real, and the useful, and without which, they assert, a man cannot please God. Let us examine these vaunted perfections, and let us see of what utility they can be to *society*; and whether they really merit the preference which is given them by their advocates.

The first of these Christian Virtues, which serves as a base for all the others is *Faith*. It consists in believing the truth of dogmas, of absurd fables, which Christianity (according to the Catechisms) orders its disciples to believe. Dogmas, as absurd and *impossible* as a *square circle!* or a *round triangle!* From which we see, that this virtue exacts an entire renunciation of common sense: an assent to incredible facts, and a blind credulity in absurd dogmas; which, yet, every Christian is required to believe, under pain of damnation.

This virtue too, though *necessary* to all men, is nevertheless the *gift* of Heaven! the effect of *special grace*. It forbids doubt and examination; it forbids a man the right to exercise his reason; it deprives him of the liberty of thinking, and degrades him into a bearded baby.

This Faith vanishes, when a man reasons: this virtue cannot sustain a tranquil scrutiny. And this is the reason why all *thorough going* Christians are naturally, and consequently, the enemies of Science. This miraculous Faith, which "believeth all things," is not given to persons enlightened by Science and Reflection, and accustomed to think.—It is not given but to those who are *afraid to think*, lest they should offend God.

The *next* Christian Virtue which flows from the first, is Hope, founded upon the promises which the New Testament makes to those who render themselves miserable in this life. It nourishes their enthusiasm, it makes them "forget the things that are on earth, and reach forward unto the things"—which are in another world. It renders them useless here below, and makes them firmly believe, that God will recompence in Heaven the pains they have taken to make themselves miserable on Earth. How can a man, occupied with such expectations of heavenly happiness, concern himself at all *with*, or *for* the actual, and present happiness of those around him, while he is *indifferent as to his own*? And how *can he help this*, when he believes, that "friendship with the world is *enmity with God?*"

The *third* Virtue is *Charity*. We have elsewhere said, that if universal love, or charity means only *general benevolence*, and a desire to make others happy, and to do them good, all this is commanded by reason and the ancient revelation; but if by this precept it is commanded, to *love* those who *hate, oppress,* or *insult* us, we do not at all scruple to assert, that the thing is *impossible*, and *unnatural*. For though we can *abstain* from *hurting* our enemy; or even *can do him good*, we cannot *really* love him. *Love* is a movement of the heart, which is governed and directed by the laws of our nature, to those whom we think worthy of it, and to those *only*.

Charity, considered as general benevolence of disposition, is virtuous and necessary. It is nothing more than a feeling which interests us in favour of our fellow beings. But how is this feeling consistent with the *peculiar* doctrines of the Gospel? According to its maxims, it is a crime to offer God a heart whose affections are shared by terrestrial objects. And besides, does not *experience* show, that devotees obliged by principle *to hate themselves*, are little disposed *to give better treatment to others*.

We should not be surprised that maxims originating with enthusiasm, should aim at, and have the effect of driving man out of himself. In the delirium of its enthusiasm, this religion forbids a man to love himself. It commands him to hate all pleasures but those of religion, and to cherish a long face. It attributes to him as meritorious all the voluntary evils he inflicts upon himself. From thence originate those austerities, those penances, destructive to health; those cruel privations by which the inhabitants of the monastic cell kill themselves by inches, in order to merit the joys of Heaven. Now how can good sense admit that God delights in seeing his creatures torment themselves?

It may be said to all this, perhaps, that this is mere declamation, for Christians now a days do not torment themselves, but live as comfortably as others. To this I answer that *Christianity* is to be *judged* not by what Christians *do*, but by what it *commands* them to do. Now I presume it will not be denied, that the New Testament commands its professors to *renounce* the world, to be *dead* to the world, to "*crucify* the flesh with its passions and desires." Certainly these directions were *literally complied with* by the *Primitive Christians*; and in doing so they acted *consistently*. In those times, the deserts, the mountains, the forests were peopled with *perfect* Christians; who withdrew from the world, deprived their families of support, and their country of citizens, in order to lead unmolested "the divine life."—It *was* the New Testament *morality* that spawned those legions of Monks, and Cenobites, who thought to secure the favour of Heaven, by burying their talents in the deserts and devoting themselves to inaction and celibacy. And at this very day, we see these very same things in those Christian countries, which are *truly faithful* to the principles of their religion.

In fine, Christianity seems from the first, to have taken pains to set itself in *point blanc opposition* to nature, and reason. If it admits and includes some virtues ordered, and appointed by God, good sense, and universal experience, it drives them beyond their bounds into extravagance. It preserves no just medium, which is the point of perfection. Voluptuousness, adultery and debauchery are forbidden by the laws of God and reason. But Christianity not content with commanding and encouraging Marriage, as did the Old Testament, must forsooth go beyond it, and therefore encourages *celibacy*, as the state of *perfection*.—God says, in Genesis, "it is *not good* that man should be alone. I will make a companion for him." And He blessed all his creatures, saying, "increase and multiply." But the Gospel annuls this law, and represents a single life to be *most pleasing*, to the very Being, whose *very first* command was, "increase and multiply!" It advises a man to die without posterity, to refuse citizens to the State, and to, himself, a support for his old age.

It is to no purpose to *deny* that Christianity recommends all this; I say, *it substantially does!* and I boldly appeal,—not to a few Protestant Divines,—but to the *New Testament*; to the *Homilies* of the *Fathers of the Church*; to the History, and *Practice* of the *Primitive Christians*; to the innumerable *Monasteries* of Europe, and Asia; to the immense multitudes who have lived and died *Hermits*; and, finally, (because I know very well, the Protestant Divines attribute these follies to the influence of *Platonism*, *Pythagoreanism*, and several other *isms* upon *pure* Christianity;) I appeal to living evidence now in the world, to the only *thorough going* Christians in it, viz. to the Society of the *Shakers*, who I maintain, and *can prove* to be true, genuine imitators of the Primitive Christians; and a perfect exemplification of their manners and modes of thinking. I adduce them the more confidently, because, being simple and unlearned, their character has been formed by the spirit of the New Testament, and perfectly represents the *effects* of its principles *fully carried out*, and acted upon. They never heard of *Platonism* or of *Pythagoras* in their lives, and consequently the Polemic tricks and evasions, which have been, as hinted just now, resorted to by Protestant Divines, to shift from the shoulders of Christianity to those of *Plato or Pythagoras*, the obnoxious principles we have been considering, are of no use in *this case*, as, whatever the characters of these Shakers *may be*, they were formed by *the New Testament, and by nothing else*; and I believe, that every scholar in Ecclesiastical History, who reads Brown's History of the Shakers,[40] will be immediately, and powerfully struck with the resemblance subsisting between *them*, and the Christians of the *two first* centuries.

As *examples* of the effects of those precepts of Christian morality, which command us to hate father, and mother, and sister, and brother, for the sake of Jesus, take the following extracts from the History referred to.

"According to their faith, natural affection must be *eradicated*; and they say they must love all equally alike, as brothers, and sisters in the gospel. It would exceed the limits of this work to give a particular account of the various schemes that have been contrived, to destroy all natural affection, and social attachment between man and wife, parent and child, brothers and sisters; especially towards such as have left the society. Two instances that occurred about this time, as specimens of others, may suffice. A mother, who had renounced the faith, (i. e. left the society,) came to Niskeuna to see *her daughter*. Eldress Hannah Matterson told the daughter to go into the room to her *carnal* mother, and say, 'What do you come here for? I don't want you to come and see me with your *carnal affections*!'

"The mother being grieved, replied, 'I did not expect that a daughter of mine would ever address me in that manner.'

"The daughter, in obedience to what she was taught, replied again, 'You have come here with your *carnal fleshly desires, and I don't want to see you*,' and left her mother.

"Some time after, one Duncan Shapley, who had belonged to the society, called to see Abigail, his sister, at Niskeuna, whom he had not seen for six or seven years: but he was not admitted; he waited some time, being loth to go away without seeing her: at length she was ordered to go to the window and address him *in the language of abuse* and *scurrility*. The words she made use of, it would be *indecent to mention*. For this she was *applauded*, and that in the author's hearing, when he belonged to the society."

This man gives a very curious account how the Elders treated "their babes" in their spiritual nursery; but I shall notice only one or two examples, which illustrate what I have advanced concerning the natural hostility of the spirit of the New Testament towards *science*. "I know of several, who, soon after they joined the Church, *have been counselled by the Elders to dispose of their Books;* and have accordingly done it. Elder Ebenezer, being at my house one day, on seeing a number of books, he said—"Ah! Thomas must put away his books if he intends to become *a good believer*."

As an instance of its effect upon the human understanding, take the following. "A short time after, being at a believer's house, at eleven o'clock at night, they all having retired to rest, and I laying awake in a dry, well finished room, in which was *a stove* and fire, there fell a large drop of water on my temples; on examination, I could not discover where the water came from. I told the believers of it in the morning."

"One said, 'Ah! it is a warning to you respecting your unbelief.'"

"I then assigned some inconclusive reason, how the drop might have become formed in the room, and its falling."

"One replied, 'Ah! that is the way, you render a *natural reason* for the cause of every thing, and so *reason away your faith*, and yourself out of the gospel.'"

As another proof that *genuine* Christianity *discourages* marriage, and considers *celibacy* as the only state of *perfection*, the Shakers *allow of no marriages at all*.

Thus you see that, among these people, to become a *"Good Believer,"* you must insult your parents, revile your brother, despise learning, and never render a *"natural reason"* for any thing, lest you should *"reason away your faith, and yourself out of the Gospel."*[41]

CHAPTER XVIII.

After having seen the uselessness, and even the danger to individuals, of the perfections, the virtues, and the duties which Christianity *peculiarly* commands, let us now see whether it has a more happy influence upon *politics*, or whether it produces real happiness among *the nations* with whom this religion is established, and the spirit of it *faithfully observed*. Let us do so, and we shall find, that wherever Christianity is established and *obeyed*, it establishes a set of laws directly opposed to those of a well ordered national society; and it soon makes this disagreement and incompatibility distinctly to be felt.

Politics are intended to maintain union and concord among the citizens. Christianity, though it preaches universal love, and commands its followers to live in peace, yet by a strange inconsistency, consequentially annihilates the effect of these excellent precepts, by the *inevitable* divisions it causes among its followers; who *necessarily* understand differently the Old and New Testaments, *because the latter* is not only irreconcilably contradictory to the *former*, but is even inconsistent with *itself*. From the *very commencement* of Christianity, we perceive very violent disputes among its founders and teachers. And through every succeeding century, we find, in the History of the Church, nothing but schism and heresy. These are followed by persecutions and quarrels, exceedingly well adapted to destroy this vaunted spirit of concord, said by its defenders to be peculiar to Christianity; and the *existence* of which is in fact *impossible* in a Religion which is one entire chaos of obscure doctrines, and impracticable precepts. In every religious dispute, both parties thought that God was on their side, and consequently they were obstinate and irreconcileable.—And how should it have been otherwise? since they confounded the cause of God, with the miserable interests of their own vanity. Thus, being little disposed to give way on one part or the other, they cut one another's throats, they tormented, they burnt each other, they tore one another to pieces; and having exterminated, or put down the obnoxious sects, they sung *Te Deum.*

It is not my intention to pursue, in this place, the horrid detail of Ecclesiastical History, as connected with that of the Roman Empire. Mr. Gibbon has exhibited in such colours this dreadful record of follies, and of crimes, that it is difficult to see how the maxim of judging the tree by its fruit, will not fatally affect the cause of the Christian Religion. I refer to Mr. Gibbon's History, as a *cool and impartial* narrative, for I am well satisfied, that so far from having reason to complain of him, the advocates of Christianity have very great reason, indeed, to thank him for his *forbearance*, since with his eloquence, he might have drawn a picture that would have made humanity shudder. For, throughout the whole history, if a man had wished to know what was then the Orthodox Faith, the best method of ascertaining it would have been, undoubtedly, to ask, *"What is the Catechism of the Public Executioner."*

The Christian Religion was, it is evident from his history, the *principal*, though by no means the *only cause*, of the Decline and Fall of the Roman Empire. Because it *degraded* the spirit of the people, and because it produced monks and hermits in abundance, but yielded no soldiers. The Heathen Adversaries of Christianity were in the right when they said, that "if it prevailed Rome was no more!" The Christians would not serve in the armies of the emperor, if they could possibly avoid it. They justly considered the profession of a *soldier* and that of a *Christian* as incompatible. Celsus accuses them of *abandoning* the empire, under whose laws they lived, to its enemies. And what is the answer of Origen to this accusation? Look at his pitiful reply! He endeavours to palliate this undutiful refusal by representing that—"the Christians had their *peculiar* camps, in which they incessantly *combatted* for the safety of the Emperor and Empire, by lifting up their right hands—IN PRAYER"!! (See Origen contra Celsum. Lib. 8, p. 427.) This is a sneaking piece of business truly! But Origen could have given another answer, if he had *dared* to avow it, which is, that his Co-religionists in his time had not ceased to expect their master momentarily to appear; and of course, it little mattered what became of the Emperor, or the Empire. This notion was the principal engine for making Proselytes; and it was by this expectation that many were frightened into Baptism.

That Christianity was considered incompatible with the military profession is evident from many passages of the Fathers. And one of them, I
believe Tertullian, ventures to *insinuate* to the Christians in the Legions,
the expediency of *deserting* to rid themselves of "their carnal employment." Nay, to such a height did this spirit prevail, that it never stopped,
till it taught the Roman youth in Italy, the expedient of cutting off the
thumbs of their right-hands in order to avoid the conscription, and that
they might be allowed to count their beads at home in quiet.

If we examine, in detail, the precepts of this religion, as they *affect
nations*, we shall see, that it interdicts every thing which can make a
nation flourishing. We have seen already the notion of imperfection which
Christianity attaches to *marriage*, and the esteem, and preference it holds
out to *celibacy*. These ideas certainly do not favour *population*, which is
without contradiction the first source of power to every state.

Commerce is not less obnoxious to the principles of a Religion whose
founder is represented as denouncing an anathema against the rich, and as
excluding them from the Kingdom of Heaven. All industry is equally
interdicted to *perfect* Christians, who are to spend their lives "as
strangers, and pilgrims upon earth," and who are "not to take care of the
morrow."

Chrysostom says, that "*a Merchant* cannot please God, and that such
a one ought to be *chased out of the Church*."

No Christian also, without being inconsistent, can serve in the army.
For a man, who is never sure of being in a state of grace, is the most
extravagant of men, if by the hazard of battle, he exposes himself to
eternal perdition.—And a Christian who ought to *love his enemies*, is he
not guilty of the greatest of crimes, when he inflicts death upon a hostile
Soldier of whose disposition he knows nothing! and whom he may at a
single stroke precipitate into hell? A Christian soldier is a monster! a non-
descript! and Lactantius affirms, that "*a Christian* cannot be either a *Soldier* or an accused in a *criminal cause*." And at this day, the Quakers and
Mennonites refuse to carry arms, and in so doing they are *consistent*
Christians.

Christianity declares war against the *sciences*; they are regarded as an
obstacle to salvation. "Science puffeth up," says Paul. And the Fathers of
the Church St. Gregory, St. Ambrose, and St. Augustine denounce vehe-

mently *Astronomy* and *Geometry*. And Jerome declares, that he was whipped by an Angel only for reading that Pagan *Cicero*!

It has been often remarked, that the most enlightened men are commonly bad Christians. For independent of its effects on *faith*, which science is exceedingly apt to subvert, it diverts the Christian from the work of his salvation, which is the only thing needful. In a word, the *peculiar* principles of Christianity *literally obeyed*, would entirely subvert from its foundations every political society now existing.—If this assertion is doubted, let the doubter read the works of the early Fathers, and he will see that their morality is totally incompatible with the preservation and prosperity of a State. He will see according to Lactantius, and others, that "no Christian can lawfully be *a Soldier*." That according to Justin, "no Christian can be *a Magistrate*."—That according to Chrysostom "no Christian ought to be a *Merchant*." And that according to several, "no Christian ought *to study*." In fine, joining these maxims together with those of the New Testament, it will follow, that a Christian, who, as he is commanded, *aims at perfection*, is a useless member of the community, useless to his family, and to all around him. He is an idle dreamer, who thinks of nothing but futurity; who has nothing in common with the interests of the world, and according to Tertullian "has no other business but *to get out of it as quick as possible*."

Let us hearken to Eusebius of Caesarea, and we shall abundantly discover the truth of what has been said.

"The manner of life, (says he,) of the Christian church surpasses our present nature, and the common life of men. It seeks neither *marriage*, nor *children*, nor *riches*. In fine, it is entirely *a stranger to human modes of living*. It is *entirely absorbed* in an insatiable love of heavenly things.—Those who follow this course of life, have only their bodies upon earth, their whole souls are in heaven, and they already dwell among pure, and celestial intelligences, and they d*espise the manner of life of other men."* Demonstrat. Evang. vol. ii. p. 29.

Indeed a man firmly persuaded of the truth of Christianity cannot attach himself to any thing here below. Every thing here is "an occasion of stumbling, a rock of offence." Every thing here diverts him from thinking of his salvation. If Christians in general, happily, for society, were not *inconsistent*, and did not *neglect* the *peculiar* precepts of their religion, no large society of them *could exist*; and the nations enlightened by the gospel would turn hermits, and nuns. All business, but fasting and prayer, would be at an end. There would be nothing but groaning in "this vale of tears;" and they would make themselves, and others, as miserable *as possible*, from the *best of motives*, viz: the desire to fulfil what they mistakenly conceived to be the will of God.

Is this a picture taken from the life, or is it a fanciful representation of something different from the *peculiar* morality of the New Testament? This serious question demands a serious answer. If it be such as it is represented above, and such it *really appears* to me, and such *I have unfortunately experienced* its operation to be on my own mind—I would respectfully ask—Can such a Religion, whose *peculiar* principles *tend* to render men hateful, and hating one another: which has often rendered Sovereigns persecutors, and subjects either rebels or slaves: A Religion, whose *peculiar* moral principles and maxims, teach the mind to grovel, and humble, and break down the energies of man; and which *divert* him from thinking of his true interests, and the true happiness of himself, and his fellow men: can such a Religion, I would respectfully ask, be *from God?* since where *fully obeyed*, it would prove *utterly destructive to society.*

CHAPTER XIX.

From the preceding chapters you may judge, Reader, of the *justice* and truth of the opinion, that "the yoke of Christian morality is *easy*, and its burthen *light*:" and also of the veracity and fairness of that constant assertion of Divines, "that Jesus came to remove the heavy yoke of the Mosaic Law, and to substitute in its room one of *easier* observance." Whether this, their assertion, be not *rash* and *ill founded*, I will cheerfully leave to be decided by any cool, and thinking man, who knows human nature, and is acquainted with the human heart. I say, I would cheerfully leave it to such a man, whether the Mosaic Law, with all its numerous rites, and ceremonial observances, nay, with all "the (ridiculous) traditions of the Elders," *superadded*, would not be much more *bearable* to human nature, and much easier to be observed and obeyed, than such precepts as these; "Sell all thou hast, and give it to the poor." "If a man ask thy cloak give him thy coat also." "Resist not the injurious person, but if a man smite thee on one cheek, turn to him the other also." "Extirpate and destroy all carnal affection, and love nothing, but religion." "Take no thought for to-morrow:"—I am confident that the decision would be given in my favour; and have no doubt, that with thinking men, the contrary opinion would be instantly rejected with the contempt it merits.

Whether the Mosaic Code be the *best possible*, or really *divine*, is of no consequence in this enquiry, and is with me, another question from that of its *inferiority* to that of the New Testament. I do by no means assert the *former*; but have no hesitation to give my opinion, after a pretty thorough examination of the subject, that the reflections of *Paul*, and those usually thrown out against the Mosaic Code by Theologians, when *comparing* it with that of the New Testament, in order to *deprecate* the former, appear to me extremely *partial* and *unjust*; and so far from *true*, that I think, that the Ancient Law has the advantage over the precepts of the New Testament, in being, at least, *practicable* and *consistent*.*

Another unfounded reproach which Theologians, in order to *magnify* the importance of the New Testament, cast upon the *Old*, is this: they say, that the Old Testament represents God only as the tutelary Deity of the Israelites, and as not so much concerned for the rest of mankind. To show that this is a very mistaken notion, and to manifest that the Jehovah of the Old Testament is *represented therein*, not as the God of the Jews only, but also of the Gentiles, I refer to these words: "The Lord thy God is God of Gods, and Lord of Lords, a great God, a mighty and a terrible, who regardeth not persons, nor taketh reward. He doth execute the judgment of the fatherless and widow, and *loveth the stranger*, in giving him food and raiment. Love ye therefore the stranger. Thou shalt neither vex a stranger nor oppress him, for ye know the heart of a stranger, seeing ye were strangers in the land of Egypt. Hear the causes between your brethren, and judge righteously between a man and his brother, *and the stranger that is with him. One law* shall be to him that his *home born, and to the stranger that sojourneth among you.* The stranger that dwelleth

---

*The author had prepared, in order to subjoin in this place, an examination of the Mosaic Code, and a development of its principles, which he thinks would have satisfied the reader of the truth of what he has said in the last paragraph. But as it would have too much increased the bulk of the volume, it has been omitted. It is an institution however curious enough to be the subject of an interesting discussion, which he should be happy to see from the hands of one able to do it justice.

with you shall be as one born among you, and thou *shalt love him as thyself.* I am the Lord your God."

Indeed, so little truth is there in the notion, that the law, and religion of the Old Testament were established with the intention of confining them to one people, *exclusive* of all others, that the Old Testament certainly *represents* them in such a manner, as shows, that they were *intended* to be as unconfined as the Christian or Mahometan; its religion, in fact, admitted every one who would receive it. And what is more, it can be proved that the Old Testament dispensation *claims*, as appears from itself, to have been given for the common advantage of all mankind. And it is asserted in it (whether truly, or not, is not the question; it is sufficient for my purpose that *it asserts it*) that the religion contained in it, will one day be the religion of all mankind. For it declares, that Jerusalem will be the centre of worship for all nations, and the temple there, be "the house of prayer for all nations;" that Jehovah will be the only God worshipped; and his laws the only laws obeyed. It represents Abraham and his posterity as merely the instruments of Jehovah to bring about these ends; it is repeatedly declared therein, that the reason of God's dispensations towards them was, "that all the earth *might know* that Jehovah is God, and that there is no other but Him." According to its history, when God threatened to destroy the Israelites for their perverseness in the Wilderness, and offers Moses, interceding for them, to raise up *his* seed to fulfil the purposes for which he designed the posterity of Abraham, he tells Moses, that his purpose should *not* be frustrated through the perverseness of the chosen instruments; "but (saith he) as surely as I live, *all the earth shall be filled with the glory of the Lord,*" Num. xiv. 21. Many passages of similar import are contained in the Psalms, and the Prophets. In fact, there is no truth at all in the statement of the Catechisms, that the Old Testament was *merely* preparatory, and *intended* merely *to prepare* the way for "a better covenant," as Paul says; even for another religion, (the Christian) which was to convert all nations; for, (if the Old Testament be suffered to tell its own story,) we shall find, that it claims, and challenges the honour of beginning, and completing this magnificent design *solely to itself.* I was going to overwhelm the patience of the reader with quotations from it to this purpose; but being willing to spare him and myself, I will only produce *one*, which, as it is direct and peremptory to this effect, is as good as a hundred, to demonstrate that the Old Testament at least *claims* what I have said. Zech. viii. 20, "Thus saith Jehovah of Hosts: it shall yet come to pass, that there shall come people, and the inhabitants of many cities; and the inhabitants of one city shall go to another, saying: 'Let us go speedily to pray before Jehovah, and to seek Jehovah of Hosts; I will go also.' Yea, many people, and strong nations shall come to seek the Jehovah of Hosts in *Jerusalem*, and to pray before Jehovah. Thus saith Jehovah of Hosts, in those days it shall come to pass, that ten men shall take hold out of all the languages of the nations, even shall take hold of the skirt of him that is a Jew, saying, 'we will go with you, for we have heard that God is with you.'"

Be it so, it may be said:—"Still it is to Christianity the world owes the consoling doctrine of a life to come. Life and immortality were brought to light by the Gospel," say the Christian Divines; and they assert that the doctrine of a resurrection was not known to Jew or Gentile, till they learned it from Christ's followers. The Old Testament, (say they,) taught the Jews nothing of the glorious truths concerning "the resurrection of the body, and the life everlasting," their *"beggarly elements"* confined their views to temporal happiness only. These assertions I shall prove from the Old Testament itself, to be contrary to fact, for the Jews both knew, and where taught by their Bibles to *expect* a resurrection, and believed it as firmly as any Christian *can or ever did*. For proof hereof, I shall in the first place quote the 37th ch. of Ezekiel, and which is as follows, "The hand of the Lord was upon me, and carried me out in the spirit of the Lord, and set me down in the midst of the valley, which was full of bones. And caused me to pass by them round about, and behold, there were very many in the open valley, and behold, they were very dry. And he said unto me, son of man, can these bones live? and I answered, O Lord God thou knowest.—Again he said unto me, prophesy upon these bones, and say unto them, O ye dry bones, hear the word of the Lord—Thus saith the Lord God unto these bones, behold, I will cause breath to enter into you, and ye shall live, and I will lay sinews upon you, and will bring up flesh upon you, and cover you with skin, and put breath into you; and ye shall live, and know that I am the Lord. So I prophesied as I was commanded, and as I prophesied there was a noise, and behold a shaking, and the bones came together, bone to his bone. And when I beheld, lo, the sinews and the flesh came up upon them, and the skin covered them above; but there was no breath in them. Then said he unto me, prophesy son of man, and say unto the wind, thus saith the Lord God, come from the four winds O breath! and breathe upon these slain, that they may live. So I prophesied as he commanded me, and the breath came into them, and they lived, and stood up upon their feet an exceeding great army."

A plainer resurrection than this is, I think never was preached either by Christ, or his followers. Again, Daniel the Prophet says, "Many of them that sleep in the dust of the earth shall awake, some to everlasting life, and some to shame, and everlasting contempt," Dan. xii. 2. Now Ezekiel lived almost *six hundred years* before Jesus, and Daniel was contemporary with the former; and is it not a little surprising, that the Jews should learn for the *first time* the doctrine of a resurrection of the followers of Jesus Christ, when they knew of the resurrection almost six hundred years before he was born? Isaiah also, (who lived before either Ezekiel, or Daniel) in the 26th ch. of his prophecies, (exciting the Jews to have confidence in God, and not to despair on account of their captivity, and the troubles and afflictions, which they should suffer therein) foretells them, that death would not deprive them of the reward of their piety, and virtue; for God would raise them from the dead, and make them happy. "Thy dead men shall live, my dead bodies (i. e. the bodies of God's servants) they shall arise. Awake! and sing! ye that dwell in the dust, for thy dew is as the dew of herbs." The meaning of the last clause is—that, as the grass, which in Oriental countries becomes brown and shrivelled by the heat of the sun, from the effects of the dew, changes, and springs up, as it were in a moment, green and fresh, and beautiful; so by the instantaneous influence of the word of God, the dry, and decayed remains of mortality shall become blooming with immortal freshness and beauty. See also Hosea xiii. 14. I might easily multiply passages from the Old Testament to prove, that the doctrine of a resurrection was familiar to the ancient Israelites, but I suppose that what I have already produced is sufficient. Those however who wish to see the subject more thoroughly examined, are referred to "Greave's Lectures on the Pentateuch," a work lately published in Europe, highly honourable to the author.[42] See also a Tract upon this subject published by Dr. Priestley, in 1801.[43]

I shall only add one observation more upon this subject; viz. that it is very singular, that Christian Divines should assert, that "life and immortality were *first brought to light* by the Gospel," when the *New Testament itself* represents the resurrection of the dead as being *perfectly well known* to the Jews, and describes *Jesus himself* as proving it to the *Sadducees out of the Old Testament!!*

CONCLUSION

I have now finished my work; which I have written in order to exculpate myself, and to do justice to others; and having re-examined every link of the chain of my argument, I think it amply strong to support the conclusions attached to it. Though there might have been drawn from the Old and New Testaments, many additional arguments corroborative of what has been said, yet, at present, I shall add no more; as I think that what has been brought forward has just claims to be considered by the impartial as quite sufficient to prove these two points—that the New Testament can neither subsist *with* the Old Testament, nor *without* it;—and, that the New Testament system was built *first* upon a *mistake*, and *afterwards* buttressed up with forged, and Apocryphal documents.

Let the candid now judge, whether the Author knowing these things, or, at least persuaded of their truth, could have persisted in affirming (in a place where sincerity is expected) in the name of the Almighty, that the claims of the New Testament *were valid*—without being a hypocrite, and an impostor.

Let them also consider, whether, after being unable to obtain a satisfactory refutation of the objections contained in this volume, his resigning a profession whose duties obliged him to say what he was convinced was false, was conduct to be reprehended. And lastly, he appeals to the good sense of the Public, for a decision, whether, with such objections, and difficulties weighing upon his mind, as he has now exposed his conduct in that respect, can reasonably be attributed to the unmanly influence of caprice, and fickleness, (as has been circulated by some who had an interest in making it believed;) or to the just influence of motives deserving a better name.

With regard to the unfortunate people whose arguments have been brought forward in this volume, we have, reader, now gone over, and distinctly felt the whole ground of the controversy between them and their persecutors, mentioned in the Preface. And as they make use of the Old Testament as a foundation, *admitted and necessarily* admitted by Christians, *to be of divine authority*, and are surrounded by the bulwarks they have raised out of the demolished entrenchments of their adversaries; I do not see but that "their castle's strength may laugh a siege to scorn." And after reviewing, and revolving over and over in my own mind the arguments *on both sides*, I am obliged to believe, that the stoutest Polemical Goliath who may venture to attack it, especially their strong hold—their arguments about the *Messiahship*, will find to his cost, that when his weak point is but *known*, the mightiest Achilles *must fall* before the feeblest Paris, whose arrow is——*aimed at his HEEL.*

The Author hopes, and thinks he has a right to *expect*, that whoever may attempt to answer his Book will do it *fairly*, like a man of candour; without trying to *evade* the main question—that of the *Messiahship of Jesus.* He fears, that he shall see an answer precisely resembling the many others he has seen upon that subject. Except two, those of *Shyes* and *Jeffries*[44] (who acknowledge that miracles have *nothing to do* with the question of the *Messiahship*, which can be decided by the Old Testament *only*;)—all that he has ever met with evade this question, and *slide over* to the ground of *miracles.* Such conduct in an answerer of this Book would be very *unfair*, and also very *absurd.* For the case is precisely resembling the following:—A father informs, by letter, his son in a foreign country that he is about to send him *a Tutor*, whom he will know by the following marks:—"He is learned in the Mathematics, and the Physical Sciences; acquainted with the learned languages, and an excellent Physician; of a *dark* complexion; *six feet high*, and with a voice *loud* and *commanding.*" By and by, a man comes to the young man, professing to be this Tutor sent to him by his Father. On examining the man, and comparing him *with the description in his Father's letter*, he finds him totally *unlike* the person he had been *taught to expect.* Instead of being acquainted with the Sciences, therein mentioned, he knows nothing about them; instead of being '*six feet* high, of a *dark* complexion, and with a voice *loud* and *commanding*,' he is a dimunitive creature of *five feet*, of a *light* complexion, with a *voice like a woman's.*

The young man, with his Father's letter in his hand, tells the pretended Tutor, that he certainly *cannot be* the person he has been told to expect. The man persists, and appeals to certain "wonderful works" he performs in order to convince the young man, that he *is* acquainted with the sciences aforesaid, and that he *is* also *six feet high*; of a *dark* complexion; and talks like *an Emperor!* The young man replies—"Friend, you are either an enthusiast, a mad man, or something worse. As to your 'signs and wonders' I have been warned in my Father's letter to pay no regard to *any such things* in *this* case. Besides, you ought to be sensible, that your *identity* with the person I am taught by my Father's letter to expect, can be *only* determined by *comparing* you with the *description* of him given therein.—Whether your 'wonderful works' are real miracles or not, I neither know, nor care. At *any rate*, they cannot, *in the nature of things*, be any thing to the purpose in *this case*.—For you to pretend, that they *prove* what you offer them to prove, is quite absurd, you might *as well*, and as *reasonably*, pretend, that they *could* prove Aristotle to have been Alexander; or the *Methodist George Whitfield* to be the *Emperor Napoleon Bonaparte!*"

To conclude, if any person should feel inclined to attempt to refute the Book, let him do it like a man, without *evading* the question, or equivocating, or *cavilling* about little things. Let him consider the *principal question*, and the *main arguments* on which he perceives that the Author *relies*, and not pass over these *silently*, and hold up a few petty mistakes, and subsidiary arguments as specimens of the whole book. Such a mode of defence would be very disingenuous, and with a *discerning reader* perfectly futile, and insufficient. It would be as if a man prostrate, and bleeding under a Lion whose teeth and claws were *infixed in his throat*, should tear *a handful of hairs* out of the animal's mane, and hold them up as proofs of *victory*.

In fine, let him, before his undertaking, carefully consider these *pungent* words of Bishop Beveridge, "Opposite answers, and downright arguments advantage a cause, but when a disputant leaves many things *untouched*, as if they were *too hot for his fingers;* and *declines* the weight of other things, and *alters the true state of the Question*: it is a shrewd sign, either that he has not weighed things maturely, or else (which is more probable,) that he *maintains a desperate Cause*."[45]

APPENDIX A

SEE Cotelerius, "Patres Apostolic," Tom. 1, p. 602.

Extracts of a letter from Peter to James prefixed to the Clementines. "For if this be not done (says Peter, after entreating James not to communicate *his preachings* to any Gentile without previous examination,) our speech of Truth will be divided into many opinions, nor do I know this thing as being a Prophet; but as seeing even now the beginning of this evil. For some from among the Gentiles have rejected my *legal* Preaching; embracing the *trifling*, and *lawless* Doctrine of a man *who is an enemy*. And these things some have endeavoured to do now in my own life time, transforming my words by various interpretations, *to the destruction of the Law*; as if *I had been of the same mind*, but dared not openly profess it; (See Gal. ii. 11, 12, &c.) which be far from me! For this were to act against the Law of God spoken by Moses, and which has the Testimony of our Lord *for its perpetual duration*; since he thus has said, 'Heaven and Earth shall pass away, yet one jot, or one tittle shall not pass from the Law.' But these, I know not how, promising to deliver my opinion, (see Gal. as above,) take upon them to explain the words they heard from me, better than I that spoke them; telling their Disciples, my sense was that of which I had not so much as thought; now if in my own life time they dare feign such things, how much more will those that come after do the same."

APPENDIX B

Extract from Dodwell's Dissertations on Irenaeus, Diss. 1. p. 38, 39. "The Canonical writings (i. e. of the New Testament,) lay *concealed* in the coffers of private Churches, or persons, till the latter *times of Trajan*, or rather perhaps of *Adrian*; so that they *could not come to the knowledge of the Church*. For if they had been *published*, they would have been overwhelmed under such a multitude *as were then of Apocryphal, and suppositious* Books, that a new examination and a new Testimony would be necessary to *distinguish them* from these false ones. And it is from this new Testimony (whereby the genuine writings of the Apostles were distinguished from the spurious pieces which went under their names,) that *depends all the authority* which the truly Apostolic writings have formerly obtained, or which *they have at present* in the Catholic Church. But this fresh attestation of the Canon is subject to the same inconveniences with those traditions of the ancient persons that I defend, and whom Irenaeus both heard and saw; for it is equally distant from the original, and could not be made except by such only as had reached those remote times. But it is very certain that *before* the period I mentioned of Trajan's time, the Canon of the sacred Books was *not yet fixed*, nor any *certain number* of books received in the Catholic Church, whose authority must ever after serve to determine matters of faith; neither were the spurious pieces of heretics *yet rejected*, nor were the faithful admonished to beware of them for the future. Likewise the true writings of the Apostles used to be so bound up in one volume *with the Apocryphal*, that it was not manifest by any mark of public censure *which of them should be preferred to the other*. We have at this day certain authentic writings of Ecclesiastical Authors of those times, as Clemens Romanus, Barnabas, Hermas, Ignatius, and Polycarp, who wrote in the same order wherein I have named them, and after all the other writers of the New Testament, except Jude, and the two Johns. But in Hermas *you shall not meet with one passage, or any mention of the New Testament*; nor in all the rest is any one of the Evangelists called by his own name. And if sometimes they cite any passages like those we read in our Gospels, yet you will find them so much changed and for the most part so interpolated, that *it cannot be known*, whether they produced them out of *ours*, or some *Apocryphal Gospels*. Nay they sometimes cite passages which it is most certain are *not in* the present Gospels. From hence therefore it is evident that *no difference* was yet put between the Apocryphal and Canonical Books of the New Testament, especially if it be considered, that they pass *no censure* on the Apocryphal, nor leave any mark whereby the reader might discern whether they attributed *less authority* to the spurious than to the genuine Gospels; from whence it may reasonably be suspected, that if they cite sometimes any passages conformable to ours, it was not done through any certain design, as if dubious things were to be confirmed *only* by the Canonical Books, so as it is very possible that both those and the like passages may have been borrowed from other Gospels besides these we now have. But what need I mention Books that are not canonical, when indeed it does not appear from those of our Canonical Books which were last written, that the Church *knew any thing of the Gospels*, or that the clergy made a common use of them.—The writers of those times do not chequer their works with texts of the New Testament, which yet is the custom of the moderns, and was also *theirs* in such Books as *they acknowledge for Scripture*; for they most frequently cite *the Books of the Old Testament*, and would doubtless have done so by those of the *New* if they had *then* been received as *Canonical*."

So far Mr. Dodwell, and (excepting the genuineness of the writings of Barnabas and the rest, for they are incontestably ancient,) it is certain that the *matters of fact* with regard to the New Testament are all true. Whoever has an inclination to write on this subject is furnished from this passage with a great many curious disquisitions wherein to show his penetration and his judgment, as—how the immediate successors, and disciples of the Apostles could so grossly *confound* the *genuine* writings of their masters with such as were *falsely* attributed to them; or, since *they* were, in the dark about these matters *so early*, how come such as followed them by *a better light*; why all those Books which are cited by the earliest

Fathers with the same respect as those now received should not be accounted *equally* authentic with them; and what stress should be laid on *the testimony* of those Fathers, who not only contradict one another, but are often inconsistent with themselves in relating the very same facts; with a great many other difficulties which deserve a clear solution from any capable person.

I have said the ancient Heretics asserted, that the present Gospels *were forgeries*. As an example of this, take the following, from the works of Faustus, quoted by Augustine, contra Faustum Lib. 32. chapter 2. "You think, (says Faustus to his adversaries,) that of all the Books in the world the Testament of the Son only could not be corrupted; that it alone contains nothing which ought to be disallowed: especially when it *appears*, that it was not written *by the Apostles*, but *a long time after them* by certain obscure persons; who, lest no credit should be given to the stories they told of what they could not know, did prefix to their writings the names of the Apostles, and partly of those who succeeded the Apostles, affirming, that what they wrote themselves was written by these. Wherein they seem to me to have been the more heinously injurious to the Disciples of Christ, by attributing to them what they wrote themselves so *dissonant*, and *repugnant*; and that they pretended to write those Gospels under their names which are so full of *mistakes*, of *contradictory relations*, and *opinions*, that they are neither *coherent with themselves*, nor consistent *with one another*. What is this therefore but to throw a calumny on good men, and to fix the accusation of *Discord* on the unanimous Society of Christ's Disciples."

ADDENDA

THERE is in the Gospel ascribed to John, a *passage* quoted as a *prophecy*, which, as it has been looked on as a proof text, ought to have been mentioned in the 7th chapter. It is this. The Evangelist (John xix. 23,) says, "Then the soldiers, when they had crucified Jesus, took his garments and made four parts, to every soldier a part; and also his coat; now *the coat* was without seam, woven from the top throughout. They said therefore among themselves, Let us not *rend it*, but cast lots for it; that the Scripture might be fulfilled, which saith, 'They parted my raiment among them, and for my *vesture* they did cast lots.'" Now however plausible this *prophecy!* may appear, it is one of the most impudent applications of passages from the Old Testament that occurs in the New. It is taken from the 18th verse of the 22d Psalm, which Psalm was probably made by David in reference to his humiliating and wretched expulsion from Jerusalem by his son Absalom, and what was done in consequence, viz. that he was hunted by ferocious enemies whom he compares to furious bulls, and roaring lions, gaping upon him to devour him; that his palace was *plundered* and that *they divided his treasured garments*; (In the East, where the fashions never change, every great man has constantly presses full of hundreds and thousands of garments, many of them very costly; they are considered as a valuable part of his riches,) *and cast lots for his robes.* This is the real meaning of this *passage* quoted as a *prophecy*. In the same Psalm there is another verse, which has been from time immemorial quoted as *a prophecy* of the crucifixion, verse 16. "They *pierced* my hands and my feet." In the original there seems to have been a word dropped importing "*they tear*," or something like it, for it is literally "Like a lion—my hands and my feet," and there is *there* no word answering to "pierced." The meaning however of the verse is not difficult to be discerned, "dogs have compassed me; the assembly of wicked men have enclosed me; like a lion—(they tear) my hands and my feet." The meaning may be discovered from the context, where David represents himself as in the utmost distress, helpless, and abandoned amidst his enemies, raging like wild beasts around him, then by a *strong*, but striking Oriental figure, he represents himself like a carcase surrounded by dogs, who are busied in tearing the flesh from his bones; their teeth *fixed in his hands and feet and pulling him asunder*. This is the import of the place, and this interpretation is at last adopted, for the first time I believe by Christians, in the new version of the Psalms used by the Unitarian Church in London.

There is not a more palpable instance of the facility with which good natured and voracious Piety is made to swallow the most flimsy arguments, if only agreeable to its wishes and wants, than the case under consideration. This Psalm containing these passages "they parted my raiment among them;" and "they pierced my hands and feet" is read, and for ages has been read, in the name of God, to the good people of the Church of England, on every Good Friday, as undoubtedly *a prophecy* of the Crucifixion; when yet the learned Divines of the Church of England (and of these it can boast a noble Catalogue indeed,) certainly *know*, and *are conscious*, that the Psalm which contains these passages has no more relation to Jesus Christ, than it has to Nebuchadnezzer.

A reference ought to have been subjoined at the end of the 10th chapter to the Dialogue called *"Philopatris"* in Lucian's Works, for an account of the customs, habits, and personal appearance of the early Christians, corroborative of what is said in the 17th and 18th chapters of this work. Lest however Lucian's testimony in this matter should be objected to, because he was a satirist, and of course may have been guilty of giving an overcharged picture of the subjects of his ridicule; I request the reader to peruse, if he can obtain it, "Lami's Account of the Domestic habits and personal appearance, and practices of the Primitive Christians." Lami was a very learned, and sincere Christian, and of course his testimony cannot be objected to, and the reader will find, on a perusal of his work, that what I have asserted in the 17th and 18th chapters is altogether true, and *not the whole truth neither*. Indeed that the statements in those chapters as to the effects of the *peculiar* maxims of the New Testament upon the *heart*, and *understanding* are substantially *correct*, will I believe be discovered by asking any honest individual among the

Methodists who is an *enthusiast*, i. e. *sincere*, and *thorough going* in his religion. I have no doubt that he, or she will avow without hesitation to the enquirer, and glory in it, that *chastity* is more honourable than *marriage*; that *Faith* is every thing; that doubt is *damnable*, and *a proof* of "*an unregenerated mind*;" that all the goods and pleasures of this world are trash; that human institutions are mere "*carnal ordinances*;" and that human science and learning is a snare to faith, and an abomination to *a true Disciple* of the cross.

FINIS

NOTE—BY THE PUBLISHER

The reader of the preceding pages cannot have failed to have observed that the Author, in many instances, has expressed his doubts as to a Divine Revelation being contained in the Old Testament. His arguments in this book are, therefore, only founded on this fact, acknowledged both by Jews and Christians, and not on his own convictions; but he has, in a subsequent Work, entitled, "Five Pebbles, from the Brook" which was written in reply to a "Defence of Christianity," by Mr. Everett,* made use of the following remarkable expressions:—

"This Book is not the work of an Infidel. I am not an Infidel; what I have learned and seen in Europe, Asia, and Africa, while it has confirmed my reasons for rejecting the New Testament, has rooted in my mind the conviction that the ancient Bible does contain a Revelation from the God of Nature, as firmly as my belief in the first proposition of Euclid."

"The whole analogy of nature, while it is in many respects opposed to the characteristics ascribed to the Divinity by the metaphysicians, yet bears witness in my opinion, that this world was made, and is governed, by just such a Being as the Jehovah of the Old Testament, while the palpable fulfillment of the predictions contained in that Book, and which is so strikingly manifest in the Old World, leaves in my mind no doubt, whatever, of the ultimate fulfillment of all that it promises, and all that it threatens."

He closes his Work with the following note:—

"I believe that the Scholar will not find any misstatement of facts, nor the Logician any flaw in the arguments, the Book lays before the public. On

---

*Mr. Everett wrote the "Defence of Christianity" in reply to the "Grounds of Christianity Examined."

these two points I feel secure in this respect; and I calmly and firmly lay my gage at the feet of all Christendom. Let him who dares to take it up, do it."

EDITOR'S NOTES

1. Richard Price (1723–1791), a Dissenting minister in England, was a prominent supporter of both the American and French Revolutions. Bethune English's citations are found on pp. 20–25 of Price's *Observations on the Importance of the American Revolution* (1784).

2. Richard Popkin noted that this comment reflected the fact that one of the leading Enlightenment explanations of religious belief was the theory that it was an imposture on the part of great religious leaders like Moses, Jesus, and Mohammed.

3. In notes that he was unable to complete, Richard Popkin commented on the fact that the miseries Christianity had inflicted on the Jews were the only human disaster George Bethune English mentioned, and wondered whether Bethune English was the first Christian author to suggest that Christianity had to be held responsible for Jewish suffering.

4. Richard Popkin suggested that Bethune English may have been familiar with eighteenth-century discussions of probability and belief by the non-Conformist theologian Thomas Bayes, Richard Price, and the French mathematician and philosopher Condorcet.

5. Richard Popkin noted that this did not apply to Rabbi Isaac, who was never in danger of persecution on account of his writings.

6. Hugo Grotius (1583–1645), Dutch jurist and scholar, best known as one of the major theorists of international law.

7. It is not clear which work of Grotius that Bethune English is referring to here. Huet's book is *Petri Danielis Huetii episcope abrincensis Demonstratio Evangelica*, 4th ed. (Leipzig: J. T. Fritsch, 1694).

8. Willem Surenhuys (Surenhusius in Latin) (1666–1729), a Dutch Bible scholar and contemporary of Spinoza, was involved in various scholarly projects relating to the Jews and was one of three scholars proposed as faculty in the College of Jewish Studies, whose founding was proposed in England in the 1640s. The "illustrious school" was an *école illustre*, the equivalent of a modern high school.

9. There had been a joint project of Jewish and Christian scholars to publish the Mishna—first in Hebrew with vowel points, then in Spanish and Latin translation. In 1646, the Hebrew volumes came out, published by Menasseh ben Israel. The

Spanish version was worked on by two rabbis, Isaac and Jacob Abendana. Isaac Abendana later moved to Cambridge, England, to work on the Latin translation, which was never completed. Surenhusius completed the editing of this and other ancient Jewish texts. He worked with several of the rabbis in Amsterdam. (—*RHP*)

10. Johann Heinrich Michaelis (1668–1738), German Hebraist, and Narcissus Marsh (1638–1713), British clergyman and Archbishop of Dublin.

11. Jean Le Clerc (1657–1736), an important journalist of the early Enlightenment.

12. Edward Stillingfleet (1635–1699), Bishop of Worcester, was a defender of the doctrine of the Trinity.

13. The Targum is an Aramaic paraphrase of the Bible, dating from around the first century of the Common Era.

14. Arthur Ashby Sykes (1683/4–1756). The reference is probably to his *Essay upon the Truth of the Christian Religion*.

15. This is a reference to Johann Christoph Wagenseil's collection of Jewish anti-Christian texts, which included Rabbi Isaac's *Chizzuk Emunah*. Stephan Rittangelius was a Dutch theological writer.

16. William Paley (1743–1805), a well-known Anglican priest and philosopher.

17. Campegius Vitringa (1659–1722), Dutch theologian.

18. This is Bethune English's first mention of Rabbi Isaac's name. (—*RHP*)

19. Another direct reference to the *Chizzuk Emunah*. (—*RHP*)

20. John Marsham (1602–1685). Entries for Wagenseil's *Tela Ignae Satanae* in the WorldCat electronic online catalogue mention his name, but I have not been able to determine his relation to the work. (—*JDP*)

21. David Levi, *Letters to Dr. Priestley in Answer to those he addressed to the Jews; inviting them to an Amicable Discussion of the Evidence of Christianity* (London, 1787).

22. Humphrey Prideaux (1648–1724) wrote a book condemning Mohammedanism. For Michaelis, see note 10, above. Benjamin Blayney (1728–1801) was another religious author.

23. Richard Popkin noted that these were the first substantial passages from Rabbi Isaac's work to be translated and published in English. (—*JDP*)

24. Probably Daniel Whitby (1638–1726), author of *A Paraphrase and Commentary on the New Testament* (1703).

25. Pierre Allix (1641–1717), theologian.

26. Probably Sebastian Muenster (1489–1552), author of a tract comparing Christian and Jewish ideas about the Messiah, *The Messias of the Christians and the Jewes*.

27. Probably Hugh Latimer (1485–1555), Anglican churchman.

28. English authors often used "Austin" to refer to St. Augustine.

29. Bethune English may have taken the notion of Mohammed as an impostor from the widely circulated work *The Three Impostors*, a denunciation of the claims of Moses, Jesus, and Mohammed, written in the late seventeenth century. See Silvia Berti, Françoise Charles-Daubert, and Richard H. Popkin, eds., *Heterodoxy, Spinozism, and Free Thought in the Early Eighteenth Century* (Dordrecht: Kluwer, 1996).

30. Thomas Brown, *An Account of the People Called Shakers: Their Faith, Doctrines, and Practice, Exemplified in the Life, Conversations, and Experience of the Author During the Time He Belonged to the Society. To Which is Affixed a History of Their Rise and Progress to the Present Day* (1812). The Shaker sect, led by a woman named Mother Ann, developed in England but migrated to the American colonies in 1774. Mother Ann died in 1784, but the group continued to spread, founding a number of communal settlements. They were noted for worship services featuring spirited singing and dancing and for their practices of celibacy and communism.

31. Conyers Middleton, *A Free Inquiry into the Miraculous Powers, which are supposed to have subsisted in the Christian Church, from the earliest ages through several successive centuries* (London, 1749).

32. Ancient Greek geographer and historian.

33. The reference is actually to the Diacre Pâris, whose tomb at the church of Saint-Merri became the center of a Jansenist cult in Paris around 1730. The extravagant behavior of the Jansenists and their claims about the miracles associated with the tomb led Louis XV's government to close down the church. (—*JDP*)

34. Edward Evanson (1731–1805), who wrote on the doctrine of the trinity.

35. It has not been possible to identify this author.

36. Probably Johann Salomon Semler (1725–1791), a German theologian.

37. Probably H. E. G. Paulus (1761–1845), a German professor.

38. Bethune English seems to be the only one who brings up the case of the Zebathai Tzevi (Shabbtai Zvi) as an indication of how religious believers can be duped no matter how ardent they are. Bethune English follows the text in Basnage's *Histoire des juifs*, which is actually factually incorrect, in reporting that Zebathai had been beheaded. (—*RHP*)

39. John Lightfoot (1602–1675), English Bible scholar.

40. See note 30.

41. Richard Popkin noted that the Shakers were the only religious group Bethune English criticized in this tone.

42. Probably Richard Graves (1763–1829), *Lectures on the Four Last Books of the Pentateuch* (London, 1807).

43. We have not been able to identify the work of Priestley referred to here.

44. We have not been able to identify these references.

45. The quoted passage appears in a work of Thomas Hobbes, *The Questions Concerning Liberty, Necessity, and Chance, Clearly Stated and Debated between Dr. Bramwell, Bishop of Derry, and Thomas Hobbes of Malmesbury*, reprinted in William Molesworth, ed., *The English Works of Thomas Hobbes*, 11 vols. (London: John Bohn, 1839–1845), vol. 5, pp. 36–37. Why Bethune English attributes it to Bishop Beveridge is unknown.

"GEORGE BETHUNE ENGLISH"

by Samuel Lorenzo Knapp

Samuel Lorenzo Knapp's article on George Bethune English, which appeared in a biographical dictionary that made up part of The Treasury of Knowledge, *a short encyclopedia, gives an idea of the contrasting reactions Bethune English's activities and personality aroused among his American contemporaries. Knapp, who knew Bethune English, appreciated his friend's originality and his remarkable linguistic abilities. He was nevertheless shocked by Bethune English's unorthodox religious ideas. Richard H. Popkin was unaware of Knapp's article at the time of his death. —JDP*

George Bethune English has filled such a particular place in our history, that he should not be omitted in American biography. He took his own path to fame, and imitated no example. He could not complain that any one had led him astray. He was original and eccentric by nature, and he followed the dictates of his own judgment, and pursued every image his fancy created at pleasure. The character of such a man is likely to be misunderstood and misrepresented, because many will hear of his singularities, when but few will have an opportunity or a disposition to read his character fairly; and it must be confessed that is somewhat difficult for those who had firm friendship for him, to do it thoroughly, as it abounded in hieroglyphics and seeming contradiction; not that he had any reserve about him, for he was as open as day, and spoke undisguisedly upon all subjects.

He was born in Boston, and received the first rudiments of his education in the excellent schools of that city. From the public school he went

Samuel Lorenzo Knapp, "George Bethune English," in Knapp, *American Biography*, Pt. VI of *The Treasury of Knowledge* (New York: Conner and Cooke, 1833), pp. 6:92–98.

to Harvard College, and was graduated with the class of 1807. In this institution he was distinguished for his love of learning, and for his lofty and
refined sentiments of honor. On leaving college he became a student of
law, and entered philosophically into the science; but it was his misfortune
to dislike some of the hard features of the common law, and he early began
to write against it: probably before he had thoroughly seen how much
these features had been softened by statutory provisions and common
sense decisions. If his criticism bore the mark of juvenility, still, it was
acknowledged by all who read them, that they discovered uncommon
research and much acuteness of mind. This was not all. He made many
objections to the practice of law; some of which, probably a greater part of
them, would have soon disappeared, and in fact, would have been
absolutely lost in a few years of respectable practice. After reading the
usual course he was admitted to the bar of Suffolk, but never appeared in
any cause before court or jury; for he had given up all thoughts of pursuing
the law as a profession. He then turned his attention to divinity, and
repaired to Cambridge to commence his studies. In the fine library of that
university, he was a book-worm for three years, and then appeared as a
preacher of the Gospel; but not as a candidate for the ministry. It was
agreed on all hands, that no one is this country had ever presented himself
as a preacher for the first time, with so much profound biblical knowledge
as Mr. English, but his eloquence was not of a high order, nor his sermons
of a very popular cast; in the former his friends were greatly disappointed,
for he was a most admirable reader of the Bible, and also of Shakespeare
and of poetry, in rhyme, or blank verse; but the loud tones of his voice had
a sharpness in them better suited to the bar or any other place than the
pulpit. That his sermons should have been too learned, metaphysical, and
controversial, might have been anticipated by those who knew how fond
he then was of disputation, and investigation. He soon discovered by the
feelings of his audience that he was not a popular preacher, and he saw that
he had disappointed the expectations of his anxious friends, and others of
a community always delighted with the first fledgings of genius in the
pulpit—and who sometimes in the yearnings of their affections for the
youthful man of God, mistake the pinions of some lesser bird for the wings
of the young Eagle. With the impression on his mind that he had not been
equal to himself, he remained in doubt whether to proceed or not, in his

profession; but probably he would have made an attempt to correct his errors, which was easily to be done, and have pursued his profession, if some doubts of the truth of the Christian Revelation had not previously insinuated themselves into his mind; and as the doubts increased, his honesty revolted at the thought of playing the hypocrite in diffusing the doctrines in which his faith was not sound and steadfast. In the Cambridge library he had found about all that is extant of the Jewish literature, and this was read with avidity until all belief in the authenticity of the New Testament was obliterated from his mind, and the inspiration of the Old more firmly established. Here was the great error of his life. Entangled in the mazes of biblical criticism, he forgot to drink deeply of the humbler spirit of the Gospel, and in the pride of human learning he followed the phosphoric light of infidelity for his guide, instead of seeking, with that light which cometh from heaven, the straight and narrow way that leadeth to life eternal; but never was there a man more honest in his deviation from the true pathway than George Bethune English. He was unfortunately not contented to stop here, and incarcerate his thoughts within his own breast, but erroneously believed it to be his duty to promulgate his opinions, which he seemed to consider as discoveries in part. In this he was in an error, for the infidels of a former age had anticipated most of his arguments; they had gone over much of the same ground, and some of them had paid more attention to the beauties of style than he had, and of course had been more dangerous to Christianity. In all this, if he had examined his own heart he would have found more of pride and vanity than he was ever willing to allow; but this cannot be remedied now; nor should it be regretted, except as it relates to himself, for his book had done more good than harm. The ignorant and vulgar could not understand it, and the wicked who were intelligent did not relish it, for it was not seasoned with the wit and ribaldry of Voltaire or Paine. There was nothing profane in the spirit of the work; the undertaking alone was the crime. Many of our young clergymen were induced to push their studies much further than they would have done if the book had not made its appearance. They had declaimed against hoaryheaded infidels, or those long since dead; but now they were obliged to follow one of their own age through the laborious labyrinth of learning, and fight him step by step. To do this they were obliged to study hard, and their parishioners reaped the fruits of their

labors. Cary and Everett, these two young clergymen, were the only opponents that the writer ever heard Mr. English mention. The productions of
their pens were extensively read, and were much admired by the public,
particularly the work of Mr. Everett. This gentleman was then a preacher
of high attainments, and the idol of a large circle of friends, and every
thing he wrote told well. English acknowledged that Everett was learned,
but complained that he was not fair, inasmuch as he treated him with the
asperity due only to those who attempt against their better judgments, to
corrupt the public mind, which was not his case. Of this, the writer will not
undertake to speak; for it is seldom that religious opponents think correctly
of each other. Mr. English did not see Mr. Everett's book until after several years from the time it was published, when he received it in Egypt. He
wrote an answer to it; but this has not been extensively circulated—Mr.
English's friends advising him to suppress it, as a revival of the controversy could not add to his reputation or to the chances of his advancement
in life. When the first burst of indignation of such opinions was over, Mr.
English looked around him for some employment. In New England, he
was shut out from every thing that depended upon public opinion. What
course to pursue for a living, he did not know until he remembered that in
his earlier days, he once thought of a military profession, and had treasured up much information to prepare himself for it. He had made himself
acquainted with both the ancient and modern tacticks, and had practiced
every manoeuvre on the black board, long before that instrument of the
education of the present day was in common use, or even hardly known
among us. In this state of his affairs, he applied for a commission in our
army; but did not receive one. After a while spent in the Western country
as an editor of a paper, he was appointed a Lieutenant in the Marine corps.
It has been said that he took a look at the South American patriots, before
he received this appointment; but they did not suit him; but of this I never
heard him speak. His office in the Marine corps, if the emolument was
small, placed him amongst gentlemen, which was gratifying to his taste;
and, it is said, he was a favorite with them. In this capacity, after some time
he sailed to the Mediterranean; but from offers made him, by Ibrahim
Pacha, he resigned his commission in the Marine corps of the United
States, and accepted a command in the Egyptian army, then preparing for
the conquest of Abyssinia. It was enough for English, that no European

foot had been imprinted in the soil of that country for more than three thousand years. He presented to the consideration of the Pacha, two plans for the campaign. In one he urged the use of a chariot armed with scythes, after the manner of the ancients, with the difference in the machine and its movements, that it was to be propelled with horses, under bullet-proof cover, in the rear, instead of being drawn by them as those of Persia, and other oriental nations. The machine was made, and in his opinion would have succeeded, if he could have found an honest whip, or if the cavalry had not been jealous of the invention. In trying the machine it was dashed against a stone house in Old Cairo, and destroyed, but he constantly maintained, that if he could have commanded an American stage driver, it would have gone well, and would have been a most destructive engine of war.

The second proposition was to form a park of artillery for the campaign, to be drawn over the sands and deserts by patient, and labor-enduring camels, instead of horses, taking horses only to be used when near or on battle ground. Camels had never before been harnessed to the draught; but on trying were found to be tractable, and by kindness easily broken to the labor. Twelve brass pieces, of from six to twelve pounders, were taken with the army, and a corps, drilled by English, were selected for this service, who made admirable artillerists. Thus equipped the invading army marched under Ismael Pacha for Abyssinia. Mr. English being general of the artillery corps, with the title and emoluments of his rank. Abyssinia is a land of romance—the cradle of man, where the swaddling bands of infant nations remain in the same fashion as they were found in the first ages of time; a region over which the Roman eagles never flew; a territory that Napoleon, in the madness of his ambition, never thought of conquering. Here were seen and noted by English, the sepulchral monuments of kings and queens, and the might of the earth who lived in the days of Solomon, or long before his time, rising in pyramids of one to two hundred feet high from the present surface of the ground. More than four hundred of these pyramids he examined, and took minutes of their size. In the first battle fought with the Abyssinian, the artillery did much execution and in fact decided the battle. This excited the envy of Ismael Pacha, and from that period, he treated English with coolness; and on his remonstrating with the Pacha, in some flagrant instances of cruelty practiced in his army—such as impaling three officers for some trivial offence, an open quarrel ensued, and English left the army with a few horsemen, as a guard, for Cairo, where new difficulties awaited him; for Ibrahim Pacha, to get rid of the reward he had promised if the army should reach a particular point at a certain time, finding that this was accomplished, had no other way of escaping from his promise than to seek a quarrel, alleging that English had left his son without a justifiable cause. The award was stipulated at twenty thousand dollars, and this was too large an amount for Asiatic avarice to part with, where there was no tribunal to enforce payment. Thrown again upon the world he sought the shores of Christendom, and doffed his Turkish dress, and was not a little weaned from his admiration of Oriental usages, and somewhat shaken in his faith of Musselman integrity and honor; but though disappointed he was not discouraged. In less than three months after English left Ismael Pacha's camp, the youthful tyrant was massacred with most of his officers; while English was with him all went on prosperously. Before he went to Egypt, he had spent some time at Constantinople, and there acquired a very considerable knowledge of the Turkish language and a better acquaintance with the state of that Empire than had ever been promulgated to France or England, and both of these nations had maintained splendid embassies there for many years. Speaking the language, and wearing the Turkish costume, he mingled with every class of people, and of course obtained in a short time, more information of the real state of affairs, political and domestic, than a legation who understood nothing of the language, could acquire in many years residence in the city. This knowledge he imparted to our government, and by them he was appointed an agent in that quarter, with letters to our public functionaries in the Mediterranean. For these services he was scantily paid, without distinction of honors: the higher representatives of a republic generally pine in obscurity abroad, for want of means to live, and the minor agents are left to supplicate for a miserable allowance on their return; and this generally dealt out to them with supercilious grudging.

In July, 1827, Mr. English returned to this country, and has spent most of his time since, until his death, in the city of Washington, waiting for employment; but he was a wretched solicitor, for favor of any kind, and government did not seem to require his services. It is said that he was about to be employed when he was taken sick, but of this the writer does not speak from authority; one thing he knows, that there is one man in power, with whom the deceased was acquainted, that knows how to measure and how to value letters and science as well as any man in this country, and that man knows, too, how accurate was the information communicated by Mr. English; and he can bear testimony that the suggestions, conjectures, and anticipations of the American agent, have proved his sagacity and foresight. It is in vain to repine; it has often happened, and will again to the end of time, that hollow-hearted and empty-headed vanity, by pertinacity and obsequiousness will snatch the bread from men of understanding, and steal away the favors intended for men of skill. Enough has been given of the history of Mr. English to show that his life was an eventful one, and his mind of no common character. His virtues were numerous; and his errors those of the head, and not of the heart. He was somewhat lofty and proud; but never overbearing or unjust to others. He was brave; but with all that prudence so necessary to personal safety. His mind was a logical one; and his passion for what he thought truth, a paramount principle; and strange as it may seem, he was naturally religious, for he had traced all things up to the Great First Cause:—the source of wisdom, power, and goodness. He delighted in demonstrating these attributes of his Maker. Although his mind was strong enough to grapple with any subject, still it must acknowledged that had no very extensive share of that exalted gift of genius, a rich and prolific imagination which creates and embellishes for posterity. His memory was well stored with facts, and reasonings upon them; but he did not possess much of what may be called taste, for vernacular thoughts and common life acquirements were mixed up with 'classical images and barbaric spoils:' he would talk with as little emotion of his resting in the shade of the great pyramid, as of a game of football in college-yard; and although his appetite for new scenes never seemed to be diminished, yet he had reached the 'nil admirare,' said to be a constituent principle of greatness. He had nothing of the traveller's fondness of display. He never poured out his streams of knowledge until the hydrant was opened by inquisitive friends who knew something of its deep reservoir. He possessed to the last, an unsophisticated mind, and an open, generous heart. His good word, his pen, his sword and purse, were all at the disposal of his friends. It was not the mere gallantry

of conventional courtesy; but a deeper and better principle. His excite-
ments for his friends were strong and lasting, and his proffering of friendship sincere and timely. It happens to weak minds, that they sometimes
forget the few in their acquaintance with many. It was not so with English;
he cherished the most ardent affection for his kindred, as those who have
heard him mourn the loss of his mother, or speak of his father's kindness,
or of his fraternal ties, can witness.

He remained firm in his creed to the last, but he long regretted that he
should ever have been induced to promulgate his doctrines, and for years
past, he has never touched upon the subject of religion, unless he was
drawn out by others, and then he defended himself manfully. In loaning
his book in answer to Mr. Everett, to a friend, he observed, 'be cautious
that your daughters do not get hold of it, for I would not shake their faith,
or interfere with their mother's pious instructions for the world—I hope
and believe that my sister has never seen it.' Nevertheless he persisted in
saying, that there was more sincerity in the worship of the mosque, and
the synagogue, than in the Christian churches.

The life of such a man is full of lessons of wisdom to those who will
profit by them. It shows more fully that the church of Christ is built on a
rock, and that nothing can move it. In the case of English, industry, talents, learning, honesty of purpose, and great zeal, have ended in nothing
but regret, disappointment, neglect, and almost ostracism and outlawry.
This is a natural consequence of the feelings and the spirit of the community in which we live, towards one who ventures to speak so freely
against our religion. We need not seek for special providences when general laws will answer to solve the difficulties in our reasonings in the
moral world. We loved the man, and sincerely deplore his premature exit.
He was fitted to have been useful to society, and an honor to the literature
of our country. Had he lived in Europe, his eccentricities would have
enhanced his fame, and with Park and Clark, and a hundred others, he
would have gone down to posterity as one of rare qualities and daring
adventures. The politicians of other countries may be as noisy as our own,
but here their obstreperous notes drown the voice, and the praises of
learning together. In other countries learning must, and will have a voice,
and she is heard and listened to wherever she speaks, whatever may be
the subject on which she treats. Mr. English left some few valuable works

that he brought from Constantinople, in the Hebrew, Turkish, and Arabic tongues, which we hope will be preserved for some public library; and he has left, also, if they have not been destroyed, several manuscripts from his own pen, on the manners and customs of the Eastern nations; one containing some particulars of the secret societies of that country, which was the birth place of letters, and science. It was truly an intellectual feast to hear him read the Old Testament in the original, and translate and commentate as he went along. He threw into the shade other translations and commentaries by the minuteness of his knowledge of the Hebrew language, as well as of the habits and manners of the Jewish nation in every age of their history. When on this subject, his whole air and character seemed to change, and he grew as enthusiastic as a Rabinical master, chaunting the pages of prophecy.

The charge of having turned Turk, which was generally spread abroad in this country, and in Europe, he constantly denied. He said that he had often joined in prayer, both with the Turks and with the Jews, as they addressed the Supreme Being alone. He was fond of reading the Koran, to improve his Arabic, and to become familiar with the Mahometan laws; but he spent ten hours on the Jewish Scriptures to one on the Koran. He valued the latter as giving a religious sanction in the minds of Islamites to an admirable code of civil law. He defended every passage of the Old Testament, while he laughed at the many singularities and the absurdities found in some of the chapters in the Mahomedan code. He frequently compared passages of Isaiah and of the other prophets, with the most sublime parts of the Koran. He has read to me the 91st chapter of the Koran, entitled 'the Sun—revealed at Mecca,' in which Mahomet makes Gabriel speak in the following truly sublime manner;—'In the name of God most merciful—I swear by the Sun, and its brightness; by the moon when she followeth him; by the day when it showeth its splendor; by the night when it covereth him with darkness; by the earth, and Him who spread it forth; by the soul, and Him who perfectly formed it, and inspired into the same its faculty of distinguishing, and power of choosing wickedness or piety— that he who hath purified himself shall be happy, and that he who has corrupted his soul is miserable.'

The passages he used to contrast with this transcript from the Koran, to show the superiority of the Jewish scriptures were numerous, from the prophets, the psalmist, and other books, one in particular from Isaiah is distinctly remembered. It is in the 40th chapter beginning at the 12th verse.

'Who hath measured the waters in the hollow of his hand, and meted out heaven with the span, and comprehended the dust of the earth in a measure, and weighed the mountains in scales, and the hills in balance?

'Who hath directed the Spirit of the Lord, or being his counsellor hath taught him.

'With whom took he counsel, and who instructed him, and taught him in the path of judgment, and taught him knowledge, and shewed to him the way of understanding.

'Behold, the nations are as a drop of a bucket, and are counted as the small dust of the balance; behold he taketh up the Isles as a very little thing.

'And Lebanon is not sufficient to him, nor the beasts thereof sufficient for a burnt offering.

'All nations before him are as nothing; and they are counted to him less than nothing and vanity.'

An anecdote of his mastery over whatever language he chose to acquire, was related to the writer of this article by a gentleman of Marseilles. The Turkish ambassador who had been residing in England, was at Marseilles on his way home—at table he contended that no foreigner could acquire the Turkish language, and speak it as vernacular. This was said when English was present,—but he took his leave next day. Soon afterwards, a Turkish gentleman arrived at the house of the consul and was introduced to the ambassador. They lived in great intimacy for several weeks, the ambassador representing his new friend as the most learned man of the East, perfectly at home in Arabic, Hebrew, and other tongues, as in his own native Turkish. The gentleman at length left for England, and shortly afterwards Mr. English made his appearance. He had played the part of a Turk during that time, without exciting a suspicion.

Another extraordinary proof of his power in the acquisition of language, was known to the writer from personal observation. The Cherokees had a delegation at Washington and took up their lodgings at a public house where English boarded, and it was observed that he was particularly fond of a bright boy that was with them. One day after the poor Cherokees had got out of patience with the government, they expressed themselves with great indignation and wrath. English heard them and reprimanded them in their own language with such eloquence and fluency as to utterly astound them. They thought the Great Spirit had sent him to reprove them and given him their language by inspiration. The fact was, he had made use first of the boy, then of the interpreter, and lastly of the whole delegation, to assist him in acquiring the Cherokee language—and then of their newspaper, which was sent to them from New Echota.

He had failings; and who is there without them? But they were not sufficient to eclipse his attainments or hide his virtues. To unforgiven severity, to persecuting zeal, to captious intolerance, to condemning rancour, and to all the hosts of evil hearts, be the language of our Saviour be applied: 'Let him that is without sin cast the first stone.'

The analysis of the mind of English, is another proof to add to the thousands already on record—that an unbeliever is the most credulous of men, and that he who doubts the revelation of Christ, must swallow innumerable absurdities, contradictions, and palpable falsehoods, to get rid of a few apparent difficulties.

Mr. English died in Washington, in August 1828—and was buried in that city. His death was deeply lamented by a large circle of acquaintances, and all who knew him became his friends. Whether there has been a monument erected to his memory or not the writer is not able to say, but this he believes, that but few of our countrymen who have died at home or abroad more unequivocally deserve such an honor.

Here repose the ashes
of
GEORGE BETHUNE ENGLISH
the
Oriental Traveller.
Of two liberal Professions
He was a distinguished Member,
But practised in neither.
He was learned
Without pedantry;
Brave, without rashness;
And determined

Without obstinacy.
Under the guise
of quietude
He cherished the spirit
of adventure;
and
Became acquainted
with war
in the
Saloons of Peace.
By opposing Bigotry,
He fell into Superstition;
By attacking the truth
of our religion,
He proved
Its Authenticity
And Holiness.
By his admiration
Of the old world
He showed the blessings
of the new.
He was fitted for
Any station in life,
But never held
A permanent place.
He was often the guide
of those
who concealed the sources
of their knowledge.
Not unfrequently
Others were paid
for service
Rendered by him.
He was neglected
by those
Who should have

Brought him succour,
And slightly noticed
by others
Bound to do him
Reverence.
His moral fortitude
Was not equal
To his natural;
And he shrunk
From simpering impudence
In the coteries
of Fashion,
When he would
Have bearded a tribe
of Exquisites
In the battle-field,
Or driven them
Fearlessly
From the Halls of Learning.
Born and educated
To all the courtesies
of good society,
He felt a loathing
To the pretenders
to gentility,
And to the Minions
of Power.
He saw honors divided
among the ignorant,
And emoluments given
To the undeserving.
While waiting for
His piece of the loaves
of Office,
As was his due;
Bustling Inanity

Snatched it from
His hand
Not leaving
A sustaining crumb.
At his disappointment
Heartlessness
Laughed aloud;
Looking around
In despair
His heart strings broke,
And he fell a victim
of Sensibility
At the early age of 39.
Go, Traveller,
Whoever you may be,
Among the mighty
Or the humble,
and
Teach your children
That departures
From the common
Paths of life,
In thinking or acting,
However chivalrous,
Are dangerous;
And that success
And happiness
Depend more
On Prudence
With mediocrity,
than on Profound acquirements
or
Transcendent Genius,
So prone
to be
Misguided.